BEYOND THE DANGER CLOSE

THE KOREAN EXPERIENCE REVEALED

2nd Battalion Princess Patricia's Canadian Light Infantry

Hub Gray
with
Grania Litwin

Published & Distributed by:
Bunker To Bunker Publishing,
4520 Crowchild Trail S. W.
Calgary, Alberta, T2T 5J4Canada.

**National Library of
Canadian Cataloguing in Publication Data**

Gray, Hub, 1928 -
Beyond the Danger Close : the Korean experience revealed :
2nd Battalion Princess Patricia's Canadian Light Infantry /
Hub Gray ; editor, Grania Litwin

Includes bibliographical references and index.

ISBN 1-894255-24-0

1.   Canada. Canadian Army - - History - - Korean War, 1950 - 1953.
2.   Canada. Canadian Army. Princess Patricia's Canadian Light Infantry - - History
3. Korean War, 1950 - 1953 - - History.
I. Litwin, Grania. II. Title.
DS919.2.G72 2003   951.904'24'0971   C2002 - 911499 - 3

Cover picture:
Lieut. Mike Levy leads The Defence at D Coy 25 April 1951.
Painting by Lindsey Newman, Victoria, British Columbia, Canada.

Book production:
Northwest Printing, Calgary, Alberta, Canada
Cover design: Geoffrey Todd

Printed in Canada

"Justice must not only be done,
but it must be seen to be done."

This record seeks to correct the inaccuracies
that have been recurring over 50 years.

Of particular interest are the actions of
D Company's 10 Platoon,
Commanded by Lieutenant Michael G Levy.

It seems unbelievable but neither
Lieutenant Mike Levy of 10 Platoon,
Lieutenant John Pearson of 11 Platoon,
nor Sergeant Bernard Holligan of 12 Platoon,
were ever consulted after the battle
or later asked to provide statements
regarding their actions.

This book is dedicated to:

All Patricias of the Second Battalion
who fought in Korea during 1951
and to all Patricias everywhere

INTRODUCTION

The vivid graphic Story of the Battle of Kapyong in which the vastly outnumbered Princess Patricias refused to retreat and broke the massive Chinese attack that threatened Seoul... told for the first time. By one who was there. A long overdue memoir of Canada's most memorable battle of the Korean War — a defensive masterpiece — and should be required reading for those who wish to understand Canada.
PETER WORTHINGTON, CAPTAIN (Ret'd), (3 PPCLI Korea), Editor Sun Newspapers

This book needed to be done and Hub Gray's done it! It is well intentioned, well researched, well written and well presented. Portrayed, "in your face," are the elements of a combat infantryman's war. You will find fright, cold, compassion, comradeship, humour, hunger, fatigue, pain, pride, glory, envy, skill, doubt and sorrow. History, re-written factually, giving credit to soldiers who fight and win our country's battles.
MGEN HC PITTS (Ret'd) MC CD. KOREA -1 & 3 PPCLI. Former COL OF THE REGIMENT.

A desperate battle in Korea and Hub Gray's honest microscope focuses on a small units critical role; he provides chilling realism, a painstaking search for the truth and timeless study of human nature under extreme stress, laced with unexpected touches of humour. Highly recommended for the food for thought it will give civilian and military readers — a valuable training vehicle for junior officers and NCOs.
COL JAMES BARRETT ~ USMC 5th MARINES, KOREA, 1952

Danger Close is the military jargon for a rarely used expedient of calling down friendly fire so close as to endanger your own soldiers. This happened, and more, at the Battle of Kapyong, which is the focal point of this book. Despite the bravery of the Chinese attackers, two under strength battalions held and defeated an offensive that could have split the UN force. A veteran of this hard fought, but decisive, battle in Korea, Hub Gray has been collecting and analyzing evidence that lead him to expand and challenge the Official History. The results are detailed, controversial, and interesting. For anyone curious about the effected of battle and privation upon the individuals involved, Mr. Gray portrays it...warts, black humour, heroism, flaws and all. He illuminates the dry and neat official version of events. This book offers the most explicit description as to what actually occurred — It is a "must read" for those interested in Canada's involvement in Korea.

MGEN B VERNON (Ret'd) CD

Too many acts of valour go unrecognized in the aftermath of battle and never make the history books. Hub Gray rights one such glaring oversight with his well researched revelations regarding the heroic leadership of Lieut Mike Levy at 2 PPCL's Battle at Kapyong, April 1951.

MGEN LEWIS MACKENZIE (Ret'd) OStJ, OOnt, MSC, CD

More than half a century after the battle the author, Hub Gray, has performed a significant service to his regiment, to Canada and to future military historians. Through painstaking research of the actions of 2PPCLI at the Battle of Kapyong he has corrected the record where corrections were needed. This very personal rendering of Canada's pivotal contribution to one of the most important segments of the Korean War brings the reader to the battlefield and it is a great read.

MGENN CW HEWSON (Ret'd) MSM,

Congratulations on a first-hand provocative and interesting account of one of the more famous and important battles in our Regimental history — Your extensive research and interviews with the veterans who were there adds credence to the details contained in the book — Well done and good luck with what obviously has been a great deal of work.

LGEN R CRABBE (Ret'd) CMM. MSC, CD

FOREWORD

In comparison to other wars of the past century, the Korean conflict produced relatively few written accounts, including few dealing with Canada's contribution to it. Non-Canadian historians have given scant coverage to this nation's military role in Korea, and some Canadian accounts contain inaccuracies resulting from their limited research. That is particularly so in the case of the Kapyong battle, in which the Second Battalion of Princess Patricia's Canadian Light Infantry distinguished itself and brought acclaim to Canada. *In Beyond the Danger Close*, Hub Gray, who fought as a Lieutenant at Kapyong, sets out to correct those inaccuracies. After years of meticulous research, and with confirmation and contributions from many of the Patricias who fought there, he has written an account that is detailed, convincing, informative and highly readable.

2 PPCLI was formed in 1950 as Canada's initial contribution to the UN action in Korea and it comprised World War Two veterans as well as newly recruited subalterns and soldiers. Its Commanding Officer, Lieutenant-Colonel Jim Stone, a much decorated veteran of the Italian and North West Europe campaigns, refused initial entreaties by senior American commanders in Korea to commit the unit to battle before he put his soldiers through a punishing but vital two-month battle-hardening program. Hub Gray describes this prelude to the Kapyong action with colourful reminiscences, both his own and those of his comrades.

The importance of the Kapyong battle derives from the strategy of the Chinese Spring Offensive of April 1951, which sought to clear the way south to Seoul as a prelude to defeating the army of the Republic of Korea and driving the UN forces from the peninsula. Overwhelming superior numbers of Chinese and North Korean soldiers, brave to the point of fanaticism, were poised to destroy the troops of General Ridgeway's Eighth Army in a series of major assaults across three sectors. Gray describes the early Chinese successes, including the routing of the 6th ROK Division and the courageous but eventually unsuccessful defence by the Gloucesters on the Imjin River, all as a prelude to the Second Patricias' defence of their sector at Kapyong.

The account of the battle evokes the atmosphere of apprehension that existed as the Patricias dug in on the high ground over the Kapyong valley, while thousands of demoralized ROK soldiers retreated through them, fleeing the advancing Chinese Divisions. The complications of laying out individual platoon and company defensive positions, and the gallows humour of soldiers who know they are facing a defining and deadly experience, are brought alive by the wealth of individual accounts and curt asides. It is these intimate and baldly stated recollections that give the book its immediacy and relevance. Soldiers who have been in similar situations will nod knowingly.

The outcome of the Kapyong battle was hugely significant as it forced a pause in the Chinese Spring offensive which, while continuing for another month, was brought to an end in late May 1951 after the loss of more than one hundred and thirty thousand Chinese and North Korean soldiers. In assessing just how important the battle was, it is difficult to imagine what the result would have been if the Patricias and their Commonwealth and American allies had not held firm at Kapyong. That they did so is testimony to their professionalism, skill, bravery and endurance, attributes that are the ingredients of so many military victories.

While the action at Kapyong is the focus of Gray's attention, he also provides intriguing accounts of other aspects of the Patricias' experience in Korea. Thus we hear of the eerie and still unresolved description of fifty-six Chinese soldiers, discovered by the Patricias deployed in a classic defensive pose, and all dead of no visible cause. We follow the experience of the Patricia officer assigned to fly with the American Mosquito pilots, whose task was to control air strikes against the enemy and to avoid "friendly fire" casualties. We hear hilarious accounts of forays to gather supplies of liquor to stock the Company mess and the experience of the soldier given a summary trial by the Commanding Officer for stealing what the CO believed was a unit vehicle, but which turned out to be one bought by the soldier from the Americans for a bottle of gin.

Beyond the Danger Close is a book about soldiers in battle, written by one who was there. It makes bold assertions and blunt comments, which is one of its virtues. Not all will agree with some of Gray's claims. He rightly comments on the paucity of decorations awarded to the officers and men of the unit after such a pivotal battle, and he names those that he and his comrades feel were particularly deserving of recognition. In doing so, and in describing so vividly their exploits, he puts his case to the reader who, he notes *"will come to his or her own conclusions"*

In writing *Beyond the Danger Close*, and in producing this compelling account of how Canadian soldiers fought a crucial battle on the other side of the world more than half a century ago, Hub Gray has made an important addition to the written history of the Korean War and the role 2 PPCLI played in it. Former and serving Patricias will welcome the book and it will enrich the Canadian public's understanding of what its soldiers achieved in one of the more important, but less celebrated, wars in our history.

General John de Chastelain OC, CMM, CD, CH
Colonel of the Regiment
Princess Patricia's Canadian Light Infantry
March 2003

TABLE OF CONTENTS

APPENDICES

ACKNOWLEDGEMENTS

I am deeply indebted to all of the veterans who made valued contributions to this publication. Without their enthusiastic co-operation this work would not have seen the light of day. I contacted and re-contacted some of the contributors over and over, and their patience was amazing. These many individuals are acknowledged at the end of this book. There were also those who assisted me in my research, encouraged me endlessly, and provided much needed guidance.

Major General CW Hewson, CMM CD (Ret'd) - A good friend, a tireless supporter. Former Colonel of the Regiment, counsel, valued contacts.
LCol Don Ardelian CD (Ret'd) who made many contributions carefully editing military correctness, significant observations. 3 PPCLI, Korea.
Major Rod Middleton CD (Ret'd), and Capt Charles Petrie CD (Ret'd) providing thoughtful comments, reading rewrites. Both 2 PPCLI, Korea.
LCol Brian Munro CD (Ret'd) - Tracing many individuals. 2PPCLI, Korea.
LCol Bud MacLeod CD (Ret'd), searching American military internet records. 2PPCLI, Korea.
Professor Steve Brodsky CD, D. Phil, (Ret'd Major), a great guiding hand. 3 PPCLI, Korea.
LCol Jeffery Williams CD (Ret'd) Military Historian. Helpful observations. 1PPCLI, Korea.
Dr. David Bercuson, PhD, FRCS, LLB, Professor, Department of Strategic Studies, University of Calgary; provided valued observations, and lent me a selection of his personal files.
The Staff - PPCLI Archives, Museum of the Regiments, Calgary, AB; Lynn Bulloch, Curator, Warrant Officer Dan Hitchcock, and Corporal Regan MacLeod.

I wish to thank General Sir Anthony Farrar-Hockley, author of "The British Part in the Korean War". I met him in London and he gave me permission to reproduce from Volume II, selected phrases from the directives of General P'eng The-haui, CIC Communist Forces, for his Spring Offensive, Korea 1951.

Mr. Ian Kelly, Marketing and Public Affairs, Australian War memorial, for permission to reproduce selected text and maps, as noted, from the book, "Australia in the Korean War".

Mr. Ian McGibbon, author of, "New Zealand in the Korean War", for a number of discussions.

I am extremely grateful to Grania Litwin, of Victoria BC, a longstanding feature writer of the Times-Colonist. She has twice come to Calgary and dedicated many hours turning raw phrases into well-turned passages. Grania, I could not have done it without you!

I must credit my partner of 50 plus years, my wife. Poor Pam, I have thought of myself as being dedicated to this project, I believe my wife viewed it as my endless obsession. We entered into many a passionate discussion. Pam endured the silly arguments of this overloaded, and at times a frustrated and stubborn, amateur research-writer. I cannot believe the hours that I dedicated being selfishly shackled to my computer and losing all track of time. Six years of it. Thanks for all of your understanding Pam, Love.

MAPS

PROLOGUE

Grossly inaccurate, that is how I would describe many of the articles and books reporting upon the actions of D Company, Second Battalion Princess Patricia's Canadian Light Infantry, at the Battle of Kapyong, Korea, which took place April 23/25, 1951. Erroneous accounts have been repeated and "enhanced" during the intervening 50 years since this battle was fought, and it is a situation that is deeply disturbing to veteran Patricias of 2PPCLI, which is the only Canadian Army unit to be awarded the United States Army Presidential Unit Citation, for valour at the Battle of Kapyong.

The most damning historical error is contained in the official history of Patricia's Regiment, Volume III, 1957, which includes reports that the Chinese overran 10 Platoon during the battle. Nothing could be further from the truth. Members of this platoon fought a well-conceived defensive battle in which they <u>surrendered not one inch of ground</u>. Another glaring error that has been repeated in many accounts is that Captain JGW (Wally) Mills originated the extraordinary order for the artillery fire to descend upon 10 Platoon. This was not the case either, but more of this later.

Having participated at Kapyong, I was also disturbed that the exceptional actions of Lieutenant Michael G. Levy, commanding 10 Platoon, were never recognized. In 1996 I contacted Government House, in Ottawa, which is Canada's ultimate awards authority, to explore the possibility of his receiving an award despite the passage of so many years. I was advised that retroactive awards are forbidden. This injustice became a further incentive for me to research and record, particularly since Canada does sanction retroactive awards for Canadians by foreign governments. (See Appendix "J", page 275). Hopefully this book will allow Canadians an opportunity to judge for themselves the actions of a true Canadian hero.

Another critical reason I decided to write this history is that many international books and articles recording the Commonwealth contributions, touch only briefly upon the Patricias' participation at Kapyong, while expanding upon the British, Australian, New Zealand and Indian participation. Even Canada's own official history of Korea, "Strange Battleground," included few interviews with original sources and battle survivors. Having been written in 1966 it was based on somewhat restricted research since many official Canadian government documents were not released until decades after the war. By contrast, the very wide-ranging British, American, Australian and New Zealand official histories - each of 1,200 to 2,000 pages, were all written years later, between 1985 - 1996, after exhaustive research of much later released official records and abundant interviews of veterans. Small wonder, that our own official histories fall far short.

In writing this book I also wanted to explore and rebut some of the comments made by Commonwealth allies regarding our presence in Korea, where our Canadian commitment mushroomed from seven per cent of the British contingent to a fully operational Infantry Brigade comprising about a third of the Commonwealth ground troops. Overnight we became a considerable force of arms, and perhaps we appeared to be more competitive. I will deal with this more thoroughly in the ensuing chapters.

During the Battle at Kapyong, I was a lieutenant and second in command of the Patricias' Mortar Platoon, and on April 26, immediately after the battle, I took command of 12 Platoon, D Company. After the battle while memories were still smoldering I spoke with many pivotal members of D Company - including Lieutenant Michael Levy, who commanded 10 Platoon; Lieutenant John Pearson, of 11 Platoon; Sergeant Bernard Holligan, who was Acting Platoon Commander of 12 Platoon - and this is how I became aware of their gallant defensive battle the night of April 24/5. This is also how I learned about the decisive actions and heroism of Levy, which deserved special recognition that never came. Why didn't I or anyone else speak up about this injustice at the time? During the Korean conflict the Government of Canada was expanding the army from an authorized 20,000 to over 60,000 and was granting officer applicants five-year and 20-year commissions. I was over the moon to be granted a long-term commission, and was not about to advise my commanding officer that he had overlooked an award to Michael Levy. Yet it remained a sore point throughout the rest of my service with the Second Patricias, and the injustice has continued to plague me and many other veterans. I assumed that with time the truth would be revealed but not one "historical" writer sought out Levy, Pearson or Holligan. Quite the contrary - with the passage of time it appeared that many authors in their desire to add greater colour, simply compounded the situation by perpetuating or adding to the inaccuracies.

These are the reasons why I determined to explore and report upon the inspiring actions of the Second Battalion, Princess Patricia's Canadian Light Infantry, at the Battle of Kapyong. In excess of six years has been dedicated to research and rewriting numerous drafts, which began with finding and interviewing survivors of Kapyong in my attempt to be as accurate as possible. Unfortunately a number of the key participants had passed on before I commenced my research: Captain JGW Mills, MC, Acting Officer Commanding of D Company; Company Sergeant Major Eddie Morris, and Sergeant Bernard W Holligan, GM, Acting Commander of 12 Platoon to name a few. It is regrettable that they are gone since their contributions would have been of inestimable value, but I have endeavoured to represent their actions to the best of my ability, consistent with the reports of the survivors I have interviewed. As I have located only one survivor who served in what I define as 12 Platoon east, I cannot report fully on the action at that location and I will not create an "assumed" report of Holligan's actions.

For those of us who fought in Korea, it was definitely our war, at times intense and at other times bloody boring. Our motivation was to defeat our enemy: to ensure that 2PPCLI was the best darn unit we could be. We were all volunteers. To say we were intent upon defeating communism only presents how we got there, it does not explain why we fought as we did. We fought because we were proud of our Regiment, proud to display the historic and widely recognized red and white PPCLI shoulder flash, one of many sacred Canadian military traditions subsequently obliterated by incompetent Liberal policies. We also fought to preserve our lives and the lives of our comrades. Under the esteemed leadership of Lieutenant-Colonel (LCol) JR Stone, a highly decorated soldier in World War II, we were resolute in our desire to carry on the finest fighting traditions of our proud Regiment, and we really wanted to be better than any other unit serving in the UN Forces, such a goal no doubt being applicable to virtually every proud fighting regiment.

In composing this book I have, from time to time, requested individuals (veterans and non-participants both military and civilian) to read the text, and to provide objective criticism. There are those who strongly believe I should strive for a sanitized version that avoids the factoring of deficiencies or mistakes. "Managed information" appears attractive to some current militarists, but not this writer. Once every two years the Patricias Regiment holds a three-day indoctrination for new officers, known as the Ric-a-Dam-Doo, named after the Regimental Colour originally designed and hand made by Lady Patricia in 1914, our Regiment's Colonel-in Chief. Rod Middleton, a Lieutenant in Korea, at one time cited mistakes made at Hill 532 on the 7th of March 1951. It was a difficult battle in which Patricia casualties were 7 killed and 28 wounded, all but one from D Company. [1] Finally he was informed that he should not deliver that lecture again as it was "demoralizing" for the new entrants. In July of 2001, at Kapyong Barracks in Winnipeg, I had a similar experience after presenting 2nd Battalion with a painting I had commissioned depicting Levy's defence at Kapyong. I was subsequently berated by the commanding officer for stating during my speech that Mills had abdicated control of the battle to his platoon commanders (a situation explored at length in this book). I take issue with this abhorrence to constructive criticism. How else do soldiers become equipped for the future, if not by revealing and discussing battle errors? How else do you truly recognize those who excelled under fire, if not by citing all the elements they had to contend with? This is carrying political correctness to an extreme, and if it prevails then God help our soldiers! To excise our failures and to focus only on our successes is to deny veterans, historians and readers the foundation of some very pertinent decisions. Every human being from time to time exhibits failings, obsessions, obstinate viewpoints that impact their thoughts and actions and rightly or wrongly, after six years of digging, I have concluded that all of the actions amassed from my research and relevant to Kapyong must, and will be revealed.

There were three leading figures at the battle of Kapyong: LCol James R Stone, Captain JG Wally Mills and Lieutenant Michael G Levy. Stone proved himself to be a complex individual, self contained, aloof, intelligent, decidedly imperious, intrepid in battle, and on occasion, unforgiving. With failing health in later years Stone became reclusive. Mills was also a distant and unapproachable man. He could never tolerate his authority being questioned, nor did he appear able to communicate freely with those under his command. He sadly under performed at Kapyong, at the same time I believe he was the victim of circumstance. Mills WWII fighting experience consisted of one day, as a Coporal at Dieppe, 1942. **Promoted to Captain in the field, he had not commanded men in combat, and was not instructed on the duties of a company commander in battle.** Levy, is a quiet and unassuming individual with a core of steel. Raised in the English community of Shanghai, China, from one year of age, he was a Japanese prisoner of war until he escaped at age 18, in 1944, to join the British Army. Although he too could be difficult to read and detached at times, he rose to great heights at Kapyong, and revealed himself to be an astute observer and a determined, skilful leader. In this history, I have endeavoured at all times to provide a balanced view of these three veteran Patricias.

I served with 2PPCLI, at Currie Barracks, Calgary, until the 14th of May 1953, when I resigned my Canadian Army Active Force Commission to enter into civilian life. In 1996 I began conducting interviews and compiling information for this book, astounded that in half a century those who had written so called "definitive" analyses of the Patricias' action at Kapyong had failed to seek out any of the key participants. Below is a list of the individuals who were central to D Company's defence, and who were available for decades.

John Pearson, an articulate individual, was medically discharged in August of 1951, and later attended law school and practised law in Winnipeg, Montreal, and Vancouver. He has never been consulted until now.

Michael Levy, quiet mannered but highly observant, retired from the

Army with the rank of Major in 1974, was then employed in Ottawa for a year, subsequently worked in Vancouver, and is now retired in Richmond BC. He has never previously been consulted, until now.

Bernard Holligan continued service with the Canadian Army. On the 14th of February 1958, he risked his life rescuing a Patricia paratrooper who became entangled on the outside exit of a C119 aircraft, and was awarded the George Medal by HM the Queen, at Ottawa in 1959. Holligan passed away shortly after retiring as a Master Warrant Officer, on the 21st of January 1972. [2]

Wally Mills contributed to the Patricias 1957 Regimental History; however, the budget was restricted, and the author who remained in Montreal, had little personal contact. Mills retired from the Army in January 1969 with the rank of Major. He joined the Edmonton School Board as a business manager from 1970 through 1984. He passed away on the 1st of February 1995.

I have assembled 24-signed statements: some are one page, others are eight to ten pages, and one is much longer. Over the years I have extensively discussed the events at Kapyong with in excess of 70 veterans of that battle. The veterans quoted in this book are scattered across Canada; they are listed at the end of book, Appendix "K" page 283. Statements contained in the text detailing Mills' decisions at D Company are not my opinions. They are derived from signed statements of veterans of the battle. Those reading my account of Kapyong will draw their own conclusions.

Redefining a long accepted historical event, such as the Battle at Kapyong will no doubt offend some, but I have undertaken my research with an earnest desire for the truth, and have reported the facts exactly as those who participated there revealed them to me. Both strengths and weaknesses hitherto unrevealed are exposed and I offer no apologies. I have endeavoured to communicate with Jim Stone on a number of occasions, and forwarded an early draft of my work inviting his participation. He has read my manuscript but has consistently denied me an audience. Thus the quotations attributed to Stone, are taken from his speeches; audio tape recordings; quoted publications and personal letters addressed to me, to Dr. David Bercuson and from Lance Corporal HR Crocker, who operated the Battalion's #19 wireless set, at 2PPCLI Tactical Headquarters, on the 27 Brigade Communications Net.

Over the years, as I talked with an expanding list of veterans, it became evident that I was accumulating a wealth of information about the Battle of Kapyong, that had never before seen the light of day. Captain

Steve Newman, then Regimental Adjutant responsible for publishing the PPCLI Association Newsletter, urged me to expand my research and write a book. This urging combined with the declining likelihood of having the Government of Canada retroactively recognize Levy's actions, and Major General Bill Hewson's strong support helped tip the scales. The ultimate deciding factor came in the form of boundless encouragement offered to me by veterans who wanted the story of Levy's heroic achievements to be revealed at last. I had no idea how much work would be required, both qualitatively and quantitatively, and I certainly never anticipated the seemingly endless searching and checking required to ensure as much accuracy as possible after almost 50 years. The hunt for veterans was a formidable and time-consuming task, as were the audio and video tapings, writing and editing that have consumed more than six years of my life - and my wife's

In conclusion this report is essentially the product of the Patricias veterans who dedicated their time to assist me. Without their valued guidance these details could never have come to light. My sincere wish is that this book will gain for Michael Levy, the men of D Company, as well as the Second Battalion Princess Patricia's Canadian Light Infantry veterans, the recognition they deserve for their gallant defence at the Battle of Kapyong.

The devastation in Seoul (photo: Hub Gray)

Chapter ONE

INTRODUCTION TO A WAR ZONE

The Patricias were committed to battle on the 17th of February 1951; temperatures were below freezing during the day and much colder at night. The second day the battalion came across some 65 slain American troops at Chuam-ni. Averse to mounting the hilltops and digging in they chose to stake their bedding down in several warm village structures in a valley setting. It appears they also neglected to set out sentries. They were later slaughtered by Chinese troops who had silently observed their movements from their hilltops. (The commander of the US unit involved did not report this slaughter of his troops to his superiors. It was later revealed in an article written by Bill Boss, a Canadian War Correspondent, who fortunately had the photographs to prove the validity of his article). Upon this revelation our commanding officer, LCol. James R. Stone, withdrew all sleeping bags and ordered that only one blanket be carried by each soldier, for additional warmth in slit trenches during cold winter nights. We also learned in short order that the parkas we had been issued were not wholly suited for fighting conditions, as their hoods were not removable. To solve that problem Stone ordered that the hoods be strapped down, so that they would not muffle the noise of the approaching enemy. In time Stone ceased the delivery of hot meals to the front line troops and American canned "C" rations became the order of the day. Due to the mountainous terrain and the lack of serviceable roads, (A Echelon was up to 10 miles behind the front lines) hot meals could not be brought forward. Stone demanded the highest form of vigilance at all times and set the conditions to ensure we adhered to his orders. It was a chilling start to our yearlong tour of duty.

I had been with the Patricias for about a month when I stumbled upon a sight that has haunted me ever since. The horrific scene floods back even now as I recall the event that I will relate. It occurred when we were out of the fighting line and happily looking forward to our first bath at a British Mobile Laundry and Bath Unit (MLBU). My anticipation was high, for the troops had lived, fought and slept in the same clothing for weeks and we were about to enjoy our first change into clean clothing. My platoon and I undressed in one tent, handed in our clothing and proceeded outside where we walked down a meandering

25-meter long portable boardwalk to the shower tent. I was last. The temperature was below freezing and the walkway was caked in ice, from the water that had dripped off the naked bodies of the returning bathers. I moved slowly, cautiously watching my footing and stepping carefully. I entered a tent with my head down and when I looked up I stood paralysed by what I saw. This was not the assigned tent! Before me was a US Army Graves Registration facility. It was the longest damn tent I have ever seen and before me was the horror of legions of horribly torn and mangled bodies, grotesquely stacked six to eight corpses high in cordwood fashion, over five rows.

In the past I had always felt a strong emotion when I viewed the masses of war graves of the Canadian soldiers who had fallen in Europe, during the First and Second World Wars. Looking down the rows it was as though all those thousands of mutilated bodies had simultaneously risen from their graves in the most macabre manner, to pierce the very depths of my soul. And now I was suddenly staring at masses of frozen, decaying and putrefying forms, my body shuddered in repulsion and I stood transfixed, fascinated and horrified. Lifeless yet hypnotic eyes stared at me conveying a frightful message: "Welcome, join with us Hub Gray. You're next to entering the frightful harvest of Korea!" The sheer magnitude of violent death before me was overwhelming. I damn near fainted, but then, summoning up strength in my weakened knees, I fled! For some time I was tormented and obsessed by the insanity of that grizzly scene and wondered if it was a preview of my own date with destiny. The reality of being in a war zone slammed into my being. Oh God, how could men commit such atrocities upon one another? I escaped that stifling tent of death and retraced my steps to the shelter of the merciful showers where I attempted to wash away the thought that my mortality was nothing more than a passing fancy. As I shuddered in the hot shower I silently wondered how I could have ended up in this morbid and demoralizing place. The reality of being involved in a foreign war, in a Godforsaken country called Korea began to sink in.

When Canada authorized the raising of the Special Force, I was 22 years old, working and living at home in Victoria, B.C. A couple of years previously I had been selected as an officer candidate while serving in a reserve army unit, The Canadian Scottish Regiment (Princess Mary's). In September of 1949, along with 26 others candidates, I enrolled in a six-month Command Contingent Course at the Royal Canadian School of Infantry, Camp Borden, Ontario. This was the first of a series of Canadian Officers Training Corps (COTC) Method D, qualifying courses, for officer candidates recruited from the reserves.

INTRODUCTION TO A WAR ZONE

A number of the 2PPCLI junior officers had been commissioned via Method D, either by attending The School of Infantry, Camp Borden, or by taking courses at their home regiment. As time went on we were to become close associates and friends. Included were Hugh Cleveland Killed in Action (KIA), Rod Middleton, Brian Munro, Charles Petrie, Angus Read, Bob Whittaker, and others. A number came through the university COTC, including Jerry Botting, Mert Entwhistle, Doug Hamilton KIA, Lee Hill, Joe Levinson KIA, Bud MacLeod, John Pearson, and George Skelly. Still others had gained their commission during WWII. In late 1943 six senior NCOs enrolled in the same Officer Cadet Training Unit (OCTU) course at Brockville, Ontario. After the war they left the service and were scattered across Canada. Amazingly they signed on to be reunited at 2nd Patricias, among them: Rick Constant, Johnny Deegan, Murray Edwards, Lorne Hurst, "Red" MacLean, Wally Mills, Jack Regan, and Harold Ross.

I first set eyes on LCol "Big" Jim Stone during Exercise Sweetbriar, a combined exercise involving 1st Battalion PPCLI and 10,000 American troops in the Yukon. It was the winter of 1949-50, and at that time I had no idea this aloof man was destined to become our commanding officer in Korea. He stood tall, walked very erect and displayed rows of ribbons. I think we had a couple of brief one-sided conversations over the many months that our exercise continued, and whenever he spoke I always listened intently for Stone demanded attention, was imperious and brusque. Needless to say Big Jim was not the least bit inclined to dedicate his energies to instructing green kids, especially those fresh out of The School of Infantry. But I was fascinated by him and often observed his moods and demeanour. It seemed to me that he showed a distinct lack of interest whenever forced to listen to the opinions of others, even if majors and colonels supplied points of view. Perhaps his look of disdain reflected the fact he was quietly assessing their worth and filing away his conclusions. I asked a few older officers about Stone and was told he possessed a sterling reputation, and was a "soldier's soldier," brave beyond words in battle. He certainly seemed to have the respect of the many generals, and politicians who came to the exercise. I also learned that Stone was a call out, like me, and that was the only thing we shared in common.

When the call for volunteers came for the Korean conflict the recruiting depots overflowed with long lines of recruits so I chose to offer my services in a more leisurely way, via a letter to Pacific Command in Vancouver. About 6 weeks later I was directed to report for a medical in Vancouver. The Patricias were stationed at Camp Wainwright,

Alberta, and had been training for some weeks. Due to my late arrival the officer complement of the Second Battalion was complete and I, along with a number of other subalterns, was declared supernumerary. Once again my session with Stone lasted about 30 seconds. We soon transferred to Fort Lewis, Washington State, where I was posted to the newly formed Third Battalion, under LCol Corbould. I liked this man because he displayed a warm and encouraging, fatherly attitude to his young subalterns. But once again all the positions had been filled and so I became an unofficial second in command of the Anti-Tank Platoon, commanded by Lieutenant Bill Sterling. On February 4, while out in the field on exercise "Ignus Bellam", commonly referred to by the troops as Ignorant Bedlam, I was ordered into the first draft of reinforcements to be sent to Kure, Japan; the Second Battalion was to be committed to battle February 17. I was overjoyed. I could not understand the reservations that more experienced officers had to my boundless enthusiasm. I even thought they might secretly be jealous of my being posted overseas ahead of them. Such was my youthful optimism and I revelled in the news that now I was to be among the first, not last, to be sent overseas. We departed on February 12, 1951.

Our draft consisted of 20 other ranks and five lieutenants: Brian Munro, Red MacLean, Charles Petrie and me. Mike Levy, who was enjoying a staff appointment at Fort Lewis, arranged to be the first off and departed a day ahead of us.

Levy possessed a unique background which qualified him to excel in Korea, and of which modern legends are made. In 1926, when Mike was one year old, his father, who was a geologist employed in the oil industry was transferred to Shanghai, where Mike remained until he was 18. Growing up in China, Mike became comfortably conversant in the Shanghai dialect and could easily recognize the many nuances of day-to-day experiences among the Chinese people. The Japanese interned him and his family in 1942, and he became a prisoner of war at Pootung, an all-male camp. In 1943 he was transferred to the mixed camp of Lunghwa, (depicted in the movie "Empire of the Sun") but he along with four others managed to escape from there in 1944. Over the next two and a half gruelling months, aided by guerrillas, 18-year-old Levy and the others made their way though occupied China. Moving through free China they reached Kunming, where the US Army Air Force flew Mike over "The Hump" to India. (The *PBS Adventure Series aired a documentary in the early 1990s called "Across the Jade Divide." The one-hour video retraced the footsteps of their escape route, interviewing many of those who aided and sheltered them*).

*1944 - **Huchow, Occupied China** - Reg Uhlich, Mike Levy (18 yrs.), Tom Huxley, Chinese soldier, Roy Scott, L. Murray. (photo: M. Levy).*

Shortly afterwards, Levy joined the British Army and was assigned to the Yorkshire Light Infantry at Redfoot, Old Delhi. After recruit training he was posted to Poona where he received a specialized education at The Far Eastern Warfare School. Here he learned jungle craft and industrial sabotage, including how to blow up railway lines, bridges and ammunition dumps. He was also instructed in hand-to-hand combat and told how to quickly, and silently, kill a man with a knife. Commissioned a 2nd Lieutenant and qualified as a parachutist, he was assigned to British Special Operations Executive Force (SOE) 136. He parachuted behind Japanese lines in Malaya in 1945, leading a band of guerrillas, and was promoted in the field to captain at age 20. Levy was awarded a "Mentioned in Dispatches" (MiD), for his bravery in fighting the enemy. After the war the British Army was engaged in fighting the guerrilla movement and this is how Levy was described in part of a personnel report dated December 3, 1945: *"Captain Mike Levy: A young chap with previous experience of Guerrillas in a recent escape from internment in China. Full of guts and really at his happiest when Japs or puppets were reported in the vicinity. Deserves full praise for his handling of the ugly situation at Salak South (reported fully in my operational report) when he led his Gurellas with flying colours."*
Appendix "B" page 225.

SOE FORCE 136 - Parachuted into Malaya. Kuala Lumpur, November 1945
Back row: Unknown, B. Lee, E. Lowe, H. Ho, W. Lee,
Front row: T. Wong, Ntl. Chinese officer, Cpt. M. Levy, H. Fung. (photo: M. Levy).

Among Levy's many extraordinary qualities, which stem perhaps from his exposure to Oriental culture from a young age, is his uncanny ability to silently and unobtrusively observe many details, assess them, and then arrive at thorough conclusions. This trait was unnerving some-times, to those around him but Levy's language ability, powers of observation and coolness in battle served the Patricias well in Korea.

Other intrepid members of the draft included Brian Munro, who gradu-ated on the second Command Contingent Course at Camp Borden. He was and still is, one hell of a great character and renowned raconteur, full of fun and passion. In his younger days he led many a girl on a merry chase, but Munro was cool under fire, and quickly gained the respect of his troops. Red McLean, one of the older in our group was comfortably overweight, a veteran of WW II, and formerly a policeman in Brockville. This generous and happy soul loved to display an article from the Brockville newspaper describing how he single-handedly captured a criminal. Charles Petrie was and is a unique character, who served in the infantry overseas during 1945-6 and whose father was Stone's commanding officer at one time in WW II. He walks with a distinct bounce, and was frequently seen sucking upon a pipe. Petrie was better read than anyone except Stone, and his mannerisms revealed a strong English influence. Initially he was thought of as a bit of an 'egg-head,' but he soon proved himself calmly effective in battle and a very good friend. Our very proper Charles gained a degree of notoriety when he accidentally shot a burning Very Light flare into the buttocks of a soldier, while celebrating the 17th of March, Lady Patricia's birthday, in Korea.

Another officer who figures prominently during the Battle at Kapyong was Captain Wally Mills, who was Acting Officer Commanding D Company, and had served as a clerk radio operator during the Dieppe raid. My assessment of Mills was garnered from the experiences related to me by soldiers of D Company who served under him during the battle, and subsequently when serving under his command in Korea. Prior to Korea, Mills was engaged in full time Army Call Outs in Winnipeg. A man of medium stature, he was prone to issue definitive directives and any questioning of them was unwelcomed.

Lieutenant John Pearson, 11 Platoon, remembers a heated exchange that occurred when one of his men, whom he particularly respected, was killed in battle. Pearson advised Mills that he would be writing the man's father and it became an intense and one-sided discussion until Mills finally decreed, "I order you not to write his family!" No explanation. Pearson never sought permission again. In all my time Mills only once visited my own platoon position and that was when Brigadier Rockingham toured our position at the front. Neither Levy nor Pearson can recollect Mills ever inspecting their entrenchments either; our orders were to see Mills at his own headquarters. Prior to commanding D Company, Mills served as battalion transport officer. Thus he had no battle experience in Korea before he took over the company when Major Bob Swinton, MC, went on leave in Japan. Mills was formerly stationed at B Echelon, along with other second-in-commands who were waiting to replace the company commander, if he needed to fulfill another assignment or became a casualty.

Those who stayed in the army and served with him in Canada and overseas in Germany, noted that he always went by the book, and was occasionally overzealous in his interpretations. Mills retired with the rank of Major,1968.

Canadian Army Call Outs supplemented the meager manpower resources of our minuscule army in the years after the Second World

War. Levy, Mills, myself and a number of the officers in the newly recruited Patricias had been employed for many months and in some cases for years on a Call Out basis. At Western Command Headquarters, Edmonton, Captain Andy Mills, Wally's older brother, managed the files of Call Outs. Andy, a dashingly handsome and extremely personable officer, was always approachable and well liked by everyone. During Exercise Sweetbriar, in the Yukon/Alaska 1949-50, a combined exercise employing the Patricias 1st Battalion alongside 10,000 American troops, reservists were required to supplement administrative aspects. Only one officer was called out in the rank of LCol - JR Stone. In the fall of 1950, the 2nd Patricias were poised to move from Wainwright to Fort Lewis, Washington State. Captain Andy Mills came to Wainwright to bid us farewell, for he was well known to so many. Standing at the bar in the Officers Mess, Mills put a hand on Stone's shoulder - an extremely rare occurrence that appeared to indicate an enduring friendship. As well as shaking hands with many of the officers and wishing them well, Andy turned to Stone saying something to the effect of, "Good luck in all that you undertake Colonel, and by the way, take care of my little brother," [1] - a reference to Lieutenant Wally Mills. Due to casualties, many officers received what is termed "Field Promotion," during the fighting in Korea. Wally Mills was the first officer promoted in the field in Korea, to the rank of Captain. Every 2nd Battalion officer promoted in Korea was demoted to his original rank upon returning to Canada - with one exception - Captain Wally Mills, MC. It was rumoured that Gordon Churchill, Mills' MP, was a factor in the confirmation of his Captaincy. Whether Stone played a part or not, has never been revealed.

Our reinforcement draft took off from McCord Field, in an American Air Force Military Air Transport Service (MATS) aircraft, a DC 4, on the 12th of February 1951. The first stop was Anchorage, Alaska. The pilot announced that passengers would deplane to eat and rest in the airport facilities. This brought about a rude awakening; US Immigration officials denied us entry, being foreigners, and we would not be allowed on hallowed American soil. The next destination was Shemya Island, one of the smallest of the last Islands in the Aleutian chain. From here one could make out Attu Island, which was occupied by the Japanese during World War II. The pilot executed an amazing landing in a frightful fog. The military employed Ground Control Approach, allowing the men in the control tower to control the landing procedure of our aircraft. This is standard procedure at all major airports today, but at the time it was not.

Stepping out of the door was a sobering experience. To our left was a high cliff, and the wing of the aircraft could not have been more than 5 meters from it. Low fog hid the top of the aircraft's tail and to the right of the plane was a sharp cliff descending at least 100 meters to the roaring and freezing Pacific Ocean. The right wing of the plane partially overhung the outer edge of the cliff! We felt blessed that the pilot was so skilled and the resident troops were only too happy to advise us that we were among the fortunate, for they had lost the odd plane over the cliff. On a clear day one could see four Bell P39 Air Cobra fighter aircraft beneath the water under the cliff. Shemya enjoyed the reputation of having a girl hiding behind every tree on the island, and you guessed it, it was completely barren. The wind off the Bering Sea could be fierce, the fogs encompassing, thus many of the facilities were built below ground. Needless to say the personnel stationed there, while enjoying hardship pay, could hardly wait to get out.

Having been well received by our hosts we took off the next morning for Tokyo, but did not make it that day. Little more than half way to our destination the far right engine of the aircraft packed it in, the propeller flew off, and pieces of engine descended for parts unknown. Minor abrasions developed in the wing skin. We sat nervously in bucket seats that ran the length of the plane, on either side of containers packed with urgently required military cargo, stacked ceiling high in the centre. Also on board was a middle-aged American war correspondent. We had tried to engage the man in conversation but having only received grunts and groans in return, we shrugged and gave up. As small pieces of damaged wing flapped violently around outside the plane, a sergeant appeared from the flight deck to inform us that while the captain was in full control and did not anticipate further problems; he wanted us to be informed of ditching procedures. At that point the previously unsociable war correspondent stood and produced some identification from his wallet. Displaying his ID, he addressed the sergeant in a firm and resounding voice: "Sergeant, I am a Brigadier General in the United States Air Force Reserve, and I am taking control of this aircraft." The sergeant came to attention, saluted and said, "Yes Sir." Our newfound General continued, "My first order to you sergeant is, stop frightening these young boys with your ditching procedure. We will now go to the flight deck." We gasped and looked at each other in disbelief, having thought the idea of learning how to evacuate a damaged aircraft in the freezing Pacific Ocean was most appropriate at that juncture - particularly as we were advised that our cargo included land mines. We sat there feeling like victims of the "senior officer's" indiscrete order. We heard about him for the last time two weeks later when reading Stars and Stripes, the US Army military paper. The ill-starred general was on an aircraft carrier's flight deck during a typhoon when he was suddenly washed overboard. His body was not recovered.

The plane made an emergency landing in northern Japan, at Matsu-shimia, a former Japanese naval air-training base during the war, now manned by a skeleton crew. There was a snow blizzard in Tokyo, and in no time at all five more aircraft had landed on the strip and deposited almost 300 personnel. The Officers Club was functioning, the well equipped bar was open for business, and the Japanese steward had posted the evening's fare on the notice board: *Sir Lion Steaks*. We transients were accommodated in former married quarters and an officious American officer, recently returned from Korea, advised us to be quiet in our shared accommodation. He slept with a loaded .45 under his pillow and told us he would shoot if anyone made any noise. Welcome to a war zone! Rollie LaPointe, one of the soldiers of our draft, learned another quick lesson that night.

He related many years later how pleased he was at the personal attention he received in exchange for a mere bar of soap.

We duly arrived in Tokyo. During the ride to our Australian administered quarters, we wondered what could be the source of a continuing scraping noise. It turned out to be the movement of the raised wooden clogs scraping along the sidewalks on the feet of the colourfully kimono draped women. The grim sight of Japanese ex-servicemen who were missing limbs, wearing threadbare uniforms and begging on the streets also struck us. Many of them were huddled in small groups. It was a pitiful sight and emotionally ominous to a group of young soldiers about to embark upon their own war.

In a couple of days we boarded an overnight train for Kure, and because the Japanese are of a shorter stature the berth posed a problem for me. Being considerably over six feet tall, I had to place my head and one shoulder in the aisle propped up on my kit bag. It was an uncomfortable night. Breakfast consisted of an ice-cold porridge of some kind without enough milk to cover it. At one stop the stationmaster exhibited a wry sense of humour when he serenaded us with a Japanese version of, "East is East and West is West, and the Wrong One I Have Chose." We all had a good laugh.

The headquarters of Australian British Commonwealth Occupation Forces, (BCOF) was in Kure, about 325 km south of Tokyo. We were stationed in a Royal Australian Army Service Corps depot. Later the 25th Canadian Reinforcement Group (25CRG) established independent facilities at the nearby town of Hiro. We joked that the Aussies served four kinds of meat at their table - lamb, ram, mutton and sheep - although we actually found the food very good.

It was a cold February and the base had an open and unheated swimming pool. The Aussies frequently asked how cold it might be in Canada at this time of year and though it was fairly cool in Kure we informed them we thought it was relatively warm, compared to Canada. To underline our point, on one cold morning we marched the troops to the pool informing them that anyone who would swim and stay in for five minutes could have a pass to go into town for the day. But they would also have to announce how amazingly warm the water was. In two minutes all the soldiers had stripped and dived into the freezing water, twenty Canadians immersed themselves loudly making the required comments, while we officers observed! The Aussies were astounded.

The shops in Kure displayed some very attractive prices for cameras, film and a variety of items. At each shop there would be one or more friendly Australian soldiers. We enquired of the Aussies if the prices were valid or if we should negotiate. The answer indicated the price was right. We came to realize that virtually every business in the town, from shops to taxis, was owned by the occupying Australian troops.

Kure was a fascinating place. Long before World War II, in 1930 or earlier, the Japanese sealed off the entire area. Any unauthorized person who entered was shot or detained until the termination of the war. There were steel mills, foundries, rolling mills, fabricating shops, tool and die machine shops, and munitions works. There was an extensive shipyard, which built destroyers, cruisers, aircraft carriers and the mammoth Yamammoto, the largest battleship in the Japanese navy. Local facilities included manufacturing and tooling of all manner of weapons for the ships, from small weapons to torpedoes as well as the massive 16-inch naval guns, and there was a huge dry dock. On a nearby Island was the Japanese naval training school for officers, an exact replica of the British Naval College, at Dartmouth. This area was so secure that it remained totally unknown to the allies and most of the Japanese until 1945 when it was accidentally discovered. An aeroplane was on a mission to photograph Hiroshima about 20 km away, prior to the atom bomb being dropped, and because their prime target was clouded over they shot other photographs in the vicinity. The allies were astounded at what they discovered and began bombing Kure intensely. A few years after the war there was a cave-in revealing miles of tunnels that contained masses of photographic equipment and other supplies. The enterprising Japanese salted all of it away out of sight of the Americans, to be reclaimed later for use in a reconstructed Japanese Navy.

At the end of February our draft prepared to join the battalion. We travelled by train to Sasebo, the American port of embarkation for Korea, and an extensive American Naval Base. One of our troops created a ruckus with the Port Authority. The troop ship we boarded held about 2,000 soldiers. Some were former casualties returning to their units, a few were deserters shackled and escorted by armed MPs, while others like ourselves were new to Korea. Adhered to a dock shed some 20 feet up, was a large yellow sign, informing all: *Through this Port pass The Best Damn Fighting Troops in the World!"* This was obviously intended for the dominating masses of American Troops but one of our men somehow cornered a can of paint, a brush, a ladder and slapped on an overlaying message - "PPCLI" in appropriate red paint. The US Movement Control Officer, a Major in the US Army, was furious. This short and cocky character stormed up the gangplank, charged at us, and demanded we arrest the culprit, and turn him over to the Port Authority. No one owned up. We officers never found out who had committed this heinous crime, and after the disgruntled major had departed we all had a good laugh, as did the US soldiers and others on the ship.

I was the only person in our group to have had experience at sea, though it was limited to the passenger ships sailing the Inland Passage between Victoria and Vancouver. As the "experienced" sailor I informed our troops that our voyage, about 125 Km to Pusan, would be a piece of cake. Unfortunately I was the only one to get sick. This was a Japanese transport built some years earlier and the convenience consisted of a rectangular basin with the top situated at ground level. Immediately forward was a strategically located bar also at ground level. For someone over six feet tall it required careful manoeuvring to attain the proper position, especially as the plumbing system had failed and the basin was overflowing. The smell was enough to nauseate a normal person. Over the remaining voyage I had the misfortune of making about five visits to the facilities and was determined never to relax my dubious grip on that important restraining bar.

We approached the harbour at Pusan at noon and soon realized that the land was cultivated with human waste. The stench wafted out in great noxious clouds: Welcome to Korea. The longshoremen who awaited our docking all appeared to be extremely youthful, even though they were in their 40s or 50s. The unwrinkled and composed character of their faces astounded us, but the war had begun to change many things.

Leaving the ship our troop train introduced us to another aspect of a country ravaged by war. The car was full of bullet holes, the coach was barren but for bench seating running the length of the car on either side. On one side at the end there was a toilet with two walls, no door, a simple seat and an open hole in the floor. Two windows were covered in plywood, one had a pane of glass, and the remainder running the length of the car were open to the air. A run-in with the commander of the troop train ensued when a US Military Policeman (MP) Corporal came to try and confiscate our rifles and pistols for the duration of the journey. Having examined the exterior damage to our car we enquired if we might encounter guerrillas who might fire on the train, "Oh, yes, but we have armed guards aboard with machine guns who will take care of them." Since they were at the head of the train and we were at the rear we decided not to give up our weapons. A little while later along came the Commander of the train who informed us we would surrender our weapons or be placed under arrest. That was definitive. We could either fight or surrender, we chose the latter.

The train commander took the time to explain there were far too many SIWs (Self Inflicted Wounds) by soldiers being transported to the front. This was news to us. We had never heard of such cowardice, but soon learned even the Patricias were not immune to such wounds when soldiers emerged for a rest from front line battles. For some, anything was preferable to going back to fight the Chinese. Twice the train was fired upon during our northward journey, particularly at Taegu, but no one in our coach was hit.

As we were about to depart the station in Pusan, two American MPs escorting a shackled prisoner boarded our car. A deserter from his unit, he was being returned for court-martial. At the station stop in Suwon the prisoner asked to use the lavatory. They uncuffed his hands, and one MP stood outside glancing at the window so he would not escape. But the MP must have looked away for a moment, because the prisoner bought a bottle of booze from one of the many Koreans peddling a variety of goods. He eventually emerged totally pissed. Within ten minutes this coloured soldier began to groan in pain on the floor, then scream and yell, thrashing about wildly, and then he went silent except for his slowly fluttering eyes. The nervous system of his body was paralysed and in fifteen minutes he suffocated to death. The MP said, "Ah well, we just lost another one, time to head back to base and report in." The hooch likely contained such unsavoury ingredients as melted down boot polish, human or animal urine, brake fluid, wood alcohol squeezed from canned heat cotton batten, as well as a great variety of additional delicacies to stretch out the contents. Oh God, we thought. Welcome to the reality of war and human failure. We experienced similar deaths in the Patricias. Later, while serving on a Board of Inquiry during March of 1951, concerning a drinking incident, I questioned a soldier named MacKenzie who had survived a bout of wild drinking while three of his alcoholic buddies suffocated from muscle paralysis. MacKenzie was about 6' 3" and a huge strong man, but with a limited education. He explained that he hadn't died because he had not drunk as much as the others. His cocktail had consisted of canned grapefruit juice, brake fluid (which he purchased from one of the transport types) hopefully Scotch, and the inevitable canned heat (which contained cotton batten soaked in alcohol to heat tinned food) as well as anything else he could scrounge. With a straight face he said that he was conservative in his habit, for he only drank a steel helmet full for breakfast every morning!

Our journey lasted two days and at the end of it we were met by British Army transport trucks that delivered us to the 27th British Commonwealth Infantry Brigade, in which our battalion served. We made a stop and were introduced to the British habit of ceasing all activity to brew tea, at the Han River. Later we retraced our steps for some time as our convoy, in error, crossed the Han at the wrong point. As we neared the front we came across 30 to 40 blackened and grotesquely twisted bodies of the enemy scattered about, their rotting bodies being feasted upon by swarms of flies and rodents. They had been Napalmed. The sight of their horribly mutilated and shrunken bodies was nauseating. I questioned how I would react, and for the first time I wondered, could I actually kill a man? I silently prayed that I would not be a coward.

We arrived late at night at what is known as B Echelon, 20 miles or so behind the front line, containing battalion administration. After being given a sandwich and tea and renewing friendships we five bedded down in a tent and were soon fast asleep. We were wakened at about 0530 hours, to the loudest bloody thunderclap I have ever experienced. It was as if the world had come to an end. In a total panic we all tore out of our sleeping bags and dashed outside in about one second flat. None of us realized we could collectively move so fast. Nothing was visible, but the banging went on and on at a lower noise level. An entire Division was involved in an attack and all the artillery guns fired their opening salvo in unison. To top things off that day the cook preparing breakfast had an accident and his tent burst into flames. One more arresting initiation for a bunch of green Canadian kids.

We were transported to A Echelon and awaited our appearance before the Colonel in the Officers Mess. One day a small fire occurred which left a few small holes over a two inch area. It added to the lore of the place since it soon became the tactic to inform new reinforcements to duck past that area as Chinese snipers had been firing upon the mess but moments earlier. As new boys we all ducked when passing the noted area, and one could detect a silent chuckle descending upon those "others" attending the mess.

Whenever a soldier became "lost" in Korea, it was prudent to check out the nearest funeral. (When a Korean husband died the family would go into mourning for three years, if a son two years, a daughter one year, and a wife six months. The husband would then take another wife. Very practical people these Koreans.) The Koreans were buried sitting up and the mourners would gather at a pre-dug grave, and then proceed to fill in the four or five foot deep hole and build a mound above and around the body. The higher and more expansive the mound, the greater their stature had been in life. Each mourner would place one shovel full of earth into the grave, then jump in and stamp it down, pay homage to the deceased and then emerge from the grave. This process was repeated over and over until the grave was filled and the mound erected. There was one additional and extremely significant procedure, which intrigued our troops. Each time one emerged from the grave one took a swig of booze provided by the deceased's family. Obviously this was genuine liquor. And so our Canadian soldiers, exhibiting unending empathy for the bereaved, joined every available funeral they could. In keeping with local tradition they were actually welcomed as the more mourners the more significant the honouring of the deceased.

During the Second World War, the Japanese employed Koreans as jailors to guard the prisoners of war. They were cruel in the extreme. Perhaps this could be partially explained when we understand the rules of an inter-village sport. The contestants, facing each other and separated by appropriate distance, were drawn up in front of defined lines. Losers were individuals who retreated behind the line; the winning team was the one having the greater number still standing forward of their line. All had a good time, for it was thought of as a test of manhood. On a signal they proceeded to launch volleys of rocks at the opposing team. We were certainly learning about the rudiments of rural

Korean life.

The people of Korea suffered terribly, and I unnecessarily added to that suffering for one family. It has long bothered me, but at the time I had no feeling for what I had done. It was March 16, and we were mercifully out of the line. In one day it would be the birthday of the Colonel-in-Chief of our Regiment, Lady Patricia Ramsay. For the PPCLI it would be a time of celebration, and there was going to be a Brigade sports day. Stone designated me to take a truck and scrounge up wood for a big bonfire, and I was ordered not to come back without the necessary ingredients.

Korea was a country devoid of trees in may areas, and larger ones were so valued that telephone poles were constructed out of cement. We travelled for some time when we came across a dilapidated and bombed out house. These dwellings are not constructed like Canadian homes; typically they consisted of one storey with a thatched roof, and two rooms at most. A long and large log, usually highly varnished and much prized formed the centre beam upon which all else depended. The mud and dung floor was unique for within it, it held an ancient and highly efficient radiant heating system. The floor had a series of hollow bamboo logs encased in it. At one end was a charcoal fire with a system of distribution allowing the heat to circulate evenly throughout the bamboo channels.

We began loading the remaining timbers onto our truck, including the large centre beam, which would become the centrepiece of our bonfire. After a few minutes along came a Korean man with his family, evidently the owner of this former dwelling. By gesturing he indicated he wanted us to leave the wood, I imagined so that he might reconstruct his home. In time he was pleading but I did not respond to his emotional despair. Eventually the man's expression was pleadingly sad, and he looked as if he were in immense pain. I have never been able to erase the scene from my memory and many times in the elapsed years, I have silently asked for his forgiveness. We were at war, in a foreign land and, by our standards it was a terribly backward country. We existed in holes in the ground 80 to 90% of the time, sharing our "accommodation" with rats, mice, lizards and lice. We watched our buddies come down with unknown devastating diseases and being killed in battle. We were intent upon killing our enemy before the bastards killed us and frequently we wondered why the hell we came to this Godforsaken country! On this day, we were gathering wood so that our buddies might relax, consume a beer and have an enjoyable time sitting by the glow of a fire. Surely for all that we were sacrificing in this strange and hostile environment we were entitled to have a celebration bonfire? One's emotions became tuned to the rudiments of existence as they were indelibly forced upon us, ensnared in the killing grounds of the Korean War.

Lieut. Murray Edwards, Capt. Del Harrison—2 PPCLI - Korea 1951.

Chapter TWO

THE COMMONWEALTH
CONTINGENT, KOREA

The Korean conflict was nothing like the actions in the Hochwald Forest of North West Europe, or akin to the intense close combat at Ortona, Italy during WWII. Every war is different, each establishing its own conflict of arms and in 1951 the Chinese infantry, heavily armed with automatic weapons, attacked en masse on a limited front hoping to conquer their enemy through suicidal thrusts. They successfully placed demands upon their troops that western nations would have found repugnant, employing a doctrine that was based upon the experiences of Mao Tse-tung in fighting the Japanese and Nationalist China. China had not developed a fully modern and diversely equipped fighting force during the Korea war, although after Korea they developed a well disciplined and a broadly equipped military. They learned their lessons in Korea.

Unlike WWII the cities of Korea did not offer the spectrum of amenities for rest and relaxation which allied troops experienced in war torn Europe. Korea was essentially a rural economy at the time, and its cities and infrastructure had been fought over so many times that they were almost totally flattened. Once a year a soldier was granted five days rest and recuperation in Japan, and the rest of the time we had to make the best of what little there was available in Korea. Conditions were repetitious, and thus we existed one on top of another both in and out of the line.

The British 27th Brigade arrived in Korea in August 1950; The 3rd Battalion Royal Australian Regiment (3RAR), formerly occupation troops in Japan, arrived in late September; the 16th Field Regiment, Royal New Zealand Artillery (16 RNZA) arrived December 15 and were committed to battle on the 25th of January, 1951. The Second Patricias arrived December 16th and went into battle, February 17, 1951. In late May our 25th Canadian Brigade took to the field. The Australians had one battalion in Korea, and much later two; New Zealand had one artillery regiment; the Indians provided a first class field ambulance, all integrated within the British Brigades. 2PPCLI fought along side the Australians, New Zealanders, British and the Indians, in both the 27th and 28th British Commonwealth Infantry Brigades. I believe we got along well. I found the New Zealanders to be warm, friendly and very supportive. The Australians were proud, slightly rough around the edges but excellent soldiers. The British, as usual, were steadfast and at all times unflappable. Fortunately I did not have occasion to require the services of the Indian Parachute Field Ambulance; however, they had the reputation of having the lowest loss of casualties of all front line medical services in Korea.

Captain RKG Porter, Adjutant of the 16th RNZA, has expressed contradictory opinions concerning the performance of Canadian troops in Korea. In Ian McGibbon's official history of New Zealand in the Korean War, Vol. II, Porter is quoted as saying the Canadians: "field performance was not greatly admired;" and that Canadians were, "unpredictable in their behaviour, sloppy in fieldwork and generally arrogant."[1] During May of 1951 the Canadian presence expanded rapidly from about 800 troops to more than 6,000. We went from one under-strength infantry battalion to the reinforced 25th Canadian Infantry Brigade; three Infantry Battalions and supporting arms and services including an Armoured Squadron, an Artillery Regiment, engineers and so on. Canada's Provost Corps (Military Police) administered the Commonwealth Field Punishment Camp (Military Prison) in Korea, and it was designed to administer harsh punishment, as are all military prisons.

But this comment of Porter's seems particularly crass, especially in light of his own behaviour. Lieut Murray Edwards, was given a terribly rude reception during a brief meeting with Porter in January. It was after the Korean National Police reported that enemy guerrillas were active in the area around Miryang, and encamped on the top of a mountain. The Police lead B Company to the base of the mountain and identified three pathways up. One platoon was assigned to each pathway, under the commands of Lieuts Murray Edwards, Bud MacLeod and Harold Ross. Ross's patrol ran into the enemy, killing two of them, the remainder got away. One of Edwards' men came across a pathway in the snow revealing a trail of blood, at the end of which they found a wallet belonging to a New Zealand Warrant Officer (WO). His driver was dead having been stripped, beaten, and bayoneted through the throat. The WO wasn't so lucky. The Chinese secured his arms to his body, but left his legs unhindered. In an act of barbaric savagery they viciously cut off one hand at the wrist and the poor man began loosing blood in rhythm with his heartbeat. He headed through the woods to seek help at a nearby village, but it was deserted. The cunning barbarians had planned it well, he soon became light headed and bled to death. Having retrieved the wallet Edwards went to the 16th HQ, full of compassion for the man and the entire regiment. He entered Porter's office, saluted, identified himself, and announced that he was returning the deceased man's wallet. Porter, did not bother to lift his head, return the salute or even pause to look up at Edwards, he simply grunted, "Put it there," [2] indicating a table, Edwards, mortified, turned on his heel and departed. Based on this interview it would appear Porter's investigative techniques for assessing our participation in Korea were severely lacking.

British Colonel (retired) Michael Hickey, who served as a 2nd Lieutenant with the Royal Army Service Corps in Korea, wrote an impressive book, "The Korean War," [3] detailing the Commonwealth experience. The book is well researched, containing great historical detail and many personal interviews, which make his work both comprehensive and historically interesting. However, it too is thin on the Canadian contribution, which amounts to about three pages out of 397. Hickey acknowledges the 2 PPCLI, stand at Kapyong in one paragraph. [4] There is no mention of other impressive Canadian military successes, such as the R22eR 84-hour defence of Hill 355, November 1951 or the RCR's four-day battle commencing October 23rd 1952. Once again, the author leaves his readers with the impression that Canada's Korean effort was somehow lacking, especially when seen in stark contrast to the extensive coverage he gives to the experiences of all other Commonwealth members. He gratuitously chooses to repeat Porter's "not fitting in" jab and then editorializes that we are "…being far more American than we (Canadians) realize." [5] I don't know what he expected of us, but we **Canadians are neither English nor American**! If one is to dedicate the time to explore our character one would find that **we are uniquely Canadian!**

In subsequent correspondence Michael informed me that while he did offshore research in both New Zealand and Australia, he did not have a budget to conduct research in Canada. I wish he had noted this unavoidable exclusion in his book. In his letter to me, of October 28, 1999, he heaped praise upon Canadian soldiers and their performance in Korea.

The English author, Max Hastings, in a much earlier book on Korea, stated it was a pity the 2PPCLI did not have greater casualties at Kapyong, for then they would have received the recognition they deserved.

A typical landscape of Korea.

1. McGibbon, page 158
2. Interview with Edwards, Victoria 1999.
3. Hickey, "The Korean War." John Murray Publisher, 1999.
4. Hickey, page 218
5. Hickey, page 283

Chapter THREE

BAPTISM UNDER FIRE
- HILL 532

It has been said that Stone's belief in his own opinions was such that, having arrived at a decision, he had a reputation for being impervious to change! Is it possible the action at D Company on Hill 532, subsequently influenced Stone's decision on recommending honours or awards in recognition of D Company's defence at Kapyong?

March 7th 1951, 2PPCLI participate in a 27th Brigade attack: Patricias objective is Hill 532, to their right 3RAR are to take Hill 410. The battalion at the conclusion of the day suffered 7 killed [1] and 28 wounded, all but one were from D Company. Almost one quarter of the company are casualties. Captain Gordon Turnbull, acting company commander, reported to Stone, that Levy under performed during the attack. [2] Such a report would represent the very antithesis of the expectation for officers serving under James Riley Stone. Is it possible Turnbull's report left Stone with a lingering concern about Levy's fighting abilities? Had Levy become Turnbull's pawn in an attempt to camouflage his own ineptness? Stone, after Hill 532 removed Turnbull from a combat command to become adjutant, the administrative officer of the battalion. Was Stone's assessment of Levy's actions at odds with Turnbull's assessment; Levy retained command of 10 Platoon. The recollection of the high rate of casualties at 532 would be ingrained in Stone's memory.

March 4th The 27th British Commonwealth Infantry Brigade occupies a salient extending into the enemy's position for nearly 8,000 meters. The 7th Calvary Regimental Combat Team (Brigade) is 5,000 meters away and well south of the battalion. The Patricias' companies are stationed in the hills but their position is relatively static. They are waiting for the 6th ROK Division on the right, to advance to straighten out the line. 2PPCLI War Diary: "Men are being rotated out of the front line for hot meals and a change of clothing. The wind-proof pants are not standing up to the wear and tear of the terrain; there will have to be a new issue if the men are to keep warm. There is only one case of frozen feet in the battalion. The American socks are too thin and the troops are having a great deal of trouble with trench foot." [3]

A Brigade Orders Group on the 6th of March defines the coming operation. Captain RK Swinton, adjutant, makes a reconnaissance (recce) of the forward access road. Company commander's recce the ground they are to assault from the forward positions held by the Argyll and Sutherland Highlanders.

On the 7th, the troops rise at 0300hrs; they descend from their dug in positions on the hills. The luxury of hot water for shaving as well as a hot breakfast is a great morale booster. The paymaster is present, allowing the men to make pay assignments in case of their death. The two padres hold small services. The administrative and spiritual preparations leave everyone a little tense; it is a certain fact that some amongst the Patricias will not live to see tomorrow; others will carry wounds for the rest of their lives.

The battalion is to advance across a broad valley floor to ascend Hill 532. From the War Diary: "At 0500 hrs Stone and his Advance Tactical HQ moved forward in jeeps to the pass at Hill 419. Advancing from the start line: D Company, Advance Tactical HQ, B, A, C, companies, Mortars, and finally Tactical Main, commanded by Major Gordon Henderson, Battle Adjutant. The Machine Gun platoon, under Captain Andy Foulds, had gone ahead earlier, and the 81 mm mortars and the 4.2" mortars (US Army) were to base plates at 0600. The attack was delayed due to road conditions until 0700." [3]

Lieut Middleton: "The radio man from the 4.2" mortars serving with the American Forward Fire Officer attached to our company, commented Korea was a hell of place to celebrate his 19th birthday, we all joined in a chorus of 'Happy Birthday.' Our spontaneous Canadian salutation touched the radioman. The soldiers each took two bandoliers of .303 ammunition, two fragmentation grenades, extra ammunition for all the Bren light machine guns, while I took 64 rounds for my 9mm pistol. I also carry red, white and green flares for the Very Pistol. I too choose to carry a rifle; it is not a time to be seen as an officer by the enemy. Magazines are loaded and the grenades charged. We form up on the road in single file, one section at a time. At the start line the pioneers cleared the mines, other booby traps and barbed wire entanglements. We cross the start line right on time, 0700 hrs." [4]

Levy's 10 Platoon leads the battalion; the ground in the valley is covered by a couple of inches of snow. The troops enter a deserted village unopposed. Two sections of 10 Platoon move from bound to bound, with the third section covering them. They emerge from the village moving along a track, a section on each side of the road when a burst of machine gun fire from the left cuts down two soldier of 10 Platoon. Levy's platoon goes to ground and returns fire. Middleton moves through the village and also comes under fire. Levy is engaged in a firefight for 15 or 20 minutes, then gathers his men and moves forward once again. The valley is very broad and open; the enemy occupies the high ground atop Hill 532. Levy: "I move my platoon to the right as there appears to be better foliage for coverage from the enemy." [8] Middleton, evacuates Levy's casualties from in front of the village and then continues his advance moving over the frozen rice paddies to the base of the hill. He presses upward assuming that 10 platoon is ahead of him. Behind Middleton are Company HQ and thereafter 11 Platoon. The ascent is through scrub trees. It becomes apparent the Chinese are not on the lower slopes and so a cautious approach is abandoned, they advance for another three hours. Still there is no sign of Levy's platoon. Middleton advises Turnbull, who orders him to keep moving. As D company moves out of the scrub into a clearing all hell broke loose, machine gun fire comes from both flanks and the men go to ground. Although the Patricias are under fire the enemy remains invisible. A Chinese soldier jumps out of his hole to run up the hill, Middleton's men pick him off; he falls and rolls downward. "It is a soldier's lot; kill or be killed! The enemy begins to mortar us, I order the men to dig in. Off to my left I see the US 4.2" mortar radioman advancing up the hill alone in the open; unaware of the enemy we try to warn him. In a flash, a Chinese soldier popped up from his hole and with his burp gun cuts him to shreds. Our communications with the 4.2" mortars to provide supporting fire is finished, the American mortar controller volunteer to join us as infantrymen. A few minutes later Levy and his platoon emerged on our right flank." [4]

Levy: "We are dog tired, the foot slogging over four hours has been arduous." [8] Levy made an error ascending a saddle between Hill 532 and the 3RAR objective, Hill 410. They have been ascending, descending and once more ascending through the snow for four hours plus, and are visibly exhausted. Turnbull, noticeably tense, immediately calls his Orders Group; directing 10 and 11 platoons to lead the advance, Middleton's 12 platoon to the rear to provide supporting fire, to advance through the lead platoons once on the objective. Middleton intervenes, "Sir, Levy and his men are obviously exhausted, my men are fresh, let me take 12 platoon to advance on the right flank and 10 to the reserve position." [4] Turnbull orders the attack to proceed as directed. Once again the bogyman of personality and authority is thrust forth, ruling out common sense; the company commander will not be seen to tolerate "interference" on the part of a junior officer. Levy observes that Turnbull was nervous, Middleton commented that at times he appeared to be shaking. Turnbull: "These are my orders and this is the way it is going to be." [4] Having studied the ground to the objective for some time Middleton once again speaks up, "Both Levy and Sergeant Holligan (commanding 11 Platoon) require more time to check out the lay of the land prior to their advance." [4] Turnbull refuses, the attack will proceed immediately. Planned air support is off, due to bad weather. The tanks in the valley cannot provide supporting fire as their 90mm guns will not elevate sufficiently. Tank dozers are called up; they grade the land so the tanks gain sufficient elevation to engage hilltop targets. They use both high explosives and armour piercing ammunition to blow large chunks off the Chinese bunkers.

By 0920hrs, D Company suffers three casualties; artillery support is called for in support of another company thrusting forward at 1107 hrs. As the attack goes on the Chinese open up with Heavy Machine guns. The enemy is well dug in; additional artillery and mortar support is called for. At 1330 D Company report a further 7 casualties; one killed six wounded. By 1410 hrs, A Company is encountering stiffening resistance, accurate heavy automatic weapon fire brought to bear from hills 443 and 532. [3]

At 1400 hrs, D Company commences their final attack, and takes the first ridge, but the enemy hold a further ridge 100 meters on. The going is tough, the snow is up to six inches deep, the ascent is very steep and the ground under the snow is wet and slippery. "The Chinese are throwing grenades at our forward elements and we are under quite a bit of fire." [4] The grenades thrown by the Chinese at this time are stun grenades, releasing highly concussive explosions, which can severely disorient an individual. Levy: "I came across six or seven men, wounded or killed, lying fairly close together. I stopped to pick up a rifle. I was holding it in front of my chest, checking the ammunition in the magazine. Either a bullet or a grenade fragment hit the rifle slamming it into my chest with a terrific force, and knocking me out. I evidently careened down the hill for some distance." [10] When Levy went down and disappeared Corporal Roy Rushton took command of 10 Platoon ordering the men to go to ground because of increasing casualties. Many of the men of 12 Platoon appear to fall in with Rushton's order. Private Henry, seeing Levy was in trouble went to his aid. Henry, the oldest man of the platoon was an interesting character. During WWII, he served as a Flight Lieutenant, navigator, RCAF Bomber Command. During a flight over Germany the pilot was killed and the co-pilot badly wounded. Henry took the controls and with instructions from the co-pilot successfully guided the plane back to England, barely making it over the Dover cliffs to a safe landing. He was awarded the Distinguished Flying Cross. It was unusual to see a private infantry soldier displaying the DFC.

Rushton: "As I neared the top of the first incline a chap comes towards me, he is wounded and falls down, he gets up but falls again, his eyes are glassy and there he dies. Captain Turnbull is standing at the bottom of the incline with Company Sergeant-Major (CSM) Larson MC. This is suicidal to keep going; we do not have enough men, covering fire or smoke. Turnbull yelling at me from some distance below, asks how does it look? I tell him it is useless to proceed without more men. CSM Larson jumped up and ordered the men to follow him, there was a limited response, privates Barton and Pearson did; Barton was wounded and Pearson was killed advancing through the Chinese trench. Captain Turnbull remained in his position well down the hill." [6]

A Canadian Press article by Bill Boss, quotes Larson … "It was impossible to estimate the enemy wounded or killed, you don't stop to talk or look." The article continues, "The Patricias were fighting against interlocking enemy automatic fire and literally torrents of grenades" Said CSM Swede Larson, "Grenades, the Chinese favourite weapon, they must have had a million of them." Middleton confirms that at this time the Chinese primarily used Stun Grenades.

Middleton: "Larson, along with Lance Corporal Roy Putnam and Private Elgin Brown, came forward with a supply of grenades, which are distributed amongst two of my sections. I reach the front trench connecting with the other enemy bunkers on the crest. Larson threw a grenade, but is hit in the shoulder by a bullet in the midst of his launch; Sergeant Holligan is 15 feet away and miraculously catches the missile to send it on its way, and is wounded by shrapnel. Sergeant McGhee of my platoon is wounded. I continued my advance against the enemy, and come across Private Wylie twice-wounded in the chest, I dress his wound and apply morphine, he dies on the hill. Farther along in the trench I kill one enemy. I turn to call for supporting fire from my platoon, but I find myself alone." Middleton in his youthful enthusiasm and desire to set an example to his men made the mistake of leading from the front; the support he sought is nonexistent. Soldiers who have gone to ground when under intense fire in battle know how difficult it can be to have them rise again, to charge into the face of their enemy. "The clouds are low and the light is fast fading. Where the hell is the rest of the company? I examine the top of the hill through my binoculars, and witness the most astounding sight, one I shall never forget. Chinese soldiers, about 400 marching as though on a parade square, in line abreast across the top of the ridge, pulling out, led by one proudly flying the red banner high above his head, only a rearguard remains. We have been severely outnumbered."

Rushton: "I don't know where he came from but late in the battle Company Quartermaster Sergeant Renwick, of Support Company, appeared at Turnbull's HQ, and he looked extremely relieved to have Renwick join with him." [5]

Middleton: "Movement 50 meters to my left reveals another Patricia, carrying a Bren light machine gun, he has about 8 to 10 rounds in his magazine. We began to leapfrog down the hill, taking turns firing at our unseen enemy. Rejoining the company we are informed the attack had been called off at 1600hrs, it is now 1630hrs. Soldiers look at me in amazement, they thought we had been killed; it is most satisfying to be resurrected from the "dead." My souvenir from all of this was an exploding grenade cutting my face and knocking apart a tooth, and I am evacuated to the Indian Field Ambulance and then to an American MASH unit. I was shocked for just outside the door is a huge pile of amputated arms and legs. Thank God I was not that badly injured." [4]
Larson: "There are bloody bayonets in Dog Company tonight." [7]

Levy: "Two soldiers come to my aid, picking me up off the ground. In my disoriented state I don't know who they are. I rolled down hill to the left of company HQ. The battle is over and the company is pulling out."

It was deemed impossible by Turnbull to recover the bodies of the men killed in the final attack. The stretcher-bearers worked until midnight evacuating the wounded men of D company. Hill 532 is taken on March 8th, by B Company and later joined by A Company; only two Chinese oppose them; 25 Chinese dead are found in the blood stained snow in the trenches and another 22 bodies on the ridge. Who knows how many dead or wounded they carried off. D Company's dead are recovered the next day, the Chinese as usual had stripped their bodies; they are devoid of boots, socks, winter clothing, weapons and ammunition. Corporal John Bishop, A Company, "A numbing sight greeted us when we arrived atop 532. The Chinese had captured the position from the Americans a few days before, and they'd left the corpses of the GI's strewn about like animal carcasses." [5] Rushton remembers; "Stone addressed us the next day giving a pep talk, which we needed because of the men we lost, in part he said, " When you are dealing out death, you have to expect death in return." [6]

Captain Bob Swinton, Military Cross WWII, is promoted to Major, to command D Company. On his first inspection he made a short speech to the troops and told them they were good men, but advised they would have to improve a great deal to satisfy him. [3]

With the advantage of insight 50 years on, the action on Hill 532 appears to have served as a "learning curve" for 2nd Patricia's in Korea, a baptism under fire.

Consider Stone's assessment of the action at D Company: Turnbull is removed from a combat command; the aggressive actions of Middleton and Larson stand out. Turnbull appears to have tried to direct his company from the rear, rather than in the midst of his fighting formation, or at the very least having a view of their battle to formulate his assessment. He delegates his evaluation to Rushton. Larson, an experienced soldier sensing an opportunity acted boldly, defying Rushton's judgment and Turnbull's inaction, ordering the company forward to reinforce Middleton. To this day Rushton believes his order to go to ground was correct. Middleton did successfully advance into the enemy's trenches against light opposition - had his platoon been advancing alongside of him, they may have taken the objective, for the main body of the Chinese were seen to be pulling out. But who knows? Levy is of the view that the attack was a cock-up right from the start. The frontal attacks up a steep hill provided the enemy with a commanding view of the Patricias' movements. For years rumours abound at veteran's gatherings that it was a folly to make the frontal attack that a flanking attack would have provided better cover. At Hill 532 D Company suffered the highest numbers of casualties of all their engagements in Korea. Turnbull's advising Stone that Levy under performed during the attack - a scapegoat? Shuler, a Med A, states that Levy was disoriented, and evacuated him. The next morning Levy met with Stone and asked to be returned to command 10 Platoon, Stone complied. Did Turbull's negative report create lingering doubt concerning Stone's assessment of Levy?

21 nd. May 1951—Lieut. M. Levy 10 Platoon.
Winter uniforms, +85 ^{O}, ascending 4,000 ft. mountain.

1. The War Diary lists 6 killed 28 wounded. The 2PPCLI Roll of Honour of those killed in Korea, lists 7 on the 7th of March 1951:

NAME	AGE	PLATOON	COMPANY
Letkeman	24	11	D
Morford	20		B
Oliver	21	10	D
Pearson	19	10	D
Spence	19	10	D
Warren	21	10	D
Wylie	20	10	D

2. Mel Canfield: A Pte, clerk, in the Intelligence Section at Kapyong, is stationed in the midst of Stone's Tactical Headquarters, taking notes of wireless communications to be written up in the Radio Logs of the battalion. He quotes Turnbull's comment made to Stone at a meeting, concerning Levy's performance, after the battle. A notarized statement is in the author's possession.
3. 2PPCLI War Diary.
4. Middleton: personal notes.
5. Bishop: "The Kings's Bishop," Mossy Knoll Enterprises, by John Bishop with GW Stephen Brodsky. 2000.
6. Rushton: Emails and phone calls with the author, March and April 2002. Also an audio interview tape concerning 532, conducted November 22,1999, PPCLI Archives.
7. Canadian Press article, by Bill Boss, War Correspondent, Korea, March 1951, authors files.
8   Phone conversation with Levy.

Chapter FOUR

HISTORICAL KOREA
THE CHINESE SPRING OFFENSIVE
OF APRIL 1951

Korea has long been known as *The Land of the Morning Calm*, but on the morning 25 of June 1950 it erupted in chaos. The North and South Korean armies had been dug in for eighteen months with troops facing each other across their mutual border. Both parties initiated frequent invasive military clashes. At 4 a.m. on that Saturday the Northern armies, suddenly launched an attack with 10 divisions supported by in excess of 1,634 artillery pieces, tanks and aircraft. [1]

Why were the two Koreas suddenly on the brink of war? It is a story that has it roots in the latter part of the 19[th]Century when Japan, China and Russia all laid various claims to the country. Details of all these political skirmishes are far beyond the scope of this book, but it is important to look at the historical context if one is to understand what took place over half a century ago: 1950 to 1953.

Korea was primarily an agricultural nation, which like Japan, desired to maintain its isolation from the rest of the world. A country of extremes, it was a deep freeze in the winter and blisteringly hot in the summer. The area of the peninsula is 222,154 km, the Republic of South Korea is 99,392 km with a population in the order of 50 million, 1999.

In 1876, Japan made a token military incursion into Korea, and then in 1894 it landed an army to strengthen its hold. Japan became a world power in 1904 upon defeating the Russian Fleet, off Pusan, at the battle of Tsushima. A year later Japan declared Korea a Japanese protectorate. Dissent peaked in 1908, followed by mass executions. Japan imposed military rule and Japanese became the official language. This was to last for 35 years.

Towards the end of WWII, the Americans realized that they would incur horrific casualties upon invading Japan. The US invited the Soviet Union to align themselves against the Japanese. Russia rose to the challenge, and under the Potsdam Agreement, declared war on Japan. With the release of the atom bomb, however, Japan collapsed and the Russians moved into the northern territory of Korea, the Americans below the 38 Parallel.

There were many factions vying for power in Korea. General John R Hodge, commanding the occupation force turned to Dr. Syngman Rhee. Born in 1875 Rhee had been imprisoned for political activities in the early 1900s. He subsequently moved to the USA, where he studied at Harvard and Princeton, and remained until 1945, and thus was free of the stigma of associating with the Japanese. About the same time Kim Il Sung, who had fought with Mao's communist forces in China, was installed as head of the government of North Korea by the Soviet Union.

In December of 1945, the United States and Soviets signed an international trusteeship at the end of which the two Koreas would be unified. Reaction in the south was negative. The US renounced its prior policy and in December of 1946 a provisional South Korean Council was established.

Rhee became a ruthless leader, and those who opposed his regime suffered terribly. In 1948 the Soviets negated the UN authority. Thus South Korea held free elections and Rhee became its first president on July 24, 1948. Being parachuted in by the Americans, Rhee had little understanding of the current power factions or the desires of the Korean people. Rhee's police force, a cruel and merciless regime trained by the Japanese, once more reigned as the "enfant terrible."

While supporting Rhee the Americans did not want to give free reign to his ambitions. In the years that followed the Soviet Union created a powerful and well-equipped military machine in the north, while the Americans refused to supply the south with armour, anti-tank weapons and artillery greater than the short-range 105mm howitzers. [2] Not only was the army of the south ill equipped to fight a war, it was corrupt and morale was sadly lacking. Before long the fighting that ensued would reveal all of the inherent weaknesses of the southern forces. While there were creditable fighting units in the ROK army, many units bugged-out over the course of the war when heavily attacked or surprised by intense enemy thrusts. [3]

Border skirmishes between the north and south became commonplace, and the North's invasion was at first viewed as another of these border raids. The United States became seriously alarmed and on June 27, 1950, sponsored a motion that called upon the UN to do everything it could to support South Korea. The Soviets were absent and the vote carried. On July 10 General Douglas MacArthur was appointed Supreme Commander, and three days later General Walton Walker was appointed to command the Eighth Army.

The UN immediately put out a call to the UK, France, Australia, New Zealand, India, Turkey, Canada, and others, to commit troops to the United Nations Forces in Korea. Within a week almost half of the South Korean Army was destroyed. There was not a moment to lose.

The devastation of WWII still hung over much of Europe and the Far East. With this thought in mind US President Harry Truman wanted to avoid any possibility that the resolution would escalate into a full-scale third world war, and hence he referred to the Korean conflict as a "UN Police Action" [4]

The US immediately deployed occupation troops stationed in Japan. Essentially peacetime occupation troops they were poorly trained, under manned, and ill equipped to fight a determined and highly disciplined army fighting for their homeland. The North Koreans waged war with fanaticism. In about 35 days, by August 1, the enemy had advanced to within 50 km of the southern port of Pusan, and thus began the Battle of the Pusan Perimeter. The discovery of American prisoners, found executed with their hands secured behind their backs with barbed wire, spurred the defenders to stiffer resistance. [5] By 17 August the tide began to turn. The artillery, air force, infantry and the Naval arm of the UN forces took horrendous tolls on the suicidal attacks by the North Koreans. During August the British 27th Brigade arrived in Korea. On August 31 North Korean armies launched coordinated attacks on UN lines. By September 5 the situation was increasingly grave. But the US-UN forces held. It was apparent that the Northern force, having stretched their supply lines, been strafed from the air, and taking heavily increasing casualties, were running out of steam.

On September 15 MacArthur executed a brilliant assault from the sea, well behind the north's front lines at Inchon, the seaport to Seoul. Virtually all of his advisors were against it, which he took as a strong endorsement of his plan because it confirmed the North's forces would never even contemplate such an action. [6] They did not. On the 16th the Eighth Army launched its offensive. By the 17th the Marines secured Kimpo Airfield and on the 27th Seoul was taken.

The occupation forces of the North were cruel in the extreme. South Korean communist sympathizers ferociously administered kangaroo courts. Whatever the harshness of Rhee's regime, it was far better than Il Sung's inhumane brutality. Some 26,000 men, women and children of the south were slaughtered over three months. [7]

MacArthur believed he had to defeat China. The allies pressed north, and by October 25, 1950, leading South Korean elements reached the border between North Korea and China: the Yalu River. MacArthur's UN command was certain that China was not going to become involved. The US government was content to stop at the Yalu, despite MacArthur's personal soundings, which continued to support ongoing aggression. October 2, Mao Tse-tung, Chairman of China, through Indian officials, stated they would become involved if the UN forces crossed the 38 Parallel, his warning was ignored. [8]

About this time the Second Battalion PPCLI boarded a troop ship in Seattle, and proceeded to Korea. It was thought the war was almost over and the Canadians would become part of the occupation force. The battalion was not as yet fully trained to fight a war.

As UN units advanced on the Yalu, they unexpectedly experienced severe clashes with a new element, Chinese soldiers. They fought well, hitting hard at leading elements but after ten days fell silent. General P'eng, Commander in Chief of the Chinese and North Korean forces, concluded he would beat the UN. China deployed 130,000 soldiers of four armies, but the UN remained totally unaware of this development. UN Forces did not appreciate the significance of these forays; stern warnings signaling China's commitment to the conflict. [8]

The winter took a terrible toll on men and equipment on both sides. Unknown to the allies was the fact that the Chinese suffered far greater casualties due to the weather than did the UN troops. [9] The Chinese were poorly equipped for winter warfare but managed to capture supply depots holding massive amounts of UN food, clothing, sleeping bags, weapons including carbines (automatic rifles), artillery, ammunition and transport - supplies that ensured the enemy's survival and continuing aggression.

The American units of the Eighth Army withdrew so fast they actually out ran the enemy. US army officers noted they had not been taught how to fight an effective retreat. [10] The average American soldier was demoralized, not sufficiently trained, and poorly led in many instances. The retreat of the Eighth Army has been defined as one of the worst episodes in the history of American forces. It became a tidal wave. Soldier for soldier, the Chinese were humiliating the Americans. They fought like guerrillas, being lightly armed, against a highly mechanized and well-equipped army possessing superior artillery and airpower - and they were winning.

Desperate to turn the tide of events there were increasing discussions about whether or not the Americans should employ an atom bomb. President Truman answering a reporter's question said, "There has always been active consideration of its use." [11] There was mounting concern in Commonwealth circles as to where MacArthur's policies would lead. US opinion was deeply concerned about the defeats in Korea, and by the New Year the general populace wanted out of Korea.

Within three months the enemy had again advanced about 40 km south of Seoul. General Walton Walker, commander of the Eighth Army, was killed on the 23 of December. General Matthew Ridgeway took command of the Eighth Army and with a herculean effort instilled new life into it. Unknown to the allies the North's depleted forces were mustering 70,000 men against Walker's 140,000 troops. [12] By February the UN forces were once again advancing. It was Truman's hope that aggression by the UN forces would force China to consider a mutually agreed upon desire end to the war.

Stone deftly summarized the situation upon Ridgeway taking over. Stone found, "a defeatist attitude when he arrived in Korea in December of 1950, and was told by General Walker's G-3, that it was doubtful if the allies would still be in Korea at the end of the eight weeks which the PPCLI required to complete their training. General Ridgeway changed tactics when he took over. Up to that time the Eighth Army had worked with combat teams on the "Patton" principle of isolated troop penetrations, in which no attempt was made to consolidate the ground gained or to line up on a wide front. The British, on the other hand, had cleaned up as they went, making small gains over a wide front. General Ridgeway adopted the latter tactics." [13]

The forgoing is an extremely condensed version of events that saw the emergence of the Republic of (South) Korea in the aftermath of WWII, and the see-saw battles that marked the ongoing conflict of 1950/51. The resurgence of the UN fighting forces in early 1951 heralded the turning of the tide. This synopsis sets the background for the entrance of Canadian troops into the war.

The Chinese Spring Offensive, in the Central Sector, April 1951

General MacArthur was relieved of his command on the 14th of April

1951. The newly appointed Supreme Commander of the UN Forces, was General Matthew B. Ridgeway, US Army. The Commander in Chief of the US 8th Army in Korea, was Lieut General James Van Fleet III. General Ridgeway believed the enemy was preparing for another offensive. Prisoners confirmed this, as well as an increasing influx of refugees. The UN Forces were uncovering caches of arms and equipment buried by the retreating enemy. This was a Russian tactic, it allowed their advancing troops to be replenished at the front as their armies advanced. Their intent was reinforced when the enemy broke contact. Timing of their offensive could not be defined, though six prisoners cited the dates of April 22/23, and that the 1st and 2nd CCF Special Artillery Divisions had crossed the Yalu 15 days ago; having 46-105mm field guns, 45-155mm guns and 40 other howitzers, and 29 Anti Aircraft guns. [14] The appreciation was that the enemy would focus their attack on South Korean Forces. UN Forces were to continue their advance to line Wyoming; a strategically defendable position. General Van Fleet was instructed to continue Ridgeway's policies in the conduct of the war.

To appreciate the Chinese offensive at Kapyong, and the strategic importance in that battle, one must be cognizant of the Chinese preparations and objectives; the strengths and determination of their forces.

The Supreme Commander of the Chinese People's Volunteer's Army and the North Korean People's Volunteer's Army, was General P'eng The-haui, an aggressive leader. P'eng had massed 10 Chinese Armies between the Imjin River and the Hawch'on Reservoir. Their main objective: Seoul. It was to be conquered by three Armies totaling 270,000 troops, in the west sector, defined as the Imjin area. Two armies, the 39 and the 40 having a combined strength of 149,000, were to attack toward Kapyong, which is in the central sector of Korea. P'eng stated the offensive must penetrate about 100 miles to succeed. Four armies were to protect their rear from possible UN amphibious landings, for P'eng was afraid that the Americans might launch an amphibious attack in their rear as they did at Inchon. P'eng amassed 700,000 troops [11] against the UN's 418,000, including administrative units: [12]

US Army	245,000
Republic of Korea	152,000
British Commonwealth	11,500
Other	10,000

P'eng's Conference - April 6th (abbreviated)

P'eng instructed that: "Stocks for 20 days were to be brought forward, with every unit to carry 5 days field rations with another 5 days at hand. Ensure that the troops are able to get uninterrupted supplies of food and ammunition. Batches of drivers would be attached to advancing troops to overcome transport shortages by capturing enemy vehicles. Make use of prisoners of war for salvage operations. Damaged roads must be repaired immediately, do not wait for the engineers to do it. Troops must assist in the unloading and concealment of vehicles; wanton damaging of vehicles and attacking drivers must be prohibited. Engineers must carry out more road repairs to main supply lines to the front.

"Medical support must be prepared to care for 40,000 to 50,000 casualties. Casualty receiving stations should be as close as possible to the front. Medical orderlies and stretcher bearing parties should be organized in advance. Injured personnel must be in suitable places of concealment.

"Each Army had Deep Reconnaissance Units of up to 300 men and some had two units. 'Carrying cash, field rations, explosives, automatic weapons, walkie-talkies and so on, they should have Korean and English interpreters, and they should be prepared to destroy roads, overturn enemy vehicles, wreck enemy depots, capture prisoners, investigate the enemy situation and terrain, and actually coordinate operations with those of the front line units." [15]

P'eng's Strength - Mao's strategy was: Attack en mass, with hundreds or thousands of troops, on a limited front. Troops should be armed with automatic weapons, and be willing to sacrifice troops as cannon fodder.

Weakness - Once committed to battle, wireless communications were almost non-existent below Divisional level. The American Walkie-talkies were not suited to the topography of Korea, when a hill intervened transmission was blocked. Battle experience proved the Chinese could maintain a strong massed offensive for only five to six days; thereafter their strength was depleted.

The Chinese believed that on April 22nd, the British 27th Brigade was still in action; however, on the 19th the Brigade had been transferred to Corps reserve, the Republic of Korea (ROK) 6 Division relieved them.

April 18 - P'eng's Operations Directive

General P'eng, a robust commander, decided to attack an hour after darkness fell on April 22, 1951. "For our Spring Offensive - We have decided to make our objective the wiping out of three divisions (less one regiment) of the American Army, three Brigades of British and Turkish Troops, and two divisions of the Puppet Army (S. Korean), the British 27 Brigade, American 3 Division (less one regiment) The Turkish Brigade, the British 29 Brigade and the 1 Division of the Puppet Army, and after this to wipe out the American 24 and 25 divisions...." [15]

For the Central Sector - Kapyong

"The three Armies of 9 Army Group will first concentrate an absolute superiority of troop strength and fire power, and quickly wipe out the British 27 Brigade, while using part of their strength to pin down the American 24 Division, and sever links between the British 27 Brigade and the American 24 Division; once they have succeeded in doing this, they will penetrate directly to (the area of P'och'on) where, attacking from the south east to the north west, they can wipe out the American 24 and 25 Division." [15]

These orders reveal a problem P'eng had maintaining a high standard of efficiency, his difficulty sustaining supply lines to his troops, and a continual concern with pillaging.

Combining the Imjin and Kapyong objectives, Gen P'eng sought to tear a breech in the UN's line and overcome 100,000 of its fighting men. The US Air Force had earlier destroyed his air capability and thus his armies would be without air support.

April 20th - Chinese Deep Reconnaissance units began infiltrating UN lines.

The Chinese Fighting Soldier

We Canadians developed a great respect for the fighting tenacity of the Chinese soldier. They were fired upon by small arms, as well as light and heavy machine guns. mortars and masses of artillery came crashing through their ranks, exploding all about them. There was an indescribable agony of napalmed bodies burning beyond recognition ... the nauseating smell of death engulfing ... comrades falling like flies ... and yet they did not fail to charge forward into the hell of battle!

How did the Chinese motivate their men to sustain such bravery? In our terms, how did they persuade their troops to commit mass suicide charges in which so many of their fellows perished? They continued to press on, wave after wave, until their numbers became one continuous assault, and their bodies littered the battlefield.

It appears there was a three-fold system of "encouragement." At the top of the Chinese Military Command there was the all-powerful Political Commissar, and in the platoon there were basic 'cells,' each comprised of three men. One, a designated and committed Communist, was assigned to kill the others should they falter in battle. Supposedly no one knew who was the appointed assassin. Within a section, there was an even more dedicated Red, and so on up the line to the battalion level, and the Political Commissar. The Chinese charged in waves about 30 meters apart, if anyone in the lead wave was to turn back, members in the ensuing wave were directed to shoot them. Opium Balls were found on Chinese bodies. Once when overtaking the point where the Chinese had formed up their troops for the attack, the ground was littered with needles.

Mao's Unique Motivation...

1) Fear of death at the hand of an unseen internal "Death Squad cadre."
2) The "Ensuing Wave" which was to kill those in front who faltered.
3) Opium or drugs - "You feel so good, who gives a damn!"

THE CHINESE 1951 SPRING OFFENSIVE

When you have millions of men under arms, the cheapest expenditure in your arsenal of weaponry is their lives. The Communist system impressed hordes of men to become cannon fodder.

The Chinese Spring Offensive took place during April and May of 1951, and it became the largest battle of the entire Korean War. Their objective was the retaking of Seoul. Initially there were two main thrusts: In the Western Sector, known as the Imjin, the Chinese had assembled three Army Groups, III, IX and XIX, comprising 270,000 troops. They launched their offensive with 80,000 men. The focal point of their onslaught was the British 29th Infantry Brigade comprising 4,000 plus troops dug in on the Imjin River. At the same time, in the Central Sector, XIII Army group, 39th and 40th Armies, had 149,000 troops assembled and launched their offensive with the intent of initially destroying the British 27th Infantry Brigade. [16] These two engagements have garnered the greatest attention from Commonwealth historians. Frequently overlooked is the Third and final phase of the enemy's Spring Offensive, commencing 16 May. This ferocious third thrust of P'eng's offensive was undertaken by Chinese and North Korean troops, in the area of Inji, which I define as the Eastern Sector. I will briefly explore the action at the Imjin, and extensively report on the Patricias' battle in the Kapyong area. After Kapyong, I will summarize how General P'eng unleashed his unscathed reserves in the Eastern Sector. Overwhelming numbers of fresh troops were set upon unsuspecting South Korean and American forces. The Chinese once again gained initial success; however, as was so often demonstrated in Korea, they could not sustain the high intensity of their major assaults.

The Chinese infantry were renowned for their ability to move 10,000 to 50,000 men, unnoticed and overnight. Although they were not highly mechanized they were able to move as much as 35 km overnight on foot through mountainous terrain - and be ready to launch their unheralded attacking forces in the ensuing dawn.

The Chinese launched their Spring Offensive, both Western and Central, on the night of April 22, 1951. By the 24 the ferocity of their onslaught sent shock waves across the Eighth Army front. Anticipating the enemy offensive, Ridgeway had already drawn up plan "Audacious", [17] to destroy the Chinese forces. He planned an orderly withdrawal of UN forces, to entice the Chinese into a trap. He then envisioned the 1st Calvary Division unleashing a surprising and devastating flanking attack in the western (Imjin) sector. This never happened because the total collapse of the 6th Republic of Korea (ROK) Division, in the central sector, opened a 16 km gap in the UN front line. This created a hemorrhaging of the UN forces. The Chinese onslaught, thrashing all in its pathway, drove headlong south 40 km in 36 hours. Combined with the 25% losses to the British 29th Brigade on Gloucester Hill, at the Imjin, the Chinese offensive placed the Eighth Army in serious peril. Van Fleet determined that the 1st Cavalry Division must be sent into action piecemeal to assist in stemming the tide of battle at its weakest points. Plan Audacious was finished.

THE BATTLE OF THE IMJIN

April 22nd - The British 29th Brigade covered a front of about 12 km: The Gloucesters were on the left; Royal Northumberland Fusiliers, in the centre; and the Belgiums on the right. The Royal Ulster rifles were in reserve. The Belgiums were north and across the Imjin River, while all the others were south, and north of the village of Kanak-san. The right flank was an axis point beyond which the American 1/65, Regimental Combat Team, had advanced some 20km farther north. Intelligence reports indicated the Chinese were preparing for a major assault, but the timing was unknown. "During the day (of the 22nd) a Communist artillery officer and staff who had lost their way and been captured confirmed that they were taking up position to support the attack to be made that night. The CCF were apparently well informed of the UN dispositions and had ample guides and their attacks aimed at striking at both flanks of the 1st USA Corps which were disposed on a wide salient some 25 miles from Seoul …. along the Imjin .. undoubtedly directed upon UIJONGBU." [22]

When the attacks began it was assumed they were preliminary forays and that the main effort was still a day or two off. The enemy launched their offensive with two Army Groups, in the area of 29th Brigade, and they charged forth with three divisions, (30,000 men). The numbers of the assaulting troops were overwhelming. The American 1/65 was withdrawn south of the British position, the Belgian Battalion pulled back across the Imjin. The Gloucester's companies, and much of the Brigade were not drawn up in mutually supporting positions, and thus the layout made it impossible to halt a well-coordinated attack by an enemy, which outnumbered the 29th by almost 8 to 1. On the right of the 29th was the 1/65th Puerto Rican Regimental Combat Team with four battalions, reinforced by the Filipino and Turkish battalion, consisting of about 10,000 men. They were attacked by 50,000 troops of the 12th and 15th Armies. The result was devastating. The Turks fell back 16 to 20 km while American units on the south bank of the Hantan formed an effective holding pattern and slaughtered thousands of Chinese. [18]

Harris commanding the 1/65th; " On our left flank we had that reliable, unflappable British Brigade and they really caught hell." [18] The swarming Chinese forces were surrounding the Gloucesters, who were defending the main road to Seoul, and the Chinese wanted it … at any price. The Gloucesters, with approximately 800 men, fought a heroic battle for three days and the extent of the area they were defending deprived them of interlocking fire positions, which are sacred to the defensive positioning of infantry. The heavy casualties suffered by the enemy in their unsuccessful February offensive combined with the ease of the recent advance led them to believe there was no need to be highly defensive. The devastating hordes forced the Gloucesters to gradually reduce their defensive perimeter and they eventually ran out of ammunition.

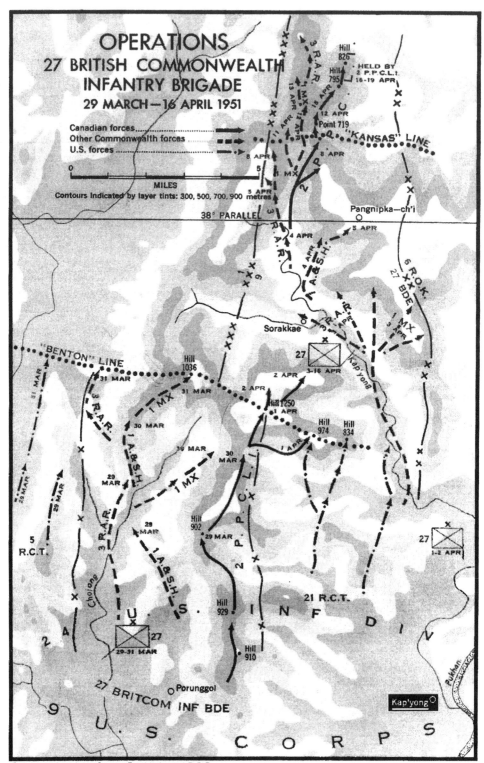

OPERATIONS
27 BRITISH COMMONWEALTH
INFANTRY BRIGADE
29 MARCH—16 APRIL 1951

Canadian forces
Other Commonwealth forces
U.S. forces

MILES
Contours indicated by layer tints: 300, 500, 700, 900 metres

The nuance of language also played a part in the demise of the Gloucesters, who were absorbing the brunt of the assault. When American General Soule, asked Brigadier Brodie of 29 Brigade, how the Gloucesters were doing, the reply was in a typically understated British stiff upper lip idiom: " A bit of a Sticky Wicket." In British terms this understatement meant things were bloody awful, but the American commander assumed, "unpleasant but sustainable." [19] General Soule ordered Colonel Carne to "hold fast," though he asked for permission to withdraw, and Soule reduced the elements of a relief column and delaying the timing of their thrust. Learning of this later, Colonel Carne delivered a blunt message, "I understand the position quite clearly: What I must make clear to you is that my command is no longer an effective fighting force. If it is required that we stay here, in spite of all this, we shall continue to hold. But I wish to make known the nature of my position." [20] They were instructed to hold.

Captain JC Gorman, an Australian, serving with the 8th Hussars Armoured relief column, defines the ferocity and determination of the Chinese Communist Forces when they arrived at the Gloucesters B echelon.: "…. Rifles and equipment lay scattered everywhere, among burned-out carriers and smoldering trucks. Dead Englishmen lolled behind shattered steering wheels, and rows of holes in the vehicles showed the line of enemy machine-gun fire. Short Chinese cartridge-cases littered the area. Dead men lay in profusion sightless eyes staring at the sky. It was definitely depressing. The thought occurred - 'That dead man, but for the grace of God, is me.' There is not a single enemy body. *It is nerve-racking to see only your own dead, for it gives the impression of disastrous defeat. Of course, the Reds have removed their own dead, as they always did.*" [21]

Only about 42 men of the Gloucesters escaped the Chinese carnage. The events surrounding the defeat of the Gloucesters lead to a debacle that should have never taken place. One of those captured was the adjutant of the Gloucesters, Captain A. Farrar-Hockley. A tenacious and determined soldier he escaped from prisoner of war camps five times, only to be recaptured, and on each occasion to suffer further under the cruelty of his jailors. He later became the Commanding General of the British Army of the Rhine, and still later the official historian of the British experience in Korea.

The significance of the defence by the Gloucesters facing overwhelming numbers of a determined enemy at the Imjin River, is defined in the following: An early report stated 29 Brigade endured 25% casualties, about 1,000 men. However they meted out an earth-shattering defeat upon the Chinese 63 Army - forcing an estimated 11,000 casualties. [22]

General Van Fleet awarded the Gloucesters a United States Presidential Unit Citation, stating their stand at Gloucester Hill was, ***"The most outstanding example of unit bravery in modern warfare."*** [22]

1. "Korean War," Max Hastings, page 53,

2. Hickey, page 27.

3. "The Forgotten War," Clay Blair, page 864.

4. Blair page 80

5. Hastings page 81.

6. Blair. Page 231

7. Hastings page 90.

8. Hastings, pages 134, 135.

9. Hastings, page 170-1

10. Hastings, page 174

11. Hastings page 179

12. Strange Battleground page 72.

13. Notes on a talk given by LCol JR Stone, Army Headquarters, 0900 hrs, 5 June 1951

14. Periodic Intelligence Report, No 284 - period covered 21-2400 to 22-2400 hrs April 1951.

15. These paragraphs are reproduced from "Official History, The British Part in the Korean War, Volume II" by the kind permission of the author, General Sir Anthony Farrar-Hockley.

16. McGibbon, Page 108

17. Farrar-Hockley, page 128

18. Blair, 825-6

19. Farrar-Hockley, page 127

20. Farrar-Hockley, page 128

21. O'Neill, page 133

22. Blair, page 847

Chapter FIVE

THE ONSLAUGHT IN THE CENTRAL SECTOR

22nd April, 2130 hrs

Terrified of the Chinese onslaught, the soldiers of 6th ROK Division fled the front lines, running south as fast as their legs could carry them. The wholesale flight of 10,000 armed and panic stricken men created a massive gap stretching 16km wide across the UN lines. Like a flood, the Chinese hordes poured into the void. It was frightening in the extreme for us, as defenders in a foreign country, to realize the soldiers of the host nation were so terrified that they ran away through the very lines that we had been ordered to defend. What on earth did they face that so undermined their will to fight for their own country? The emotional effect on the remaining defending troops cannot be described in words except to say the experience was devastating. **Thousands of enemy armed soldiers were advancing in columns six abreast - an arrogant blitzkrieg thrusting forward at the double, not even pausing when strafed or bombed!** "Oh My God, was this how the Roman Legions looked, disciplined and seemingly unconquerable ... left alone to face the enemy, our soldiers wonder where the hell their fate lies ... in this God forsaken country...." [1]   Intelligence reports of April 11th revealed that enemy resistance had stiffened. Information from prisoners, and refugees going south, and other intelligence indicated the enemy were rapidly preparing for another offensive.

A report by Lieutenant-General Sir HCH Robertson, KBE, DSO, released by the CIC British Commonwealth Forces, speculates how the Chinese broke through on the central front. "The second thrust of the night ... using a Corps of three Divisions (30,000 troops) was through the 6th ROK Division, and it is possible there was some treachery for during the night the whole Division broke and streamed in panic to the rear, thereby opening the right flank of the 1st Corps and the left flank of 9th Corps." [2]

On the 15th 2PPCLI took Hill Turbot, which was almost 800 meters high. They endeavored to take Trout, 826 meters elevation, though 10 Platoon took the forward slope about 1500hrs, they did not secure the crest until the next day. Hill Salmon was taken by 3RAR. [3]   The

Brigade's objective, Line Utah, was now in hand. Over the past few months the 27th Brigade had advanced about 100 km. The Northern Armies' February winter offensive had been defeated, and they suffered heavy losses. But here they had massed hundreds of thousands of fresh troops determined to annihilate our army and to throw us out of Korea.

Four days later 27th Brigade moved into Corps reserve just north of Kapyong. Commencing on the 19th two battalions of the Brigade were being rotated out of Korea. The Argylls and the Middlesex were posted to Hong Kong, to be replaced by the King's Own Scottish Borderers (KOSB) and the King's Shropshire Light Infantry (KSLI). The advance party of the Argylls had departed for Hong Kong.

By the 22nd the 6 Republic of Korea (ROK) Division, having relieved the 27th Brigade, advanced about 12 km and were continuing their advance north to Line Wyoming. [4] Motorized patrols, ranging in front of the Main Line of Resistance did not distinguish enemy activity. The Northern forces had intentionally pulled back in an attempt to weaken the UN's supply line and to foster an attitude of relaxed confidence in our forces. They certainly succeeded in the latter.

A IX Corps Air Observation Post picked up very large bodies of enemy moving south and immediately notified the Eighth Army. At about 1800 hrs many units became less defensively focused, after all, we had hammered the enemy in February and once again had them on the run! Brigadier General Chang Do-young ordered his 6 ROK Division into defensive positions. They were slow to take action and many units lacked effective leadership. [5]

The 16th Field Regiment Royal New Zealand Artillery (16 RNZA) had been supporting the 6th ROK advance. Early in the evening the 16 RNZA were released from supporting the 19th ROK Regiment, to be attached to 27th Brigade. The 16 RNZA are north of Karim, just south of Line Kansas. [6]

An hour after dark, the Chinese Offensive struck the 6th ROK Division, with the effectiveness of a sledgehammer. The Chinese 60 Division of the newly formed III Field Army, swept over the left forward battalion of the ROK 2nd Regiment. Within an hour the remaining units of the 2nd and all of the 19th had been defeated and were running helter skelter south as fast as they could. The ROK 7th Regiment was committed to battle, but within an hour they too collapsed. [7] The CO of the 92nd US Field Artillery Battalion (FAB) advised IX Corps HQ of the total

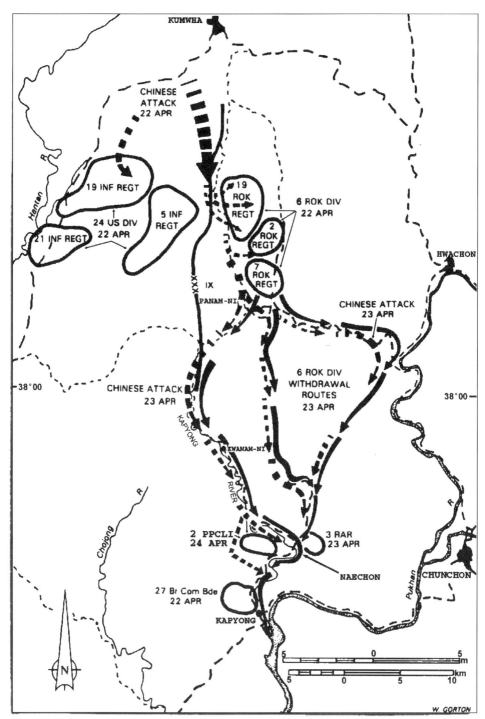

The Chinese Attack on the 6th ROK Division, 22/24 April 1951
Source: Australia in the Korean War, Vol II — Robert O'Neil 1985

demise of the 6th Division. The ROK 27th Field Artillery fled, leaving their guns and ammunition stocks to the Chinese. [8]

With the front collapsing around him LCol Moodie, 16th RNZA, was advised to move to Kapyong forthwith. The 6th ROK Divisional HQ, informed Moodie that the 19th ROK Regiment was moving forward to stem the tide so he decided to move the next day. [9]

The Chinese expected to confront the British 27th Brigade. They found instead the lines being quickly deserted by the 6th ROK Division, and they took time to check out the abandoned trenches. They could hardly believe the extent of their overwhelming success. South Korean officers tried to form a temporary blocking position and requested 16th RNZA support. Because there were no ROK forward artillery officers among the scattered infantry, there were no calls for fire support. In their bug-out the retreating soldiers outran their foes and it saved the division from being destroyed. [10]

1. Pte Don Worsfield, 2PPCLI - Interview 1998
2. "Impressions by Lieutenant General Sir HCH Robertson, KBE, DSO," released by CIC British Commonwealth Force.
3. 2PPCLI War Diary
4. O'Neill 134
5. Farrar-Hockley 139
6. McGibbon 110
7. McGibbon 111
8. McGibbon 111
8. McGibbon 110
10. It was not uncommon for the ROK troops to break when hit hard by the enemy. Later in the war, reinforced by American advisors and a scattering of US unit, the ROK army performed to a higher standard. The treachery factor remains a speculation.

Chapter SIX

CHAOS AND DEFEAT
South Korean 6th Division

27 BRIGADE MOVE INTO CORPS RESERVE
AND THEN TO KAPYONG

(Less 16th RNZ Artillery, positioned at Karim, just south of Line Kansas)

Second Battalion
Princess Patricia's Canadian Light Infantry

27th British Commonwealth Infantry Brigade

24th US Infantry Division

IX Corps, US Eighth Army

April 18
        Captain Andy Foulds and the advance party were the first to take R&R (Rest and Recuperation) leave to Japan. The War Diary incorrectly states the date was April 11th and I make the point here to stress that the War Diary contains a number of errors relating to timing. From time to time the diary suffers from time lapses between actual events and the subsequent date of recorded entries. I mention this because future researchers may question occasional differences between stated timings of the 2PPCLI War Diary and the results of my research. Much of the time diary entries are short on detail.

War Diary - Extracts.

April 14 - "At 1510 hrs, D Company led an attack on Hill 795, Turbot. Lieut Lee Hill of 12 Platoon was immediately wounded. At 1610 Lieut MG Levy led the attack with Great Spirit. Five were wounded including Lieut Hill.

April 16 - "27th Brigade HQ notified all battalions at 1900 hrs, that they were due to be relieved by the 19th Regiment Combat Team (RCT) of the 6th ROK Division on or about 17th of April. It now remained for the 6 ROK to complete their advance in order that the 27th Brigade could be relieved. Early on the 18th, there was no sign of the leading elements of the 2nd Battalion, 19 RCT. 1630 hrs, Major Tighe, Acting Commanding Officer 2PPCLI, had Lieut AP McKenzie, conduct officers of 1st Battalion, ROK 19 RCT, on a tour of Patricia's positions. At 1630hrs Tighe advised the proposed relief is to take place 0900hrs on the 19th, we are to move to Corps reserve near the town of CHUNGCHON-NI, to be completed by 1830hrs.

19 April - "Relief started with the arrival of the ROKs at 1100 hrs; however the relief for D Company did not commence until 1730 hrs, and they did not arrive at the assigned rest area until 2330 hrs." The ROKs were rather slow to move, reflecting a degree of disorganization, foretelling a disturbing element of the upcoming events.

April 20, 21 - "Battalion activities: laying out the camp, cleaning equipment, servicing weapons, kit inspection, submitting lists of shortages to Captain PM Pyne, Quartermaster. A shortage of uniforms made it necessary to issue British battle dress in place of our own. Vehicles inspection: lack of maintenance and extremely rough roads has led to serious deterioration. In the afternoon sports were conducted under the supervision of Lieut. Levy. Due to an outbreak of several cases of malaria Paludrine tablets are to be issued henceforth on a scale of one per day per man. A ceremonial guard is to be mounted each night by companies, consisting of 60 men, commanded by the junior officer of the assigned company.

April 22nd - "Troops on five days in Japan on R&R, returned in the morning. At that time others departed for their "rest" in Japan". Among those departing was Major Bob Swinton MC, commanding D Company. "The troops enjoyed hot meals, sports, showers, clean clothes and maintaining their equipment. We were fully prepared to go back into the line. LCol Stone returned to the battalion after recovering from an attack of Smallpox, which he contacted on or about the 20th of March. At 0930hrs The Intelligence Officer takes a recce to examine the various road approaches that were critical to the front."

An hour after dark, the Chinese Communist Forces commenced their Spring Offensive. There were 10 Armies comprising 700,000 men, of which 419,000 were allocated to the attacking forces. Over the prior two weeks, 2PPCLI had fought their way to the Utah Line. The 10,000 soldiers of the Republic of Korea (ROK) 6 Division had relieved British 27th Brigade. Faced with the concentrated onslaught of the Chinese offensive, the 6 ROK Division ran away. This was a common event for many units of the ROK army. It usually took three to five days for them to regroup. Each time this occurred they left behind massive amounts of equipment, **and by May 1951 they had thrown away enough gear to arm 10 complete Divisions, 100,000 men - ironically re-equipping the enemy.** [1]

By the time the UN Line was stabilized on the 30 of April, UN Forces had withdrawn south 52 - 70km. Our new position was called Line Golden (also referred to as Line Lincoln), and was in the vicinity of the Han River near the village of Tokso-ri, about 4 km northeast of Seoul. Kapyong was about 40km south of the farthest point of advance of the 6 ROK Division.

During the afternoon of the 22nd, the Gunners 162nd Battery, 16RNZA, hosted a farewell party for the departing Argylls. Among those attending were Lieut Rod Middleton, 2PPCLI Liaison Officer (LO) at 27 Brigade HQ, along with a major, two captains and the Australian LO. In an offhanded way they observed there were Korean refugees passing by when the field telephone rang. The white jacketed bar steward answered and then enquired if there was anyone from Brigade HQ present, Rod answered. **"Middleton. Duty Officer here. A bit of a sticky wicket is developing at the front, gather all Brigade officers and return at once**." [2] They raced back to Brigade.

April 23 - 0300 hrs - South Korean Officers are trying to stem the retreat, and are even shooting their own troops, but to no avail. Retreating ROKs are passing through the New Zealand gun Lines. At 0400 hrs the 16RNZA gunners are pulling out, as they have no means of obtaining targets. It is difficult to prepare to move as they are engulfed by masses of fleeing civilians enjoined with the flight of the 6th ROK troops and infiltrating Chinese forces, "... you could not see the guns or limbers for the blasted gooks, every trailer was alive with them." [3] At first compassionate, it soon becomes a case of survival as the Kiwis cast the South Koreans off, striking them with boots and rifle butts to ensure their own survival. As a result some are run over by following vehicles and others are buried under the feet of their retreating comrades. Panic-stricken, it is every man for himself. The gunner's Regimental HQ withdraws by 0630 hrs.

0700 hrs - BRIGADIER BURKE: THE COMMANDER,
27th BRITISH COMMONWEALTH INFANTRY BRIGADE
He learns of the offensive as he is shaving and listening to the Armed Forces Radio from Japan at 0700hrs. Captain Murray Edwards, newly

appointed 2PPCLI Quartermaster, related this. "Burke studies his maps and concludes that the two main thrusts will be across the Imjin River (British 29 Brigade) and down the Kapyong Valley. Burke orders a Brigade reconnaissance (recce or "R" group) to Kapyong without instructions from higher command." Eighth Army HQ issues their order for the 27th Brigade to recce Kapyong at 0830hrs. [4]

O800 hrs

The RNZA batteries are in the area of Naech'on, at the foot of Hill 677, Kapyong where they had been a month ago. The US 987 Field Artillery (FA) and the 2nd Rocket FA Battery (both having 105 mm howitzers) are ensnarled by a collapsing road. C Company, 2nd Chemical Heavy Mortar Battalion is overrun, and 92nd US FA Battalion extracts their 155 howitzers.[5]

Stone goes to 27th Brigade HQ for Brigadier Burke's Orders Group.[6] Orders: "The 27th, is to take up blocking positions just north of the junction of the Kapyong and Pukham rivers (map page 87), which is south of the Kapyong Gorge. Middlesex (MX) will occupy Hill 794. 2 PPCLI Hill 677; 3 RAR and Company A, US 72nd Heavy Tank Battalion to Hill 504; 1 KOSB Hill 225 in reserve just north of the bombed out village of Kapyong." [6] The MX, under strength, were to occupy Hill 794, but instead provided protective cover for 16RNZA, and were subsequently in reserve near 27th Brigade HQ. [7]

The Kapyong area is an important junction point for east - west communications as it is south of the main line of resistance. There are three hills that would provide the ideal defensive layout. On the east Hill 504, to the west Hill 677 [4] and to the northwest Sundok San, a large feature rising 794 meters. The Argylls are on their way out of Korea. The MX battalion is forward protecting the 16RNZA, their experienced Commanding Officer has departed for Hong Kong, the battalion is not fully operational. It is impossible to construct a continuous defensive line. Burke has only two operational battalions: 3RAR and the Patricia's. He chooses to establish positions on hills 504 and 677. [5] It is believed these positions may only be staging points in the further advance of the 27th Brigade and if they were to be fully defended, they would establish stronger fortifications the next day. [5] IX Corps HQ does not appreciate the extent of the 6ROK division collapse, because they do not know where the South Koreans or Chinese are.

0900 hrs - Stone leaves 27th Brigade HQ returning to the Patricia's rest area at 1100 hrs. Stone organizes a battalion recce group to move to Kapyong. [6] Second in commands are to remain and have the battalion prepared to move into the front line. Stone: "When I heard what we had to do I took forward a large reconnaissance party of company commanders, platoon commanders, the mortar platoon commander and the machine gun fellow, (signals) and we went to the enemy side of the hill and looked at it from the enemy's point of view, which gave us a good idea of the possible attack approaches. I then decided which way the attack would come and deployed my battalion accordingly." [8] Because of the terrain, companies cannot be in the classical position of mutual support. As all companies are to be in individually defended localities, Stone instructs his officers: **all platoons must be mutually supporting.**

Intelligence Officer (IO) Lieut AP Peter MacKenzie leads the officers up Hill 677, which rises 600 meters above the valley floor. Lieut Chas Petrie recalls: "He read the map incorrectly leading us to the wrong position. When we finally got to where we could view the valley below we got properly oriented. The lot of us seemed quite tired from the climb and very thirsty from the heat. Only Major George and myself brought along water bottles, which we shared with everyone.

"Lieut Mike Levy had recently acquired from the enemy a weighty Thompson sub-machine gun, and a magazine carrier with a number of magazines. It grew heavier on Mike as the day wore on. Having climbed to the top of the mountain to orient ourselves, we then descend halfway down the northern slopes along the spurs that our company would occupy. We are assigned our platoon positions and disperse to reconnoiter them. We review our appreciations with Major Lilley and check how we tie in with one another in covering the ground with fire. This is necessary for we will not move into position until after dark." [9]

"It is about 80+ degrees, an exhausting day climbing over the entire hill. At B Company the ground on the ridges proves to be unsuitable for digging, but there is sufficient shale and gravel to form parapets. We are about 350 meters north and east of D Company. Major Vince Lilley ensures that each of his platoons will be mutually supporting." [9] Upon descending the hill Lieut Petrie and Major George, the two officers carrying water bottles, make for the river to refill their bottles. They wait for 15 minutes after inserting the purification tablets. [9] Captain Andy Foulds: "I had just returned from leave in Japan. Surveying each company position sighting the Vickers medium machine gun positions at every company. At the end of the day I can hardly walk, my knees are swollen from the intensive climbing. [10] There is a tremendous explosion as the engineers destroy the Kapyong Bridge.

The valley in the area north of the town of Kapyong is about 3,000 meters wide, but to the North the hills on either side converge becoming very narrow. Beyond Kapyong the river turns northeast for 6 ½ Km. Beyond 504 the valley forms a "Y", one arm turns sharply east for 5 Km, and an unnamed tributary reaches out to the NE, with an accompanying ridge line. At Hill 667 the main body of the Kapyong turns west and then to the northwest. Almost due North of 677 across the river is Hill 794, between these hills the valley narrows sharply to become a gorge.

HILL 677. The area defended by 2PPCLI is about 2 km across, gently curving from a northerly direction to an eastern face. The Australians aptly described it as shaped like a boomerang. Company locations are 300 to 500 meters apart. They are so far apart that the gaps have to be covered by defensive fire tasks of the machine guns and mortars of the battalion plus the 16 RNZA. D Company holds the highest position on the west flank of the battalion-facing north up the narrowing Kapyong Valley, which develops into a slender gorge. C Company is in the centre, being northern most. A Company is to their right. B Company is initially sighted forward of D Company, between D and C, but was later relocated on to the right flank of the battalion facing NNE, while support company platoons and Tactical HQ, are overlooking the broadening Kapyong and Pukhan River Valleys to the east, south of the relocated B Company position.

Our hill is much larger than the Australian Hill 504. The face of 677 alternates between re-entrants 5 to 20 meters in depth and up to 200 meters across, the walls are generally steep. The rising ridges range from 60 to 100 meters across. Soil covering is thin and underneath it is very rocky, thus our slit trenches are restricted in depth. During the morning of the 24 the average slit at 10 Platoon is narrow and about two feet deep. As the day wears on D Company observes the intensity of the firefights between the 3RAR and the enemy. Soon the men are cursing and swearing as they force their trenches to three or four feet in depth, and begin erecting parapets. Hills 15 meters or higher, rise steeply behind each platoon. At intervals the face of Hill 677 falls sharply away and rock faces with steep descents are not uncommon. Growth consists of scrub grass, shrubbery 1 to 2 meters high and fir trees of 3 to 5 meters. [11] There are many large open spaces throughout the battalion area.

KAPYONG

THE FRONT WAS 7 KM ACROSS

2PPCLI FRONT - 2 KM

3RAR FRONT - 2 KM

DISTANCE BETWEEN - 3 KM

EACH COY 'CLUSTER', 200 - 400 METERS ACROSS

EIGHT CLUSTERS

DISTANCE BETWEEN COMPANIES, 300 - 500 METERS
MAP following page 86

NO FLANK PROTECTION

CENTRAL SECTOR UNOCCUPIED

NO WIRE - NO MINES

PIONEERS LAID OUT BOOBY TRAPS

UNTIL 16RNZA RETURNED, 27th BRIGADE HAS
REDUCED ARTILLERY SUPPORT.
THE MIDDLESEX BATTALION IS PROTECTING
FORWARD 16RNZA BATTERIES.
27th BRIGADE ONLY HAS TWO FULLY
OPERATIONAL BATTALIONS.

SUPPORTING ARMS:

2PPCLI & 3RAR - EACH

ONE US HEAVY MORTAR COMPANY, 4.2" MORTARS

2 CHEMICAL MORTAR BATTALION

3RAR

15 M4A3 SHERMAN TANKS

COMPANY A, US 72 HEAVY TANK BATTALION [11]

Due to the rapid advance of the Chinese over some 30 km, there is unchecked confusion in UN formations. Divisional Intelligence cannot define the Main Line of Resistance because they do not know where the enemy or the South Korean front lines are. Army supply points are disrupted, and there are no mines or wire available to strengthen our defences. 2PPCLI pioneers lay flares and booby-traps along our front. [12]

Hill 677 dominates the narrowing Kapyong Gorge to the North, and the Chinese have to conquer the Patricias, to open their gateway to Seoul. Hill 667, rising 600 meters above the valley floor, is about 6km north of Kapyong, facing Naech'on to the east. Kapyong has been so heavily bombarded both from the ground and the air that it has been destroyed.

2PPCLI, depending on the company location, are to dig in between 400 and 500 meters above the valley floor, D Company being the highest. The Kapyong River is not very big but the Pukhan is a major drainage system of central Korea. To the east the valley is quite broad, to the north the Kapyong River Valley becomes a narrow gorge. Hill 677 appears to offer the Patricias and the artillery an effective killing ground. The narrow valley favours concentrated artillery and air strikes.

1200 hrs - Brigadier General Chang, Commanding 6th ROK Division, gathers some 4 - 5,000 men in the upper Kapyong Valley and General Hodges orders them to take up a position roughly on Line Kansas by 1700 hrs.[13] Two batteries (16 - 25 pounder field artillery) of 16RNZA are ordered forward to provide fire support. The Koreans, shattered of all confidence, lose heart once again and pursue their headlong route - South! The US 24 Division west of the ROKs and the 1st US Marines on their right, have their flanks bent. An Air Observation aircraft of the Marines, at noon, reports the chaos of the ROK troops. Harry Honnor of the 16RNZA in an IX Corps artillery observation flight advises of "… the fantastic spectacle of Chinese … marching six abreast ... heading south and going." Though they were savaged by Artillery fire, ".. they hardly broke ranks until they suffered tremendous casualties." [14] **These reports were discounted at Corps HQ, and are not conveyed to LCol Moodie.** [15]

1300 hrs - The 16RNZA reconnaissance party moves north to the Kwanamni area, about 8 km South of where they had been earlier. Two batteries subsequently move north. Moodie, relying upon his earlier experience is uncertain of the deteriorating situation. He demands his orders in writing and insists upon a protecting force. Brigadier Burke, commanding 27th Brigade, complies to both requests.[16]

The MX Battalion accompanies the gunners who push through narrow roads clogged with refugees, deserters, some HQ groups, and God knows how many Chinese infiltrators.

1500 hrs: - The Commander of the IX Corps visits Brigade HQ to discuss the situation.

1400 hrs - British 27th Brigade HQ - 4 km south of Hill 677. Lieut Rod Middleton who is Duty Officer, is in the operations van. There is a knock on the door and, he recalls: "The American LCol, commanding A and B companies of the 74th Engineer Combat Battalion, which includes a searchlight platoon, stands at the doorway. He is agitated, with a .45 loosely slung on his hip, he states the front has been broken; the Chinese are coming headlong south! Where is he to go? Brigade Major JD Stewart, in his understated and laconic English manner notes his unit is not under British control but he would presume … possibly South? The LCol says, "I'm hauling ass outta here!" [17]

In their cowardly panic to scramble south the engineers abandon vehicles and equipment. 2PPCLI acquires a water trailer. 3RAR liberates tentage and a considerable amount of military supplies. Days later US Military Police arrived at our Brigade seeking their missing equipment and amazingly none with appropriate US Army markings is found.

1500 hrs - 3RAR begin moving on truck transports as well as 15 tanks of the American 72nd Heavy Tank Battalion. **The Brigade Orders Group advise they would "settle in for a quiet night" on Hill 504**, to move forward the next day or develop defensive positions at 504. [18] The extent of the collapse at the front of the 6ROK Division, streaming south, is still not appreciated. The 3RAR occupy Hill 504 and one other feature on the east side of the Kapyong River. Battalion HQ is astride the main north-south road, about 1.5 km behind the four rifle companies. They try to form a blocking position, [19] in an endeavour to stem the 6th ROK fearful retreat, which is putting the entire 8th Army at risk. The situation is so fluid and chaotic that the IX Corps is incapable of conceiving the speed with which the Chinese juggernaut is overwhelming the 6th ROK.

1700hrs - The US 213 Armoured (self propelled) Field Artillery Battalion having 155mm howitzers, are set up in the neighboring valley, but have no infantry support. [20] IX Corps HQ erroneously assures them the ROK 19th Regiment is occupying the hills to their front. South Korean Military Police are shooting their own troops, trying to stop them escaping. The South Koreans lose momentum as the newly committed Chinese 118th Division of the 40th Army infiltrates their ranks and the whole becomes a disorganized mob and heads full bore toward Kapyong.

1730 hrs - 2PPCLI Reconnaissance Group returns late from Kapyong, delayed because the lead driver got lost after taking a wrong turn going north. MacKenzie, the Intelligence Officer, leads them astray on the mountain. The battalion is ready for an early move. The men have eaten and the Company Quartermaster Sergeants have a meal held for the officers on the recce.[21]

Captain M Edwards, Quartermaster - "Everyone is acutely aware of the gravity of the situation. Rifle companies are swamping us with requests for extra allotments of ammunition and grenades. The mortar platoon takes all the 81mm bombs we had, possibly approaching twice their normal allotment. The pioneers are accumulating extra inventory, the entire battalion wants to be ready for a continuing engagement." [22]

1800 hrs - Stone's Orders Group: "It is estimated that two battalions are still holding the enemy, about 23km north of Kapyong. Two batteries of Self Propelled guns and a battery of mortars are feared lost. The 16RNZA batteries are north of Kapyong, and supporting the remaining UN troops. Because of the topography and the extent of the battalion area to be defended, Patricias' companies cannot be deployed in the classical manner to be mutually supportive of each other." [23]

Stone reiterates:

"My defensive plan necessitates Company Platoons be Mutually Supporting"

1800hrs - B Company Orders Group:
      Stand To 0500 - 0600hrs
      1900 - 2000hrs
      Daytime look-out established.
      No standing on the skyline.
      Forward Platoon position rotation : 50% on guard all times.
      Trip flares to be issued in the morning. [22]

Canadian Army
Duties of a Company Commander in Battle

- Establish a company fighting Observation Post, so that the commander can move amongst his platoons, **and be at the vital point of battle at the right time**.

- The company commander's signalers ensure that at all times he is in contact with both Tactical HQ signalers and the company to all platoons radio net.

- In this manner the commander can immediately communicate with Tactical HQ, and receive/send such vital information as: situation reports; requests for firing defensive tasks for artillery and mortars etc. He can also maintain vital links with: his other platoons, tanks in support, mortar mobile fire controller, artillery or whomever is tied into the company radio net, **whilst visiting the platoon that requires his immediate influence**.

- The Company Sergeant Major (CSM), at Company HQ, would be handling casualties, prisoners, ammo supply etc.

- At every opportunity it is important to keep the CSM informed of the company situation. Should the company commander become a casualty the CSM becomes the de facto acting commander until one of the platoon commanders moves to company HQ to take command.

1900 hrs - Kwanamni

The Middlesex Battalion supporting the 16RNZA descends from the hills protecting the gun position as darkness falls. The Chinese are flooding the valley and Moodie orders intensive firing up the valley, even though no artillery Forward Observation Officers are with the ROK infantry. Eventually Moodie issues a 15-minute warning order to pull out. The road is choked with retreating ROKs, masses of men are streaming south as fast as their legs can convey them. The gunners commence firing at "7,000 - and then 4,000 yards - then open sights at 300 yards." [24] The terrifying sight of an army in chaotic retreat, running south as fast as they can from the enemy is unnerving, the aura of fear is pervasive. The Kiwis put down a barrage of fire as the Middlesex descend from the hills. For a short time a ghostlike silence prevails. Two batteries pull out taking the infantry with them, hanging on to anything that would support them. Their enemy is so numerous it is like shooting fish in a barrel. Every shot is a grim reaper of death. "Panic stricken ROKs try to climb on board our overloaded vehicles but are clubbed off, self-preservation" [25] In the confusion and darkness one cannot distinguish between friend and foe - masses of onrushing Orientals all look alike. The struggling stream engulfing the road frequently refuse to give way to the convoy, thus many ensure their own demise. An army that degenerates into a panic stricken mob presents an indescribable sight. Blind to all around them, they care only for their own survival. Run Away! Run Away! Run away to escape the grasp of the fearful deathly hoards descending from the north!

---

1. Blair 864, The 8th Army in April, undertook a survey of ROK losses of arms & equipment. In early May Sigman Rhee began a public campaign to have the US equip more ROK divisions. The US refused, and told Rhee "to stiffen the backs of his commanders". I do not know if the losses of the 6 ROK Division and the horrendous losses at the Inji were included in the report of May 1951.

2. Middleton personal notes

3. McGibbon 112

4. O'Neill 136

5. McGibbon 113

6. 2PPCLI War Diary

7. McGibbon 114

8. Speech by Col Stone to 3PPCLI officers, 18 December 1973

9. Petrie: Statement, 26 November 1996, from Filed Notes made at the time of the battle.

10. Andy Foulds interview, March 18, 1998

11. A report written by the Intelligence Officer, Lieut APP MacKenzie, dated 26 NOVEMBER 1954, provides misleading descriptions in the area of Hill 677, portraying the grass being about knee high. It is very short scrub grass. Further stating trees in the valley being six to 10 inches in girth and about 30 feet high, Lieut John Pearson led a patrol in the valley below 677on the 25th, the trees averaged about six to eight feet in height on the upper slope while in the valley the average was about 15 feet. Along the bank of the river there were very occasionally a taller tree or two. There are a number of other misconceptions in MacKenzie's report.

12. Interview Lieut Herst. Pioneer Platoon Commander., 1999

13. Farrar-Hockley 140

14. McGibbon 115

15. McGibbon 115

16. McGibbon 114

17. Middleton interview May 1999

18. O'Neill 138, Breen 137

19. O'Neill 138

20. McGibbon 116

21. 2PPCLI War Diary

22. Edwards interview 1998

23. Field Notes Petrie

24. McGibbon 118

25. McGibbon 119

Chapter SEVEN

2ND PATRICIAS PREPARE TO DO BATTLE AT KAPYONG

23rd of April, 1930 hrs

The 2nd Patricias' under strength at 800-plus, are transported to Kapyong and take up defensive positions at Hill 677. Leaving the Patricias rest area where the highway turns north, the South Korean Army has established a stopping point for the masses fleeing from the front. There are soldiers, civilians, deserters masquerading as civilians, and Chinese infiltrators. Anyone going beyond the demarcation point is shot. The area is ringed by the ROK's .50 caliber heavy machine guns, their periodic firing echoes throughout the valley and brings to a shattering halt the masses fleeing south. The area is strewn with a considerable number of bodies.

12 Platoon, D Company - Lance Corporal Jimmy Wanniandy, a full-blooded Canadian Indian, reports that: "On the drive to Kapyong it is as though the troops are on their way to a celebration. Being well fed, supplied with clean uniforms and fully armed they appear carefree and are happily singing and telling jokes all the way to the base of the Hill 677." [1]

C Company - Corporal Rollie LaPointe: "We are just approaching our position and I am stunned to see an unending line of ROK soldiers, walking in single file, filing through our position. We have not even begun to dig in. It reminds me of the photographs that I have seen of the Yukon, during the gold rush, of the miners hiking over the Chilkoot trail mountain pass. These men are armed and intent on going in only one direction, South! I shudder in disbelief at seeing our allies running hell-bent away from the advancing enemy; they are a disorganized rabble! Leaving us to face their enemy, to fight for their bloody country! Anger rages through out my being watching these cowardly deserters running away, and at the same time a piercing fear begins to gnaw slowly in the pit of my stomach. I think of Genghis Kahn and the oriental hordes feasting on the empire of Rome. God Help us, for what the hell are we about to face? I do not show my concern to my men, for I must stand tall in their eyes." [2] LaPointe is an aggressive rough diamond with a deep commanding voice that penetrates like a foghorn.

He is from a French Canadian family that lives in The Pas, Manitoba. He left home at the age of 15, to work surveying for the Department of Highways. A farmer, trapper and an avid hunter, he inspires his men who unwaveringly trust his leadership. A month earlier he had taken the battalion's Jr NCOs course, and coming last of 31 candidates, he failed it. But his platoon commander, Lieut Mert Entwhistle, recognized LaPoint's leadership qualities and immediately promoted him. This contrary decision was fully justified by LaPoint's outstanding battle performance.

Pioneer Platoon

The track up Hill 677 is rough and constricted. Lieut Hurst tells Captain Lloyd Hill the halftracks cannot make it up the narrow track. Stone overhears the conversation, turns with a hard glare and growls, "Hurst, get the halftracks up that bloody hill!" Hurst recalled: "For a moment I stand in awe of Stone, yet my mind turns to the explosions we will make, will they attract enemy fire? As his glare penetrates my being I mobilize myself. An order is an order regardless of the possible conse-quences. I gather my men, Private Tommy Powell brings forward the required equipment, and we break open the rock at three sites with pick-axes to make holes. It is the more difficult because of the darkness. We place plastic explosive at the bottom, then cordite to ignite it and finally the fuse. The entire platoon works long and hard. I constantly worry throughout our preparations the explosions will attract enemy, and that we are inviting the devastation of being fired upon, but it does not hap-pen." [3]

2030 hrs [40] - Stones Tactical HQ, ascends the rough track up Hill 677 from the Kapyong Valley. Two-thirds of the way up, the leading mortar platoon halftrack breaks down. Darkness envelops us. Stone, frustrated, is threatening to have the offending halftrack thrown over the side of the hill, but Captain Hill pleads with him to let it be for a time. A starter motor failed? Bob Hoffman, a Royal Canadian Electrical and Mechani-cal Engineers (RCEME) Craftsman (mechanic) eventually arrives from B Echelon, with a new starter motor, only to find that the problem is a dead battery.[4] It could have been replaced at any time. Stones restrained wrath, if one can ever think of Stone being restrained, impacts upon the unfortunate Hill. It is time consuming widening the road and clearing the rock by hand. We are ever mindful that our stalled formation is vulnerable. For two hours or more, the stalled half-track and widening of the ledge, immobilize the nerve centre of the Patricias; Tactical HQ, as well as the Mortar, Anti-Tank and Pioneers platoons.

2ND PATRICIAS PREPARE TO DO BATTLE AT KAPYONG

The tension increases. All our thoughts centre upon our Colonel, and we are anxiously anticipating his commands. The heightened nervous tension is overwhelming; there is a feeling of pervading paralysis. The urge to move infects everyone but we sit powerless while our infantry companies, now out of sight, are moving into their exposed forward positions.

Movements

The Patricias move to Kapyong as supply dumps are being destroyed, ammunition dumps are being fired, and supply depots are being torched - IX Corps had been accumulating supplies for the next stage of their offensive. Wanniandy, Section Commander 12 Platoon, reports that descending from the trucks the euphoria of the party mood of the troops evaporates. His thought - "Which of my men will not be around once this battle is over? It always seems to be D Company that gets it in the neck." [1]

Lieut. Brian Munro, A Company. For the second time today he is climbing to the top of Hill 677. "I become so exhausted my knees seem to buckle, every step is agonizing, I damn near do not make it. The last 100 meters is a dreadful struggle for me. I finally take off my very heavy pack. I fall to the ground exhausted. I am incensed to discover my batman, Ron Bourgon, has stuffed my pack with about 25 comic books, a large bottle of ketchup and a package of cookies! Bourgon has covertly appointed me his bloody porter! It is one of the two occasions I want to 'get Bourgon.' The cookies and ketchup later feed my hungry platoon." [5]

1st Middlesex Battalion

The enemy's rapid advance necessitates three companies to abandon their planned position, in front of 27th Brigade, at hill Sundok San, which is 794 meters high. They locate just forward of Brigade HQ, in reserve, south of Hill 677. [6] At the 3RAR Battalion HQ defensive position the ROK soldiers are rushing by in torrents. The withdrawal of the 6th ROK Division is developing into a total frenzy, reflecting a complete collapse at the front.

The firing line of the 81mm mortars is designated, they are base plated and zero in about 0300hrs the 24th. Four halftracks of the platoon are positioned midway between the mortar line and battalion Tactical HQ. [41] Private Michael Czuboka, recalls, " My number one, Robbie Roberts and I set up our mortar in an abandoned rice paddy. The ground is soft for two feet thereafter it is solid rock. We are dug in on open ground; the remaining mortars are close to us and in a similar position. Unfortunately much of our ammunition has to be stored above ground instead of being secured in the mortar pit. While the paddy walls provided a degree of added protection we are vulnerable to any kind of enemy fire. The mortar below us is very exposed. I dismount the .30 caliber browning machine gun from the halftrack, as I usually do, to provide added protection.[41] During the night hundreds of shadowy figures poured past us in a southerly direction. We are told these pathetic figures were remnants of the 6 Republic of Korea Division, but we are uncertain. They could be Chinese or North Koreans. They come to within 50 to 100 meters of our position they make us very nervous. During the aggressive Chinese attacks the sky is full of lights and explosions, but fortunately for us, no bombs or shells land in our immediate area.

"After setting up we are allotted "Defensive Fire" (DF) tasks, to zone in on locations where the Chinese might be expected to attack. These targets are designated "Fox1, Fox, 2, Fox 3, etc. When we go into action we are given commands such as; "Rapid Fire, Fox 3." [7]

Tactical HQ is not fully operational until 0400 hrs on the 24th.[7] PPCLI companies ascending in total darkness, move to their assigned areas. Formations visible during the day are obscured; this generates a degree of confusion. It is impossible to define features associated with the recce made earlier in the day. At D Company, 10 Platoon is the first to drop off as they ascend the hill. The rest of the company moves quietly upward, their destination unseen.

The Anti-Tank Platoon. Sergeant A. Sim: "We are located on a little pimple feature. It is dark and I don't know where our fields of fire are. We are told to do the best we can, to lie down on our bellies. We spend a restless and somewhat anxious night trying to sleep lying on the cold and open ground; we do not dig in until the next day. I keep one eye open all night." [8]

10 Platoon - Says Levy: "Our area is awash in smoke, I assume it has been recently napalmed. About 20 meters to our front there is scrub growth. I discover a large number of mud ovens over a wide area. They are in operation making charcoal. Sergeant Rushton was posted from my platoon immediately prior to Kapyong, when I learned in an earlier action that being deaf and in receipt of a disability pension for it stemming from WW II, he was unable to hear distant rifle fire. Corporal

Watson is acting Sergeant, but actually fulfills the role of a section commander at Kapyong." [9]

The Chinese are slowly building up their strength behind the Patricias. The halftrack ambulance, carrying Private Don Copley, Stretcher Bearer, does not have the power to make it up the hill. Everyone inside falls asleep. They are awakened by a soldier who is sent from above, banging his rifle on their vehicle: "Get the hell out of here! The valley is crawling with the enemy." [10] The driver hurriedly wheels around heading for A Echelon.

Masses of Chinese troops are seen in the moonlight advancing South from Hanamjong, a village east and north of Hill 504 situated on a northern tributary of the Kapyong River. A few shots ring out and soon it becomes an intense firefight as the Chinese press their attacks upon 3RAR. We witness the heavy machine guns and mortars joining the fray to become a crescendo. Flares light up the carnage. Tracer bullets of varying colours, whistles and varied bugle calls define the Chinese lines of attacks. Patricias stand-to, we are not attacked - yet.

Captain O. Browne, A Company: "The early night was quiet and fairly bright, and I was unaware the battle was about to be joined, until my company signaler, Corporal Dunbar, called me to the radio to listen in. "The Aussies were on our radio net," Dunbar was monitoring - "He had just overheard them report the enemy were in the valley to their front. Later I heard, 'There's about 200 of them now. About 600 yards away. They've stopped and seem to be forming up. Don't fire! I don't know which direction they are going.' I sent a warning to Tactical HQ and all sections. The Australia voice continues, 'There's more than 200, they are all approaching. They are passing to the left of the copse SHARK TRAIL. They are about 400 yards away. DON'T FIRE.' After a long pause, with utter silence throughout the night, 'They're about 200 yards away. They have reached WHALE BONE. FIRE!" [35]

2130 hrs - The Chinese 118 Division's 354 Regiment are engaging 3RAR, across the river by a tributary of the Kapyong River about 4 km distant. This attack results in three Company A, US 72nd Heavy Tank Battalion Tank commanders being killed. One tank is knocked out. They withdraw from in front of the Aussies to re-arm. A US 4.2 inch mortar barrage supporting A and B companies, helps repel the attackers. The 16 RNZA is in place at Naech'on, about midway between the Patricias and the 3RAR, on the west side of the Kapyong River. An American heavy 4.2-inch mortar battery assigned to 2PPCLI is nearby.

1 Platoon, A Company: Lance Corporal Bill Lee. "Watching the Australian and the Chinese fight is like watching the Movietone News in a theatre. It is a tremendous battle. There is one unique aspect. American tanks are going in circles firing at each other with their machine guns. It continues for some time, we do not understand what is taking place. Later we learn that advance Chinese infiltration troops are amongst the retreating ROK soldiers and they mount the American tanks to attack them. Three tank commanders are killed and one tank destroyed. The 72nd tankers get rid of the enemy by shooting them off of each other's tanks with their interior mounted .30 caliber medium machine guns. The Chinese are persistent, the circling continues for some time." [11]

2300 hrs - Copley and the others in the halftrack unable to climb Hill 677, arrive at A Echelon. Few staff are present and they stand-to all night observing the tracers flying through the night sky interspersed with artillery barrages.

2330 hrs - The Chinese's 354 Regiment is probing forward infantry positions, moving between the 2PPCLI and 3RAR. An Aussie scout is sent to check on the US 4.2 inch mortar battery that is assigned to support them. Fifty vehicles are loaded and waiting to move. Some mortars are still in emplacements and an entire field kitchen is abandoned. The troops, feel the "heat," and have bugged out. Running hard they scramble 16 km east of their position. They recover most of their vehicles and equipment the next day. [12]

About this time Brigadier Chung establishes his 6th ROK Div HQ, at Chuktun-ni, and again turns his machine guns on his panicked troops to restore order. But once more his soldiers lose their will to fight and stream past the RNZA gun positions. **General Chung, his troops reeling in full retreat, observes he cannot stop the Chinese and neither would the British 27th Brigade, for they are invincible.** Chung, however, reconstructs his Division and has them back in action 48 hrs later.[13] It has been rumoured they lined up certain of the officers, shot them in front of the assembled division and commenced to reorganize.

April 24 - 0100 hrs

B Company is in position, 350 to 400 meters northeast of D Company. Lieut Petrie is awakened, about 0200, to hear Major Lilley swearing and then saying: "Corporal shoot that man!" [15] The night passes without further disturbance.

Four more attacks are launched upon the Australians, the heaviest at 0130 hrs. The Chinese attackers, having vast numerical superiority, concentrate their forces so that 3RAR are engaging one continuous flow of the enemy. There are counter attacks. The Australians are literally slaughtering the enemy gross upon gross. The 72nd US tanks play a vital role in supporting, supplying the 3RAR and in saving many wounded from dying on the battlefield.[16] Retreating ROK vehicles and enemy mortar fire cut the 3RAR telephone landlines, running from the companies to Battalion HQ. As well A, B and D companies are denied wireless communication due to the intervening hills. They have to function through C Company to communicate with Battalion HQ, and the artillery support. At the same time Battalion HQ is heavily engaged defending themselves from the increasing numbers of infiltrating Chinese troops. Because of the assault on Battalion HQ, there is a lack of communication with the 16RNZA gun line, and thus an absence of artillery support for the rifle companies.

At about 0130 hrs, leading elements of the Chinese forces are nearing the 16 RNZA gun position. Two batteries are ordered farther south while the remaining battery continues supporting the Australians. The retiring batteries run a gauntlet of Chinese machine gun fire without incident. The two batteries are relocated south of Brigade HQ and are firing by 0300. The forward battery disengages to rejoin the regiment.[17]

0400 hrs - Reports are coming in about enemy movements, from Patricias units. The Chinese 354 Regiment is probing behind the forward infantry positions, moving in between the 2PPCLI and 3RAR. 16 RNZA: Major RJ Moore MBE, Battery Commander 162 Battery and Major RE Mason MC, Forward Observation Officer depart their gun line for 2PPCLI Tactical HQ. They become lost, almost stumbling upon an enemy formation. They return to their gun line to receive further direction and depart again at 0530.[18]

0400 - A company of the Middlesex is dispatched to relieve 3RAR Battalion HQ and they initially succeed in pushing the Chinese back but soon have to withdraw. By dawn the Chinese occupy the high ground behind the 2PPCLI, overlooking the 3RAR Battalion Headquarters (BHQ) and continue to strengthen their position. By 0600 the 3RAR BHQ start withdrawing in batches under cover of the 72nd tanks, and continue over three to four hours. At Headquarters Company, half a km to the southeast, they become aware of the pull out as an RAR jeep driver goes by shouting "Bug Out!" [14]

O530 hrs - B Echelon Lieut. Bud MacLeod: "Hoards of retreating ROK troops stream by, many disorganized, some in formation, and they carry arms and equipment. A few are pushing a railroad handcart loaded with weapons and equipment up a hill. A mile or more on they tire as the gradient increases. They off-load their equipment letting the cart run free, cascading down the long rising hillside to create havoc and devastation among those following. Bodies fly through the air. In the midst of the spectacle of a retreating army the situation bears its own humour akin to the Keystone Cops, we laugh heartily."[19] Private Gord Croucher remembers: "We are ordered to burn what supplies cannot be taken. We fire some tents, supplies and Stone's caravan, which was always breaking down. The instructions specify destroying our supply of booze, and somehow we salvage these refreshments." [20]

"The canteen officer has two squad tents. Cases of beer are stacked as high as they can go. We have been hauling it for days. I tell Corporal G Voth to go out and to stop the first American vehicle he sees and tell them there is beer here for $5 a case. The first vehicle is a Yank, a meathead (military policeman). They come down and fill the front of their jeep, then they fill the back with cases. We never lose a case." [21]

"I am burning junk that we are carrying around. There are sleeping bags we aren't allowed to use in the line and greatcoats we'd got rid of when they issued us parkas. We are soaking them with gasoline when this young Lieut comes up and says, "Stop, you can't do that!" I reply, "Just stand well back," and fire a Varey pistol into this heap. It was raining greatcoat buttons for days after." [21]

0545 hrs - Hill 677
Sergeant Sim, Anti-Tank Platoon has this memory: "After a fidgety night of periodic sleep, keeping one eye and one ear ever open for the Chinese, I call Corporals Nobby Clarke and Sterling MacAuley together. I lay out our defensive positions and have the men dig in. In the midst of my orders a Chinese medium machine gun opens fire from our rear. What the hell is that bloody machine gun doing there? Are the bloody Chinese here in force? It is situated on the high ground on the ridge to the west, just forward of Tactical HQ. I dive behind a wooden ration carton, which really provides little or no protection. At the very least my head is hidden behind something even though my legs and body are fully exposed. The men are diving behind scrub bushes, anything that might at least hide a portion of their bodies. I slowly inch my head around the corner of the box in the hope of spotting the point of originating fire, but I cannot. Some alert soul in the Mortar Platoon,

which is dug in nearby, sights the enemy and puts them out of action. No one is wounded." [22]

0600 hrs - The firing further alerts Stone, who has been assessing the intensity of the Chinese attacks on the Australians. He orders B Company to move east in 20 minutes, to protect the northeast flank of the battalion, including Tactical HQ. The new position is at a point north of the road track leading up from the valley below, and forward of the Mortar and Pioneer platoons and Tactical HQ. The area is under fire periodically and is too large to be defended by the Anti-Tank Platoon. [23] This proves to be an astute decision.

D Company now holds the forward most position on the west shoulder of the battalion. Levy, 10 Platoon: "At first light we stand-to, whilst doing another inspection of our area, I am surprised to discover we are isolated from the remainder of the company. We cannot achieve mutually supporting fire with 11 and 12 Platoons. There are a large number of well worn pathways in the area leading to the various charcoal mud ovens." [9]

0615 hrs - Majors Moore and Mason, 16 RNZA, arrive at 2PPCLI. Mason, the Forward Observation Officer, hikes to C Company to register artillery targets for the Patricias. Periodically, Chinese sightings are reported to the rear of Tactical HQ.[18]

B Company moves, Petrie: "....6 Platoon will move off through 5 and Company HQ, to take the lead, followed by Company HQ. Number 4 Platoon will make its way up the spur of the mountain to follow Company HQ. Number 5 would bring up the rear with the MMG section. Hastily such breakfast as can be eaten is taken and the withdrawal to the new position commences." [15] Daylight reveals that the 3RAR Rifle companies are four km behind enemy lines. 3RAR B Company launches a counter attack and hand-to-hand fighting ensues.

10 Platoon - Levy begins his ascent up the hill to the 12 Platoon position. "It is a steep incline, I am out of breath as I reach the Vickers machine gun position at 12 Platoon. Captain Mills, Acting Officer Commanding D Company, is positioning the Vickers along with one section. When he finishes I inform Mills that we are badly out of position being up to 300 meters or more down hill. I want to relocate to ensure mutually supporting fire with the other platoons." A heated discussion takes place. Mills addresses Levy bluntly: "Those are my orders, stay there!" [9] Although Levy had not attended Stone's orders

group, he points out tactically it is vital to ensure mutual supporting fire within the company platoons. Mills reiterates that Levy is to return to his position and stay there. The clash of personalities becomes intense. Mills with rising impatience glares at Levy, "Those are my orders, follow them or I will charge you with disobeying an order."

Levy the more experienced battle officer, has correctly assessed the tactical situation, and his observations are consistent with orders issued only hours earlier by Stone. But Mills cannot admit that a junior officer has greater insight into the impending conflict and appears to be more concerned with the preservation of his dignity and authority, in the face of the enemy - even if he endangers the lives of his men he is responsible for, and hence the battalion.

Mills locates his HQ out of sight of all of his platoons, 100 to 200 meters to the rear of the hills rising 15 meters or higher behind each of his platoons, and thus abdicates control of the battle to his platoon commanders. In essence, during the battle Mills relegates his position to that of a wireless relay operator between battalion Tactical HQ and his platoons. At Kapyong Mills does not coordinate his layout or his defensive plan; he does not: [24]

Visit the positions of 10 or 11 Platoons
Hold Orders Groups at Kapyong.
Issue contingency orders
Advise platoon commanders of the location of Company HQ.
Inform platoon commanders of the on going battle situation.
Later assess/discuss the performance at Kapyong
with his platoon commanders.

Mills, D Company Second-in-Command was formerly transport officer. Kapyong is his first time in the line and thus his first experience commanding a company in action. Major Bob Swinton MC, Officer Commanding D Company, is enjoying 5 days R & R in Japan. Mills, while awaiting his call to the front along with the other second in command of companies is at A echelon. Captain Del Harrison advises, "At A Echelon, we officers are not assigned other duties, and there is not a training programme designed to prepare for our eventual command of a company. Only once did I briefly visit my company in the line. We just sit around." [25] Mills had not previously served in action as an officer.

B Echelon - Carrying a white flag and dressed in South Korean army uniforms, a platoon size group of soldiers approaches. A guard is mounted, but the group proves to be ROK soldiers. They are fed and continue south.

B Company, Petrie - "As we set out to relocate we can see a great deal of movement in the valley of the Kapyong River to the northeast and organized groups of enemy soldiers coming across the valley toward the base of our mountain. They are six abreast and advancing at their ever aggressive solid trot. US Navy Corsair aircraft maintain a continuing attack on the Chinese, at the base of the mountain and up the Kapyong River Valley to the north supporting 3RAR. Patricias B Company passes over a steep mass of scree and the going is hard. The MMG crew with their heavy loads find the going even more tiring." [15]

0700 hrs - On two separate hillocks Mills sights the two positions of 12 Platoon, the only D Company positions he visits. One section supports the MMG in the West location, designed to provide inter platoon support, under Lance Corporal Jimmy Wanniandy. The other two sections dig in 75 meters to the east, under Sergeant BW Holligan, thus weakening their integrated firepower. The curve at the base of the hill behind them protrudes slightly so that only a segment of the east slits are visible to the West position.

0730 hrs - About 30 to 40 Chinese soldiers positioned five to eight meters apart are sighted moving along the base of Hill 677, advancing on either side of the road and moving at a steady trot. They scatter as two US T-33s jet aircraft strafe their ranks, but soon continue their relentless and rapid advance. Mills orders the medium machine gun at 12 west to engage the enemy. The line of fire is directly over the heads of 10 Platoon, so its trajectory endangers 10's soldiers. Mills then allows Levy to relocate, and given a free hand, he repositions his men to gain and offer a measure of mutually supporting fire.

10 Platoon, Levy - "My new position is on a spur, west of and on slightly higher ground than the section of 12 Platoon west. Our new location is separated from 12's west slits by a gully about 50 meters across; only two of 12's slits are visible. They are on slightly lower ground, dug in on a small rising hillock. The nearest trench holds the MMG. The remainder of 12 west and all of 12 east, due to the curving base of the hill behind them, are out of sight. I place two sections of my platoon forward in an inverted "V" formation. My HQ is centered about 13 meters behind the forward trench and 20 meters forward of the base

of the hill. The rear of the hill is a steep incline and I conclude there is little danger of an attack from that quarter. However, I place the reserve section under Lance Corporal Bill White on the reverse slope at the top of the hill, 15 or more meters above, ensuring an all around defence. Our front covers about 65 to 70 meters. The land falls sharply away to the front of our position. From below a well-defined pathway comes up a sharp incline into the centre of our position, the angle of descent continues for a considerable distance. To the west there is a spur leading to another feature. There are clumps of scrub growth in the general area. Our position is perfect for grenading the enemy as it advances up the steep hill.

"During the last offensive I had a number of casualties and recently sent two deserving chaps to the Junior NCOs School. I am down to 11 experienced men, with the remainder being newly arrived reinforcements from Japan, whom I have not had the opportunity to evaluate. There are 24 of us, not 40, which is the army establishment for a platoon." [9] Had Levy and his men remained isolated in their original position it is likely they would have been annihilated.

Private John Grison, D Company HQ: "All the hills to our front, between us and the platoon positions, look to be about equal in height. We cannot see any of the platoon positions." [26]

12 Platoon is under the command of Sergeant BW Holligan. A veteran of WW II in Europe, he fought with the 51st Highland Division. Lieut Lee Hill was wounded on the 14 of April; Holligan has been seconded from 11 Platoon. They are dug in on a hillock only a meter high and barely large enough for two sections to dig in. The curve of the hill allows them only a partial view of their detached section. At 12 west, the hillock is low and just large enough for only four slits.

11 Platoon - Pearson: "We are about 200 meters east of 12 Platoon's east position, separated by a precipice with a near vertical drop of about 20 meters. They are situated on a higher ridge west of us. We occupy a narrow ledge, behind which the embankment rises about 10 meters. To the right (east) is a broad sloping hillside descending to the valley floor. It is either barren and rocky, or covered in small scrub. If the Chinese are to form up a mass attack from this direction it makes an ideal killing ground. We have an unspoiled view of the valley below. I have a 9mm pistol that has the distressing habit of misfiring or jamming every three or four times I try to fire it. Hence it is only to be used in a dire emergency, because of this I also carry a Lee-Enfield Mark 4 bolt-action

rifle. Regrettably no one has short-range rapid-fire weapons, such as the US Carbine, the reliable Australian Owen Gun or the Chinese Burp Gun, all of which would have be useful in nighttime close combat. Mills does not visit my location. From the time we descend from the transport at the base of Hill 677, until Mills issues our withdrawal orders on the 26th, I do not attend a company orders group." [27]

16 RNZA - Major Ron Mason of the 162 Battery, at C Company, zeros in his artillery guns to register targets on likely enemy approaches to the sharp ridges held by the 2PPCLI. [18]

A group of five soldiers, who were left out of battle and stationed at A Echelon, are ordered to Tactical HQ, to form part of a Tactical HQ Defence Detachment. Their first assignment is to dig a protective trench so that Stone's jeep, containing the #19 radio set connected on the 27 Brigade net, would be "hulled down." Private Bill O'Dale, one of the five, was formerly with 10 Platoon when late one January night, in Miryang he: "came off guard duty at 0200 and returned to my quarters, the troops are quartered 14 to a tent. As I open the flap, a soldier inside fires a sudden burst of five rounds from a Bren machine gun at a distance of six inches. A nervous Corporal Smith has fired without warning and at point blank range, but miraculously only one round hit me. It penetrated my hand wounding my trigger finger, which has remained limp ever since." [28] At the tent wall where he had been standing there was a sinister cluster of five small bullet holes. Smith was immediately returned to Canada, while O'Dale was hospitalized in Japan. He soon recovered and was posted to 25 Canadian Reinforcement Group, Japan. In early March, at his request, he was posted to the Patricias at A Echelon, but now at last he is at the centre of the action.

At dawn Lance Corporal HR Crocker is in a jeep at Tactical HQ, operating the #19 wireless set on the 27th Brigade communications radio net. 3RAR, Middlesex, and American units are transmitting enemy reference points to Brigade Intelligence, and where possible they are providing estimates of men and weapons. For two hours Private Crocker plots these points on a map. As Crocker continues making entries he realizes the Chinese are encircling the Patricias. Crocker reports: "I called Captain Ed Coombe, Patricias Signals Officer, requesting he bring over Stone. Stone studies the map, then turns to Crocker, 'Soldier are you sure of those grid references?' Yes Sir." Stone studies the map running his finger over the enemy positions and his Patricias locations. After a silence Stone says, "By God, we could get run over." [29]

Stone orders Regimental Sergeant Major Les Grimes to remove the jerry cans from all vehicles. They are to be placed on the ground at the vehicles' fronts with matches on top. Should the enemy approach all vehicles are to be torched. The RSM orders all nonessential personnel to form an all around defence of Tactical HQ. Stone commands: "It is about 4km south to friendly territory, should we be overrun everyone is on their own." [29]

Years later, in March 1999, Les wrote me a letter, from his home in Cornwall, England, in answer to my enquiries. In part he stated: "For the last eight years I have been in and out of hospital for bladder and tumor surgery. I am 85 years of age and almost completely immobilized with arthritis, and I sometimes look at these old legs of mine, that have marched over the rocky wastes of India's North West Frontier, slogged through the sands of the desert, marched the breadth of Germany and over the hills of Korea, fighting for freedom and say, 'Was it worth it?' And the answer is yes, it sure as hell was! Even to the point of this letter I must reach a mail box about fifty yards from my door but this journey is as arduous as a Mount Everest Expedition." Mr. Grimes was nick-named "Daddy Grimes," by the men of the Patricias, and was much liked and respected. As has been said so many times, Old Soldiers Never Die, they just fade away....

As Crocker goes off duty at 0700 hrs, he walks a few yards and is shot in the foot by an enemy sniper. Two soldiers at Tactical HQ spot a Chinese machine gun nest close by and they prepare to attack the position. Just then, the enemy is fired upon by an American tank in the valley and is destroyed. The soldiers are hit with shrapnel and one later loses an arm.

0900 hrs - Stone orders Capt Murray Edwards, Quartermaster, to A Echelon, to bring forward all available ammunition. During the night the Chinese take control of the road leading south. As they are encircling the Australians, they are also building up their numbers to the Patricias' rear. Company A, 72 US Heavy Tank Battalion is evacuating 3 RAR casualties and bringing supplies forward. The road is open although the enemy now controls the high ground overlooking the road. It is a case of 'go like hell.' Edwards: "Time is of the essence as the road could be closed at any time. Staff Sergeant PD McLennan and I take two deuce and a halfs, at A Echelon, one truck takes on 60mm mortar bombs then loads .303 ammunition. Captain Gordon Turnbull, Adjutant, is outfitting 17 reinforcements and they, including Copley and other stretcher-bearers, are loaded into the second truck. Major Tighe second in command of the battalion leads the group in a jeep, racing to Tactical HQ. " [30]

0900 hrs - Headquarters IX Corps informed the 27th Brigade that the 6th ROK Division had ceased to be operational. [42]

1000 hrs - B Echelon commences the first of six withdrawals. Captain Chub Hanway MC, legal officer, (Armoured Corps WWII) has acquired an M8 Greyhound Armoured Car, with a turret mounted 37mm Gun. Hanway moves out swiveling the turret as his driver, Private Wagaczyk a legal clerk leads the charge south.

Major Don Grant, commands HQ Company - He is also known as the "Proprietor of Banglestein's Bar;" where an array of UN officers pause for refreshment whether they are going North or South. Banglestein's and Grant became famous throughout the 27th Brigade, and especially with attached American forces. Amazingly the bar was usually well supplied with "refreshments" - hard liquor. It has been suggested that senior American Commanders, who were only allowed to refresh the palates of their officers and soldiers with Coca Cola and ice cream, were upset with Banglestein's "permissiveness." Banglestein's was developing a growing recognition amongst UN officers. Stone, it was believed, had to bear the brunt of some harsh words from senior US officers.

1030 hrs - Crocker, earlier wounded in the foot, is evacuated by jeep, along with another wounded man and Major Jack George is riding in the front passenger seat. George informs Crocker that the Chinese snipers have been picking off the drivers while they are descending the hill and crossing the rice paddy to the main road. If their driver is hit they agree that George will press down on the accelerator with his hand and Crocker will steer. They make a safe passage and the wounded are delivered to the 60 Indian Parachute Field Ambulance. They are striking tents to evacuate farther South. Crocker remembers: "I waited an hour for a helicopter ride to a US MASH unit, and later spent two weeks in an American hospital in Tokyo before being transferred to an Australian medical facility at Ebisu, Yokohama." [31]

George is returning to Canada, we are informed, to instruct troops on the fighting tactics employed in Korea. There are suggestions that Stone believes C Company is not in the best condition to fight a battle. This is possibly underlined when Stone, appoints Captain Del Harrison, then second in command of B Company, to relieve George. Harrison had been a company commander in WWII and takes over a company with which he has no familiarity, just as they are about to dig in. It is not a decision that would normally be deemed desirable just as you are about to enter battle. Conversely, 27th Brigade, just prior to the battle, postponed a pending change of command. Brigadier Burke is to be relieved by Brigadier Taylor; however, as Burke had earned the respect of the battalion commanders, it is deemed prudent to have him commanding the Brigade during the forthcoming battle. Taylor took command on the 26th.

Petrie subsequently took command of 8 Platoon. He notes, "C was in surprisingly poor shape with respect to a number of practices. I found there was a dearth of effective junior NCOs, poor passing of orders and vague understanding of platoon tactical drills. The platoon had no idea of the succession of command if they lost their commander, or even a section commander. We had a hectic couple of weeks training in the line before I felt safe at all. For my money, after Vince Lilly, Del Harrison was an excellent Company Commander with whom to work." [32] Is it possible Stone's actions served to stimulate George's future performance?

[On December 10[th]1951, Major Jack George, commanding D Company, 1 PPCLI, was awarded a Distinguished Service Order (DSO), for a company patrol he led west of Hill 227. This decoration is usually awarded to LCols and above. George at one point in the action: "Several times he rushed and grenaded a particularly bothersome enemy machine gun while covered by a Bren gun." [33] During the battle George was wounded in the neck by a grenade fragment, but refused medical care until the battle was terminated. George was the last man of the patrol to return, he ensured every man of D Company had returned to base. He certainly proved his mettle in battle.]

Hill 677, Mortar Platoon. There are a number of large re-entrants, south of the track and ascending the hill that leads into our position. There is one that is about 250 meters across. On the south side there is a knoll that reaches out about 150 meters east. Company Sergeant Major Jack Rudd and this author take a recce to get a better understanding of the terrain. Approaching the eastern-most point we come under rifle fire. We assume it is a sniper because we are only targeted when we put our heads up. By trying to analyze the 'crack-thump' we hope to locate the firing point of our assailant. We do not.

2ND PATRICIAS PREPARE TO DO BATTLE AT KAPYONG

1100 hrs - Brigadier Burke addresses the 2PPCLI through a loud hailer from a US DC-3 aircraft, flying slowly and low overhead. He states that he knows the Patricias will do their duty that we will fight and be a credit to our Regiment. Rather than a harsh order, it is delivered as a confident expectation, extended between trusted friends. It is a warmly reassuring and inspiring gesture; the troops are impressed that their Brigadier, responsible for so many decisions, would take the time to personally address them.

1130 hrs B Company - They arrive at their new location to take a short rest and fill their water bottles. The enemy in the Valley below is observed advancing along the road. The officers go to Tactical HQ for a briefing. The men dig in facing north and northeast. A Vickers machine gun section attached to Company HQ. Five Platoon takes up a position on a spur between 6 Platoon and Company HQ. Six Platoon is on the forward spur, and to their extreme right (south) is Support company. About 200 meters farther south and up a gentle incline, is Tactical HQ. To the west the ridge rises 20 meters or more, while on the other side there is a medium grade slope leading to D Company. Private Paul Lamey and Corporal Webaska share a slit trench at 6 Platoon.

1200 hrs. 3RAR, LCol Ferguson ordered his companies to withdraw to the Middlesex Battalion area. For two more hours the enemy attacks their D Company. After 16 hours of engaging the enemy 3RAR receive withdrawal instructions to get out as best they can. The US 72 tankers make 11 trips evacuating 3 RAR wounded. Their fight is far from over. The 3 RAR BHQ, two km south of the various company positions, is in danger of being overrun by the Chinese and the rifle companies at times engage in hand to hand fighting. The Patricias observe that the Chinese follow Mao's dictates to the letter, massing their forces on a limited front facing 3RAR. The Australians are engaging overwhelming odds; their battle extends well into the night.

During the battle, the 16RNZA, provides 3RAR with invaluable artillery support, in spite of the restricted communications with BHQ and subsequently the companies. The battery at Kapyong sends a Second Lieut Forward Observation Officer to 3RAR, and he is almost instantly killed. [34] The Australians, heavily embattled, evidently do not call for "pinpoint" artillery fire on the attacking enemy, as a map of pre-registered targets is thought invalid. The topography interferes with wireless communication and only C Company is able to communicate with Battalion HQ. Wireless contact is also a problem for 16RNZA forward personnel.

1230 hrs - Just north of Hill 677, Major Tighe, Patricias Second-in-Command, penetrates enemy lines. In his jeep are the two padres, and following in a deuce and a half are reinforcements and stretcher-bearers and lastly Edwards. The Chinese open fire. Staff Sergeant McLennan fires a warning shot over Tighe's head and he quickly 'U' turns, high-tailing it back to our lines leaving the transport behind.[30] The truck stops in an exposed field to turn around, and the troops immediately pile out. Edwards and McLennan dash to the truck ordering the men back in. One reinforcement is shot in the chest while on the truck. For whatever reason when Edwards reaches the truck the Chinese cease firing and, curiously, stop to observe events. All make it to Tactical HQ and the wounded man is evacuated.

At Tactical HQ a Sergeant orders Copley and the others to surrender all their .303 ammunition except 10 rounds each. Copley: "I first give up only one bandoleer. The Sergeant takes my second one leaving me with but 10 rounds. I have not even fired a shot. I go to the Regimental Aid Post (RAP) and stay there for the remainder of the battle." [32]

1300 hrs - There are continuing reports of increasing numbers of the enemy moving south, always advancing at a intimidating trot, six abreast. Major Mason, 16RNZA Forward Observation Officer is at C Company: "The Chinese camouflaged with pine branches were moving on the road in the valley and every time a plane flew over they would lie still." [18] Mason brings down fire until the enemy disappears under the brow of a hill. Contrary to standard practice he then drops in shells on an almost perpendicular trajectory.

1400 hrs - B Company. 6 Platoon is under small arms fire from a knoll slightly below them. Major Vince Lilley is present, ensuring his platoons are mutually supporting. Lilley orders: "Fix bayonets." He draws his 9 mm pistol and orders "Charge" as he leads the attack. In the valley, an American tank mistakes the movement of the Patricias for the enemy and opens fire. Pte Wayne Mitchell is knocked to the ground by concussion, injuring his back. The Patricias take the knoll but do not locate the enemy. (Although Mitchell's back bothered him for years, the Department of Veterans Affairs (DVA) denied his application for a disability pension for his injury. No medical record of the injury was taken at the time of the battle).[32]

11 Platoon - A Vickers machine gun is moved into position and soon opens fire on the Chinese moving along the valley floor. There are no

tracers in the ammunition so they cannot define the point of impact, and the Vickers is removed.[27]

1500 hrs - The Patricias witness a US Navy Corsair aircraft Napalm Australian troops at their D Company. It is demoralizing as hell to witness one's supporting aircraft burning our allies. The troops look at each other and ask, 'Holy shit, what a bloody rotten deal! Are these flyers going to get us next?' The Chinese observe the napalming and choose that moment to attack. They are cut down by another RAR platoon. At 3RAR: "A man having no flesh, hands dripping flesh, completely naked, walks past. Sticks and stones are coming through his feet." [34] The horrors of being napalmed are inconceivable to the layman and must be witnessed to be comprehended. The horrific sight is heightened by the odious reeks of burning human flesh, he passes by in total silence.

An American Chemical 4.2 inch mortar battery is assigned to 2PPCLI. "Snuffy" Harrison's C Company receives their controlling Forward Fire Officer, Lieut Robert E Bundy, a Texan who is accompanied by his signalman Joe Schuller. C's position is northern most, and from there the spotters range in to support all Patricia's company positions.

1700 hrs - B Company 0rders Group.[15]

> The action witnessed earlier in the morning has been a heavy attack on 3RAR Hill 504, 30 killed, 40 are wounded.
> Extra ammo is to be kept about each soldier's neck.
> Wireless watch maintained at all times.
> All soldiers to remain in slit trenches.
> Shoot anything that moves.
> Prepare for continuous engagement without relief.

Captain Owen Browne Acting Commander A Company gave a speech to officers of the PPCLI in the 1970s during which he said: "From my arrival until mid afternoon the main Kapyong valley and the subsidiary valley cutting across the front had been empty of people. Then suddenly, down the road through the subsidiary valley came hordes of men, running, walking, running, interspaced with military vehicles - totally disorganized mobs. They were elements of the 6th ROK Division, which were supposed to be 10 miles forward engaging the Chinese. But they were not engaging the Chinese. They were fleeing. I was witnessing a rout. The valley was filled with men. Some left the road and fled over the forward edges of A Company positions. Some killed themselves on the various booby-traps we had lain, and that component of my defensive layout became worthless. I saw drivers of military vehicles run over their own men, willfully. I saw one man shoot the driver of a vehicle, pull him out to the ground, take over the vehicle and proceed. I would be ghoulish to continue with examples. Between 1530 hrs and 1800 hrs, all of A Company speeded up its defence preparations and digging as it watched, helpless to intervene, while approximately 4,000 - 5,000 troops fled in disorganized panic across and through the forward edges of our position. But we knew then that we were no longer 10 - 12 miles behind the line, we were the front line." [35]

Company Sergeant Major Mike Melnechuck, C Company. - "Regrettably I have seen fear on men's faces many times before, but none that has burned in my memory as that on the faces of the retreating Republic of Korea (ROK) troops fleeing in the face of the fast advancing Chinese juggernaut. ROK troops appeared over the very steep and seeming insurmountable rock face to our front. **Their eyes were wide open but they appeared not to see anything in front of them.**" [36]

Our troops are visibly anxious when facing the masses of retreating South Korean's taking flight through our positions. Are they really ROKs or are they Chinese infiltration troops - are they suddenly going to open fire shooting us in the back? They are carrying weapons. How do we differentiate between the enemy and the ROKs? What an unholy muddle this is. We cannot be certain who is passing through. It is unnerving, and everyone has their hidden finger on the trigger. The officers and NCOs are continuously ordering and ensuring the Patricias do not open fire on the terrified and uncontrollable fleeing troops. Browne: "War is won by the will to win and the determination of the participants. The erstwhile participants I had watched flee had no such will. This sudden meaning of Kapyong, is also the principle of war, it's called 'morale.' I watched the evening approach with confidence, because I knew the morale of A Company, and it was good - despite the shock of what we had just seen." [35]

A Company - Lance Corporal Bill Lee - "There are two well worn pathways leading into our position. All day long streams of panicked South Korean soldiers run away from the Chinese and retreat through our position. We let them pass. There are hundreds even thousands of them. The mortar men are carrying 81mm mortars; there are troops with machine guns; there are officers and NCOs alike fleeing from the front lines. At 1700 hrs Owen Brown orders us to close the passage. On the prior night the Australians had let the retreating South Korean's pass through. They were intermixed with infiltrating Chinese soldiers who then attacked the Aussies. Their numbers dry up, I don't know where the others go." [37]

Canadian authorities have always taken pride in citing how superior the Lee-Enfield is under any and all conditions but Melnechuck has a problem with his rifle. "I cannot close the bolt fully. If I had to fire it I would have to hold the bolt down, nearly in position. I am concerned that if I do fire I might have a blow back which will take half my head off." [36] The next day he discovers a speck of dirt caught in the bolt head, it takes a pointed knife to get it out. Luckily he did not have to put his Lee-Enfield to the test.

1730 hrs - The enemy, despite heavy losses, pressed their attacks against 3RAR. And it became clear they could not hold out another night. Supported by A Company 72nd Heavy Tank battalion, they began to withdraw under cover of smoke and High Explosive fire. Vehicle columns were protected by the tanks and the infantry had to fight the enemy as they came out on foot. [42]

1800 hrs - The artillery support is to be augmented by three American artillery units. The 27th Brigade now has under its command:

16 RNZA	24 - 25 pounders
213 Armoured Support Battalion	17 - 155mm Self Propelled Howitzers
(ASB) A new unit, they have been in action 24 hours.	
1 Field Artillery Battalion (FAB)	18 - 105mm
5 Regimental Combat Team (5RCT)	
17 Field Artillery Battery	18 - 105 mm
Attch'd, firing from 1650 hrs.	4 - 8inch Howitzrs

At Kapyong the American allotment of 57 howitzers, added to the New Zealand 24 field guns, a total of 81 artillery pieces. In addition the 16 RNZA were supported by one battery of 8 inch howitzers attached to the 17th Field Artillery Battalion. [39] This thunderous might was too late for the 3RAR, but sustains overwhelming support to the 2PPCLI that night. This underlines how effective the Chinese offensive has been as well as the necessity to ensure that IX Corps, is able to withdraw in an orderly fashion to over extend the enemy's supply line. The 213 ASB and the 5RCT are sent from the First Cavalry Division to reinforce 27 Brigade. The available artillery, now under the control of the 16 RNZA, is more than four times greater than normally allocated to a Brigade.

Mason, 16RNZA FOO at C Company is exhausted having engaged the enemy continuously over the prior 72 hours and is ordered by Major Moore, Battery Commander, at 2PPCLI Tactical HQ, to come to his position. Mason sleeps peacefully through the night until early the next morning. [18]

1900 hrs - B Company, Petrie recalls: "As dusk approaches 6 Platoon reports the enemy forming up in an re-entrant, preparing for an attack on the Middlesex. With darkness falling our battalion mortars open fire upon this force and decimate it." [15]

Private Don Worsfold C Coy - "Dusk is settling in. Republic of Korea soldiers have been coming through our position all day. What have they experienced that has so terrified them? The unknown makes me and my mates very nervous. A larger group of 250 to 300 men, appearing to be under the control of a ROK officer, begin their ascent toward our trenches. They are all armed. As they are about to come through Lieut Johnny Deegan approaches the officer to ask that his men stand and fight alongside us. They ignore him. Deegan, one of the quietest officers in the Patricias, is beside himself with anger, his patience exasperated he smashes the officer in the face. It makes no impression upon the officer, or upon the troops. They are a disorganized mob, paralyzed with fear, running hard, going south. Nothing is going to stand in their way." [38]

It is a most serious offence within the South Korean Army to lose one's weapon; It is punishable by death. Though they have their weapons the men have thrown away their ammunition so that they will not be forced to fight. This is why the deserting troops are so often well armed.

Private Don Worsfold - "The Chinese are advancing at a solid trot, six abreast, descending from the north out of the Kapyong Gorge. It is as if we are witnessing disciplined Roman Legions advancing, advancing, advancing... in stark contrast to the mobs of panic-stricken South Koreans fleeing from their aggressors. The Chinese are intent upon destroying us. Could nothing stop the descending hordes? Are they Invincible!? I'll tell you, this is no morale builder. I witness thousands of terrorized soldiers, fully armed running away, heralding the onrush of the oncoming legions. I am scared as Hell!" [38]

The 27th Brigade HQ is situated about four kilometers south of the Patricias, on the west side of the Pukhan River. (Map following page 86). The Australians have fought one hell of a battle against overwhelming odds. The 3RAR have put up an incredible fight! Casualties are 32 Killed, 59 wounded, 3 captured; total 94. They captured 32 Prisoners of War.

By 2240 hrs the Middlesex Battalion is forward of Brigade HQ and the 3RAR are badly weakened after their hard fought battle, and are south of the Middlesex Battalion. The US 5 Regimental Combat Team, attached to 27th Brigade, is being held in reserve. They are about to play a key part in relieving 2PPCLI on April 25. The Chinese are encircling the Patricias, and consolidating their strength prior to continuing their attack.

The unit holding back the farther advance of the main body of the Chinese 60 and 118 Divisions are Canada's Patricias.

The 2PPCLI are dug in on the dominating Hill 677, and have a clear view of their killing ground to the north and east. Chinese forces advancing from the narrow valley of the Kapyong to the north are vulnerable as are those moving through the eastern access. General P'eng has to eliminate the Patricia's before he can realize his objective of advancing upon Seoul. The Patricias battle at Kapyong is about to begin in earnest.

1. Wanniandy: Signed statement, March 30, 1998
2. LaPointe: Telephone interview, and meeting Victoria, 1999
3. Hurst: Meeting in Edmonton 1999
4. Hoffman: Telephone interview 1999
5. Munro: Video tape interview 1997
6. 2PPCLI War Diary

7. Czuboka:Exchange of e/mails, July 2001

8. Sim: Interview, Kamloops, April 2000

9. Levy: Signed statement 17 October 1997, and later conversations.

10. Copley - telephone interview 2000

11. Lee: Telephone interview September 1999

12. O'Neill 145

13. McGibbon 120

14. Breen 72

15. Petrie, Field notes, 1951

16. Breen 83

17. McGibbon 125

18. Major Mason, telephone conversation, New Zealand, 99 01 21.

19. MacLeod: memorandum, February 16 1997

20. Croucher; Telephone interview May 2000. Edwards advises the Caravan was not destroyed.

21. Speakers are unknown… taken from unidentified notes of the 1985 PPCLI reunion.

22. Sim: Interview Kamloops, 10 May 2000

23. 2PPCLI War diary

24. Pearson: Letter April 1997; Levy statement 17 Oct 1997.

25. Harrison; Telephone Feb 2002. Normally a second in command would make periodic visits to the front. 2PPCLI only had one officer who had taken staff courses, Major Vince Lilley

26. Grison, letter May 28, 1998

27. Pearson: Memorandum April 1997

28. O'Dale: telephone interview 2000

29. Crocker: telephone interview 2000

30. Edwards: telephone interview 1998

31. Copley: telephone interview Aug 2000

32. Petrie: memo 20 Sep 1996

33. 1PPCLI War Diary, Lieut R Frost, Intelligence Officer

34. Breen; 97

35. Speech by Browne: to PPCLI officers, sometime during the 1970s.

36. Melenchuck, Interview Kamloops April 1999

37. Lee: telephone interview May 2000

38. Worsfold: Interview May 01, 2000

39. McGibbon, page 132, 133,

40. MacKenzie cites a later time in his memorandum made1954, 2130 hrs.

41. Mackenzie cites all the machine guns of the halftracks being dismounted. Some of the MMGs were dismounted by those manning the mortar line. The remaining MMGs on four halftrack all remained mounted on the vehicles.

42. 27th Brigade War Diary, April 1951.

MAPS - KAPYONG - 27th BRIGADE DISPOSITIONS
......Editor's Note : Abbreviations are key to map locations ....

Description of D Company's positions

Colour Map 1

Sketch of D Company layout

Colour Map 2

Map - 2 Battalion PPCLI (2PPCLI)

27th Brigade Headquarters (27 Bde HQ)

16 Field Artillery Regiment, Royal New Zealand Artillery
(16 RNZA)

3 Battalion The Royal Australian Regiment (3RAR)

1 Battalion The Middlesex Regiment (1 MX)

1 Battalion King's Own Scottish Borderers Regiment (1 KOSB)

Attached 27th Brigade, 1800 hrs April 24:
5 Regimental Combat Team (5RCT - Equivalent to a British Brigade)

17 Field Artillery Battery, (17 FAB) 18 - 105mm howitzers

1 Calvary Division, US Army

Colour map 3

Topographical Map, Kapyong

Diagram, D Company Disposition, Kapyong.
Not drawn to scale.
Hill 677

D Company occupies the west flank of the battalion. They are also at the highest point, being about 500 meters above the valley floor. The other companies are about 400 meters or less above the valley.

D Company HQ, Captain Wally Mills, Acting Commander - No casualties
Mills locates his HQ 100 to 200 meters to the rear of his platoons. Due to the rising curving spurs 15 meters or more behind each platoon, they are not visible to Company HQ. Mills thus abdicates control of the battle to his platoon commanders. The platoons are not wholly mutually supporting.

10 Platoon Lieut Michael G. Levy - 24 men - later 28 - 8 wounded.
Western most, covering a front of about 65 - 70 meters. The forward slit is occupied by Corporal Clouthier, along with Baxter and his #2 on the Bren Gun. A major pathway from down below leads into their slit. The land gently slopes for about three meters to their front then falls steeply downward. The other slits are in an inverted "V" formation fanning out behind Clouthier. Levy's HQ is 10 to 13 meters to the rear of Clouthiers slit. This position is 7 meters higher than 12west. For all round defence Levy places a section on the reverse slope. The initial attacking Chinese troops ascend the pathway unaware of 10's presence.

12 Platoon - Sergeant Holligan - 24 men - then 34+(e), still later 26(e)
2 killed, none wounded.
Sighted in two locations. Situated on ground about 7 meters lower than 10 Platoon. Dug in on two low-rising hillocks, about 75 meters apart, referred to as 'west' and 'east.' Holligan, with 2 sections at 12east, is about 125 meters to the east or right of 10, which is out of sight. 12west, one section plus the medium machine gun, are 50 meters east of 10 Platoon and 20 meters forward, only two slits are visible to 10. 12west accommodates only four slits. The Vickers machine gun slit is in the western most slit, forward of 10. The view 12west has of 12east, a further 75 meters east, is partially obscured by the curve of the hill. About 0700/24, Mills sights the positioning of 12west. It is believed that Mills determined the sighting of both of 12's locations, and the Vickers medium machine gun.

11 Platoon Lieut Pearson - 25 men - later 13.
2 killed in action, none wounded.
They are situated 200 meters to the east of 12 Platoon east, on slightly lower ground. There is a steeply walled reentrant of 20 meters deep in between 11 and 12 Platoon. Dug in on a narrow ledge, the hill behind rises 10 meters or so. A Bren Gun is situated in the north slit, and receives a direct hit by an enemy mortar bomb, killing the two man crew.

D Company at Kapyong

This representation is not drawn to scale.

The Chinese assault commenced at 0130 hrs, April 25

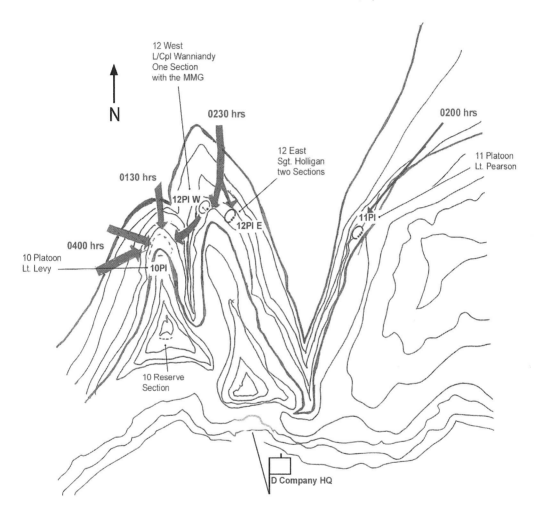

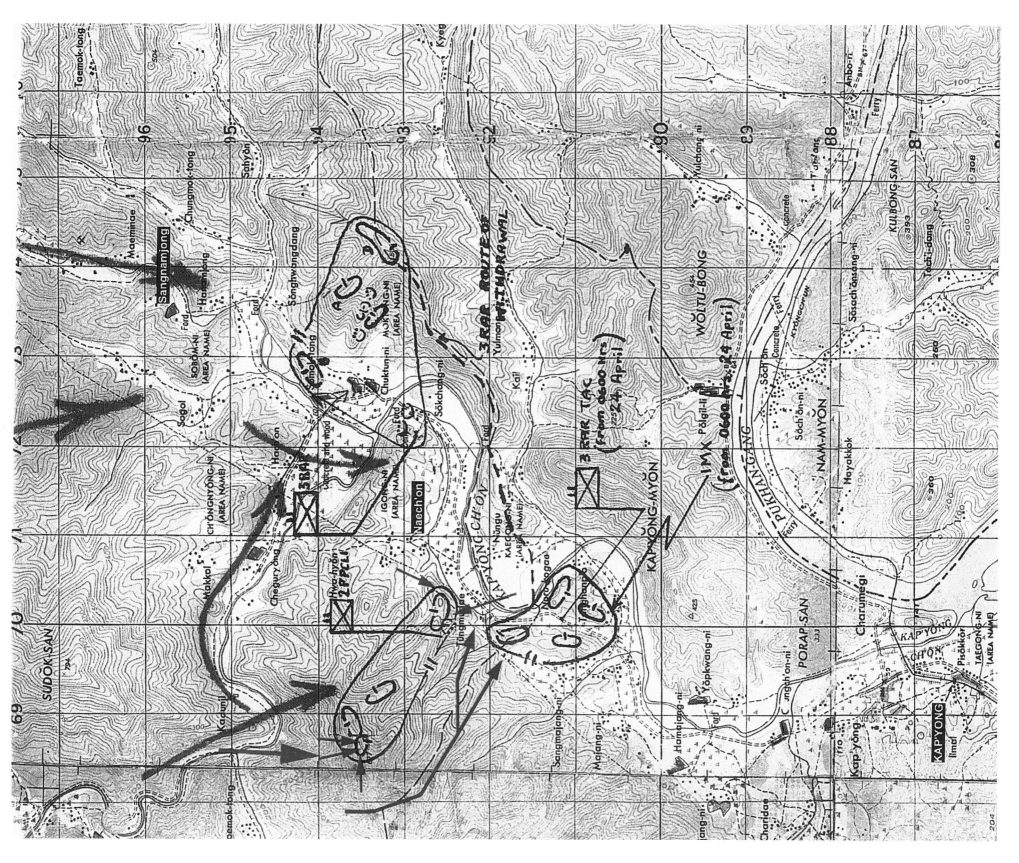

Chapter EIGHT

A PIVOTAL BATTLE

April 24 - 2130 hrs

B Company reports that 400 Chinese are massing below their forward 6 Platoon. Major Vince Lilley calls for artillery and mortar concentrations on the enemy. The Chinese commence mortaring B Company and enemy heavy machine guns open up. Dug in on a spur, 6 Platoon is 60 meters in front of 5, which in turn is forward of Company HQ. The Chinese guide their attacking formations by red and green tracer fire and bugle calls. Petrie at 5 Platoon spends much of the night directing machine gun and mortar fire on the Chinese attackers.

2330hrs - The position of the American 2 Chemical Battalion, 4.2" Heavy Mortars, Company B, assigned to provide supporting fire to the 3RAR is deserted. The soldiers bugged out, departing before the Chinese occupy the position. In their haste they left their mortars and most of their equipment behind.[1] Company A Forward Fire Officer Lieut Robert E Bundy, nicknamed

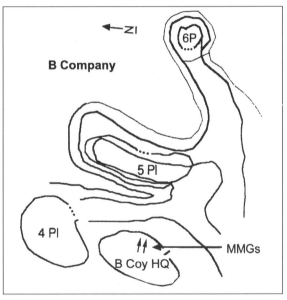

"Tex", is attached to the Patricias at C Company. He later told 2PPCLI Corporal Shuler, Med A: "Those dammed incoming mortar bombs bombarding the Pats were ours for Chris' sake! The Chinese turned our mortars on us. A company carries an inventory of 1,800 bombs, they remained in place and were being used by the enemy to hammer the Patricias!"[2]

Evidently the retreating troops did not spike their mortars, thus rendering them useless to the enemy. The Chinese took over the inventory of bombs, turned the base plates to direct their fire at the Patricias.

(There are a variety of conflicting reports concerning the actions of the 2 Chemical Battalion 4.2 inch heavy mortar crews, please refer to appendix 7, at the end of this chapter). [17]

The Patricias Medical Assistants (Med A) and stretcher-bearers are pooled. They are holding at Tactical HQ, to be dispatched as required. Early in the battle, Corporal Bill Shuler, Med A, who is normally assigned to C Company, is sent to B Company, where the fighting is underway. Major Vince Lilley, MC, nicknamed "The Black Prince" by the troops, tells Shuler, "As usual we are under strength, I need everyone to fight." Lilley continues, "The men who are wounded and able to walk and can continue to fight are not to be sent to the Regimental Aid Post. Patch them up and return them to battle." [2] Shuler later attends to Private Wayne Mitchell, who is wounded around the eye, he sends him back to continue manning his Bren light machine gun.

During the firefight Shuler runs to attend to a number of casualties at 6 Platoon. In desperate hand-to-hand combat, he kills two enemy soldiers who have infiltrated behind our lines. "It is a hell of a mess. Retreating South Korean troops are coming through our position; the Chinese are mixed in with them. In the dark I can't tell a northerner from a southerner. I club one Oriental with a rifle butt knocking him out, only to find out that he is a South Korean. Each time I go back and forth to attend to a casualty I am continually shot at. Tracer bullets following your every movement are bloody alarming; however, it's not a time to think of your own safety. There are many wounded to be cared for. I am inspired by the performance of our Patricias. Canadian kids in their late teens and early twenties; their discipline and determination stand out in stark contrast to the torrents of cowardly Koreans running away in their ruinous panic. We too are frightened, who the hell wouldn't be! We are well disciplined in the best traditions of the Patricias. When you are fighting in the front line you are fighting to preserve your life and those of your buddies. And the pride of your Regiment is always a strong factor in one's performance. I am 'wounded' twice, but only from falling on jagged rocks in the dark." [2]

Shuler: "Vince Lilly is everywhere during the battle. I bump into him a number of times. He is constantly moving about the company positions checking on his platoons, inspiring his men. Lilly's example is an inspiration to every man under his command; his calm attitude under fire reinforces the confidence of our harassed troops. I really respect him for what he is doing." [2]

2200 hrs - Lieut Hub Gray states: "A soldier arrives at the mortar platoon halftracks, and he descends from the high ridge to the west behind us. The man tells me that they have a weak spot in their defensive fire plan, and asks if they can borrow a machine gun to strengthen their firepower. It may be a platoon initiative, for a company request would no doubt come through Tactical HQ. I believe the soldier came from D Company, the other side of the ridge. As we had eight machine guns I agree and begin to dismantle a .30 caliber weapon. Just then Captain Lloyd Hill comes along escorting a prisoner who is thought to be Chinese, waving his 9mm pistol in a continuing arc. On being informed of my actions he shouted for me to put the blankety blank gun back and went on with his prisoner, who turned out to be a Korean.

Lieut Harold Ross, Commanding 6 Platoon - They are engaging the Chinese 354 Regiment, reinforced with elements from another regiment. The battle develops with increasing ferocity and hand-to-hand fighting ensues. Private Tolver, 7 Section, in the lead trench is killed. Two more companies of the Chinese attack members of 6 Platoon. Enemy formations are controlled by heavy tracer fire and varying bugle calls. Their fighting strategy reflects the "gorilla warfare" line of massed troops who are used as a "battering ram" to defeat their enemy. The Chinese fight with a fanatical determination even though their tactics of massing men and sacrificing torrents of charging troops is archaic. These are the tactics that brought them victory in China. The Mao Doctrine is followed to the letter and enforced by the ever-dominant Political Commissars. A section is overrun. Don Morrow, Richardson, Mitchell and their mates are forced to withdraw to another section's trenches. Mitchell, wounded about the eye, fights throughout the night. At one point he is almost overrun by the enemy, but by firing his Bren gun the Chinese bodies fall around him. Mitchell charges the enemy three times with his Bren. He inflicts maximum casualties to the enemy, even though he suffers a second wound in the chest. He is awarded the Distinguished Conduct Medal (DCM). Chinese mortars, medium and heavy machine guns lay down intensive fire. After an hour or so number 6 Platoon with fixed bayonets retake their position in a bloody fight. The Chinese do not easily give up their ground, but when they see the Patricias are not to be denied they turn and run, firing wildly. During the charge you try to stay close to your buddy, to kill as many of the bastards as you can. It is a matter of ensuring your own safety and survival. During the intensity of a close quarter killing ground a soldier functions like a well-trained machine, having automatic reflex actions. If you stop to think, to assess what you are committing, the horror of it all saturates you - the killing, killing, killing. Your stomach may churn, acid fear rising into you throat... "Will I be next?" Such a thought can immobilize you. The supporting fire of the battalion mortars and the16RNZA artillery cut wide swaths into the Chinese ranks. It is a relief to see your enemy being crushed by an artillery barrage!

Ross, who previously hurt his back tumbling down a winter mountainside in Korea, is a patient in the Military Hospital, Kure, Japan. He hears of the Chinese Spring offensive on the Armed Forces Radio, and feels terrible being separated from his men in their time of great need. Ross musters the strength to get out of bed to silently retrieve his uniform and to quietly walk out of the hospital. He goes to the airport and thumbs a ride back to Korea. Landing at Kimpo airport, he joins an artillery re-supply convoy which delivers him right to the Patricias' doorstep. He immediately resumes his command of 6 Platoon but is evacuated once again on the 26th.

Private Ed Richardson sights vehicle lights moving in the valley below Hill 677. Ross orders Mitchell and Richardson to open fire with their Bren light machine gun. The enemy return mortar fire impacting between slit trenches. Lance Corporal Bill Denne remembers, "The concentration of all the incoming enemy fire appears to be centered on me, I am absolutely scared out of my wits. The noise is deafening and the zing of the flying shrapnel gives the impression of coming ever closer. Some of those bombs are phosphorus; the white plums are an invitation to be severely burned. You really hate your enemy at times like this." [3]

D Company HQ - Mills advises his platoons that B Company is engaging the enemy. Thereafter no advisory information concerning the Battalion's situation is passed to his individual platoon commanders.

2230 hrs - The second enemy attack at 6 Platoon overruns two sections. Company HQ having two Vickers MMG, is lacing the enemy with fire, but ammunition is running low. Lance Corporal John Cook takes a four-man patrol to Tactical HQ, to pick up as much .303 ammunition as possible. The trenches are too near the edge and because the enemy is so close it is impossible to use our grenades. Menard states that: "This is the worst nightmare of my life. The Vickers machine guns are behind and above us, firing continuously over our heads. They are killing hundreds and hundreds of Chinese. They are charging in rows; hundreds are lined up behind each other, incessantly blowing their bloody bugles. They are being killed off like flies. Where the hell do they keep coming from? How many more thousands do we have to kill just to survive? They charge at us in everlasting bloody f…ing relays." [4]

Chinese attack in the rear of the Battalion -

The Chinese launch an assault from the valley floor to the east, centering on the Mortar, Anti-Tank and Pioneer platoons, which are a couple of hundred meters forward of Tactical HQ. Lieut Hurst's trench mate, Corporal Bob McQuaig, nudges Hurst and in a whisper asks, "Do you see what I see?" [6] Up to 500 Chinese are silently crawling up the hill toward them. "Where the hell have these bastards come from? It is incredible that they have suddenly materialized in front of us." [5] Hurst and McQaig are extremely vulnerable and feel terribly alone. Between them they have only one rifle and one Sten Gun, which may or may not fire. The soldiers of B Company are 200 meters north; to the south are the mortars and Tactical HQ. In their immediate area there is no infantry support.

Capt Murray Edwards relates: "The Sten Gun was developed by the British. Australia improved upon it, by designing the Owen Gun. Canada went cheap substituting a wire coil spring for the original 'w' spring. This resulted in a magazine that invariably failed because the coil spring would bind against the sides of the magazine. The mistake was committed during WWII, and in Korea years later the government arms us with relics from the past. A cost saving measure? One of my first duties as Quartermaster, is to obtain American Carbines for everyone in 2PPCLI who has been issued with a Sten Gun." [6] Re-arming with American carbines took place after Kapyong.

Mortar Platoon, Lieut Hub Gray: "Private Jim Wall, a pioneer driver, comes to pick up a load of grenades for booby-traps. At this time I spot the enemy ascending the hill to the east. It is an eerie sight; 500 men advancing toward us and not a discernable sound from any of them. Their silence is surreal, and for a moment I wonder if my nerves are getting the better of me. In the half-light of the night it is easy to make an error. I blink and they are still advancing ever closer, heading into our vulnerable underbelly. It is unbelievable to be observing the enemy advancing ever upward, yet remaining implausibly silent. They appear to be somewhat bunched up, but it is difficult to be certain for we are almost at right angles to them. It is as though we are watching unheralded ghosts silently floating up the hill intent upon harvesting their prey. The sobering reality is that these aren't ghosts, they are very real soldiers carrying automatic weapons, and they are hell-bent on killing us. I shout softly to Capt Hill who is on the mortar line, which is obscured from view being located on the other side of the face of the hill: "Here come the little Green men." He does not hear me.

"I alert the men manning the eight machine guns, telling them where the enemy is located, and to quietly cock their guns and take aim, but not to fire until I give the order. I allot fields of fire to each MMG to avoid bunching our fire in one area, thus maximizing our killing ground. Then I pause; transfixed until the enemy is a mere 100 meters off to my left front. Their leading formation is about 40 meters short of the crest, their objective. After what seems an eternity, I order the machine guns to open fire. Hurst recalls: 'When Hub's fire order drifted over our position, it is the sweetest sound I hear at Kapyong.' [7] The hammering fire of eight machine guns and the reverberation of the half-tracks echo through the valley. In a short time the mortars begin firing on an almost perpendicular trajectory. The enfilading fire of the machine guns unleashes a flying curtain of death, ensnarling the enemy in a blood bath, smashing huge swaths throughout the Chinese ranks. The .50 caliber bullets are about the size of a man's thumb, and when they thrust into the head it is literally blown apart; disintegrating into severed segments. The sight is one of an almost decapitated body splurging blood, limbs in their death throes, thrashing uselessly... It is a time of victorious relief combined with gut wrenching fear. 'Oh My God... please, may I never be the victim!'

Driver Private Bill Chrysler is manning one of the .50 caliber guns: "In rapid succession I fire off a number of boxes of ammunition. It is like shooting tin ducks in a gallery, they are so bloody close I simply cannot miss. It is such a relief to feel pumped up, victorious! To know that you are actually going to live another day." [8] This engagement lasts ten to 12 intense minutes. The impacting slugs rip through successive bodies in the path of their trajectory, turning men into masses of bleeding flesh and hanging entrails. The horrific reality of war is forever engraved in the recess of your mind. Then suddenly it is over. The continuing screams of the wounded and dying enemy are piercing, and once again; Thanks to God, that is not I."

Mortar Platoon - Private Michael Czuboka states. "I am totally unaware of the oncoming enemy as is everyone else, until Hub Gray opens fire. We are continuously firing various defensive fire tasks; the barrels of our mortars are burning hot. We cease firing in support of the companies to turn our mortars around 180 degrees, and fire at an almost perpendicular angle. With the enemy on our doorstep we are in overdrive, everyone is moving at breakneck speed, and I am worried that in our haste there is the possibility of a bomb exploding prematurely - as in the case of a "double feed." Being number two, it is my job to feed the bombs into the barrel quickly and with precise timing. Two bombs at once would produce an instant disaster. During a training session in Canada, a double feed occurred and the mortar crew was killed. If that were to happen our closely stored inventory of mortar bombs on the open ground would no doubt detonate. I must remain calm and precise. The firing of the eight machine guns is devastating, slaughtering everything in their pathway. In my opinion the .50 and .30 caliber machine guns firing in unison from near Tactical HQ save all of us at Kapyong. Their vicious firepower is thunderous and overwhelming. It is fascinating observing the various fire patterns, the trajectory of the machine gun tracers is so close they are almost firing upon us. The Chinese, having already suffered heavy losses, must have felt that they had suddenly encountered a powerful and well-armed enemy. I feel very relieved when it is over, for they were advancing uphill in the rear of our position, totally unexpected. Engulfed in an unbelievable silence! God only knows; these bastards might have been upon us before we even knew they were there. It is a very close thing." [9]

Private Jim Wall recalls: "Approaching our position in the dull light of night they look like a bunch of ants groping their way up the hill. It is frightening watching them slowly ascend, and to realize they are coming to kill us. When Gray orders the machine guns to fire it is as though someone had kicked the top off the anthill. There are masses of the fallen, dead and wounded. Those left standing grab what they can of their casualties and are running and tumbling down the hill as fast as their legs can carry them, heading for the river. They are panic stricken. I am one happy soldier when the enemy turn and run away." [10] The attack is beaten back, inflicting extremely heavy losses. We are not attacked again on this front."

Sergeant Sim, Anti-Tank Platoon: "The previous night we had occupied the ground now held by B Company. During the day we relocated south of Tactical HQ, about 1,000 meters behind our former position. We are not aware of the approaching enemy until the machine guns commence firing. Most of us are in our slit trenches. When the firing begins Lieut Rick Constance stays in his slit trench with his batman-signaler, Private Doan, who begins shouting, "The Chinese are coming. Sergeant Sim, the Chinese are coming!" He keeps this useless, hysterical banter up from the bottom of his slit for three minutes or so. I finally get out of my trench and go to Constant's slit and shout: 'Doan, shut up that God damn noise, it's bugging the troops.' Suddenly it ends, Constant does not emerge from his slit." [11]

The next day a soldier ventures forth seeking souvenirs, he also takes a body count of the dead and stops at 100. The trees and shrubbery are leveled, as though a lawn mower had cropped and shaved the ground. Again, how many dead and wounded did the Chinese carry off? The eight machine guns and the mortars settled the matter. Lilley, commanding B Company reports the enemy were out of his line of fire.

Stone classifies the attack as a diversion. Possibly he is correct. I cannot judge how long the mortars are engaged firing to their rear, but it demands a 180 degree turn. Afterwards they once again reposition the mortars to their front in the confusion of darkness, and once more zero in on the targets. Possibly these quick moves result in a 15 minute or more delay, denying vital mortar supporting fire to the front line troops engaging the enemy at B Company. The diversion is significant for those mounting the defences at 6 Platoon.

If the Mortar Platoon's eight machine guns were not positioned as they were, and if the Chinese thrust had succeeded in smashing the nerve centre of Second Patricias, things may have been very different... With the enemy gaining the high ground and all of our companies in isolated locations, 400 to 500 meters apart... I leave it to the reader to surmise how significant this diversion would have been.

One may question why your author, second in command of the mortars, was not on the actual mortar line, as would normally be the case. Eighteen months prior I had graduated from the 3" Mortar course at the School of Infantry, at Camp Borden. Hill, commanding the platoon, is christened "Mother Hill," by Captain Andy Foulds, MMG Officer. In a sense it summed up Hill's overly possessive attitude to "his" platoon. I was posted to the mortars, in early March, a reinforcement. Hill had been in charge since the formation of the platoon the prior summer, and they were 'his boys." He laid it on the line; he wanted absolutely nothing to do with me. No matter how I tried to improve the relationship Hill was immoveable. What the hell was I here for? My duties are restricted to everything but the mortar line. When I finally advise Hill I am going to the Adjutant to lodge a redress of grievance to request a transfer, he proposes a compromise and ensures I will be posted to a rifle company ASAP. The transfer took longer than anticipated. On the

17 of March I was granted a temporary reprieve. I became a Liaison Officer at 27th Brigade, and subsequently attached to the American Regimental Combat Team, on our Brigade's right flank. The sole purpose of my posting was to report to Brigade HQ immediately should they bug out. That was a revealing experience. After Kapyong I was transferred to D Company. An ugly confrontation in front of the Colonel was avoided, which would not have been helpful to the careers of either Hill or myself. Personality conflicts in armies have been recorded since time immemorial.

D Company HQ - Mills orders Private Jean Grison, operating the 300 wireless set to Tactical HQ, to move to his own trench. Mills then operates the 300 set in communication with Tactical HQ for the remainder of the night. Major Henderson, Battle Adjutant, at Tactical HQ, confirms this. [13]

Midnight

Tactical HQ - Private Mel Canfield, Intelligence Section, takes his turn on guard duty. There is a pathway leading up from the valley below and he hears voices, Chinese voices. "We throw a grenade and open fire, a few minutes later there is silence. No more voices." [13]

April 25th

B Coy - A third attack is launched on 6 Platoon from their forward positions. Private Lamey reports; "Private Disobato fires his rocket launcher into our abandoned slit trenches, these are now held by the Chinese. He inflicts many casualties. The flash of light from the launcher allows the Chinese, who are manning captured American 4.2 inch mortars, to range in and shell our position. The Chinese attackers cover a front of about 70 meters. Our section guards Platoon HQ, which is on the highest part of the knoll. We have been under constant attack. I throw a flare to illuminate the enemy who seem to be everywhere, but it is a dud." [15] Petrie of 5 Platoon, crawls to his Rocket Launcher Crew, and orders them to keep their heads down. The machine gun fire is then directed at the Chinese, tight over their heads. Petrie is also correcting the mortar fire in defence of 6 Platoon. "Artillery and mortar support is helping to slow the enemy attacks, but in spite of this continuing firepower they press forward. It is as if they are totally unconscious of their mounting casualties. In the midst of battle one cannot help but wonder how meaningless it is for the Chinese commanders to employ tactics that try to ensure as much as possible, the preservation of their troops -

as we slaughter them by the hundreds." [14]

Sergeant Ulmer at 6 Platoon HQ. He shouts: "Luchi Ho Ho," [16] and immediately their HQ are peppered with enemy grenades and they are pinned down. The Patricias fight while running out of ammunition. Ross: "We are being overrun. Fire what ammunition you have left while the wounded are being evacuated." [16] Private Ed Richardson fires his remaining three rounds, and is wounded in the jaw. Corporal Shuler and Lance Corporal Marsh, dodging incessant enemy fire, take Richardson to the main body of B Company. Private Morrow is wounded in the arm and face losing many teeth. Shuler escorts more casualties to the Regimental Aid Post.

During the battle Shuler observes Corporal CR Evans who is lying some distance in front of a trench but he cannot get to him as the Chinese control the area. The next morning his death is confirmed and Evans' body is recovered. He is found gripping his rifle, his bayonet piercing the body of his enemy. The dead Chinese soldier is still clutching his rifle and his bayonet is run through Evans' body. This grizzly scene marks the last bayonet engagement of the Canadian Army on Active Service.

Lamey recollects that; "With fixed bayonets we charge to Platoon HQ, for we do not know where the hell the enemy is located. Mitchell has suffered a grenade wound in the chest. In the midst of the platoon's withdrawal, Mitchell stands his ground, faces the enemy firing his Bren Light machine gun from the hip, allowing his comrades to successfully retire to company HQ. Ross calls for supporting fire directly upon our position." [6] Battalion 81mm mortars and the artillery bombard the enemy. Ross reports the Chinese have done the unexpected. They have silently clawed their way up the face of a precipitous rock spur. Once on top the enemy is a short distance from his leading section, well within grenade range. They shower 6 Platoon with grenades. Ross has 4 killed, 10 wounded.

---

1. O'Neill page 145
2. Shuler: telephone interview 11 June 1998. He remembers this conversation for the signaler with the 4.2 FFO, was named Schuller.
3. Denne: Phone interview
4. Speech By Capt (then LCol) Browne to PPCLI officers in Canada, not dated, late 1960s.
5. Menard: Letter March 28, 1998
6. Hurst, Telephone interview, November 21, 2000

6. Edwards, Interview Victoria, May 1999
7. Hurst: Interview, Edmonton, 1999
8. Chrysler, Telephone interview, e/mail exchanges, March 1998
9. Czuboka: e/mail July 2001
10. Wall: telephone, letter, August 16, 2000
11. Sim: Interview, Kamloops, April 2000
12. Grison: Written statement
13. Canfieled: Interview April 1998
14. Lamey: Phone calls, letter, April 1997
15. Morrow; Phone calls
16. Lamey, Richardson, Morrow
17. Conflicting Reports

Stone: "a company of US 120 mm (4.2 inch) mortars supported with defensive fire tasks, but when the battle got hot on the Australian front.... never a 'pop' did we get from them."

AUSTRALIAN OFFICIAL HISTORY: At 2330 hrs April 23, a runner was dispatched to check on the 4.2 mortar company supporting 3RAR. He found the position abandoned, mortars in place, a complete field kitchen set up and about 50 deserted vehicles. The men of the 4.2s ran 16 km to the east.

NEW ZEALAND OFFICIAL HISTORY: Company B, 4.2 mortars are set up behind 3RAR BHQ. Pulling out at dawn (24th) the lead driver was killed causing a blockage. 35 Vehicles were abandoned. An American Engineer company abandoned their vehicles and proceed south.

July 25th, 1999, A letter from Carl H. Hulsman, enclosing **report APO 301.** *His letter was complimentary to the Patricias.*

"HQ 2nd CHEMICAL MORTAR BATTALION: APO 301, DATED 12 JULY, 1951 (condensed) *COMPANY A* - Commander Paul A. Morton, "0510 hrs, 23rd communication with FOO Lieut. Bundy (at PPCLI C Company) failed. Harassing and interdiction fire ceased. Chinese firing .30 MG fire into our position. It was the decision of the company commanders to withdraw to the higher ground and buy time to return to their positions and destroy their equipment. Company assembled 3 miles south. Afternoon April 24, we moved back into line supporting Canadians, until dawn the 25th. Broke all company record firing 1,600 rounds HW and WP ammunition."

COMPANY B - Commander Captain TB Elliott. "FOOs dispatched to 3RAR A, B, & C companies. Shortly after dark, ROKs and refugees and undoubtedly infiltrators streaming by. Midnight, FOOs report probing attacks - hesitant to call for mortar fire because of retreating ROKs. 0230 hrs 24th, 16 RNZA pull out (2 batteries only). 0500-0600 hrs fired about 90 rounds. 0545 hrs 3RAR HQ pulling out, Company of MX Regt pulling out to higher ground. 0600 24th 3RAR Exec Officer orders our company south. After 75 yards lead vehicle shot up, column halted. Chinese within 50 feet. Company B joined MX and arrived at Kapyong road about 0830 hrs. 1730 hrs moved by Battalion transport to south of Kapyong. The following day April 25th, Company B, went into firing position in support of the 3RAR."

"THE RED DRAGON ASSOCIATION" - *Veteran's Association of 2nd Chemical Battalion.* **AUGUST 2002,** *I enquired of Bruce Elliott, founder and editor of The Red Dragon Assn if the APO* **reports were written as dated (12 July 1951) - or later reconstructed - No reply.**

<u>**CONFLICTING AREAS:**</u>

a) Stone cites no fire support from 4.2s the nights of April 24-25, once the Chinese joined the battle with 3RAR.

b) 3RAR report a 4.2 position deserted at 2330 hrs April 23rd. US report Company B, moving south dawn the next day.

c) Lieut Bundy, 4.2 FOO at PPCLI C Company, reports incoming mortar bombs are US 4.2 inch bombs, the night of April 24-25 - advising they were coming from American abandoned position. (4.2s contain 8.5 pounds of TNT, vs 105mm having only 3.5 pounds TNT).

d) Patricias were largely exempt from battle the night of April 23 - 24.

e) The withdrawal movements of 2nd Chemical companies are varied - Companies A & B report moving south. The 3RAR and New Zealand histories cite them withdrawing 16 km to the east.

Mortar Platoon around the camp fire. (photo: M. Czuboka)

Chapter NINE

CHINESE SUICIDE THRUSTS
AT DOG COMPANY

APRIL 25 - 0130 hrs.

There are two men to a trench and one man must always stay awake. The night is long, and it is extremely quiet with no wind. You can hear a whisper from trench to trench. "We look forward to the coming daylight and dread the night," says Corporal Clouthier, who is awakened with the news that "the Chinks are coming." [1] At 10 Platoon Clouthier commands the leading section. Privates Gifford and Nash are dug in to the left, Hughes and Walker to the right. One of the many paths in the area rising from the steep descent down below leads into the middle of Clouthier's slit trench. He dashes to Platoon HQ, and reports, "The enemy is moving up the path talking freely, evidently unaware of our position." [1]

The leading element of the enemy force is estimated at 200 plus and they are 30 meters off. Levy sends Clouthier forward to his position and calls for a FOX III Defensive Fire (DF) task by the artillery and the battalion's mortars. Levy then moves to Clouthier's section where they have engaged the enemy before he arrives. The shoot was long, said Levy: "Down 50. The enemy is charging en masse, coming at us in continuing waves of 30 to 50 men at a time. As the battle becomes intense I keep calling for more artillery and mortar fire. In spite of their devastating casualties the Chinese maintain the violent flow of their attacks. I have to adjust the fire gradually creeping closer and closer to our lines as the Chinese are pressing ever more upon us I move from position to position to encourage my troops and to direct the fire where it is most needed.

"It is inconceivable that despite the intense supporting artillery fire shredding their lines and the firing of my platoon the enemy is closing in on us, seemingly oblivious of their increasing casualties. We are engaging a fanatical blitzkrieg. The attack becomes so concentrated it develops into a continuous assault. My God, how long can we endure this never-ending saturation? How do you conquer an army bent on mass suicide? There are a multitude of details demanding my attention, I must stay focused on defeating them" [2]

Mills has located his company HQ out of sight of all of his platoons, and has not visited the positions of either 10 or 11 platoons. **If you are unfamiliar with the particulars of your formations, and do not have a clear line of sight... you cannot assess the flow of the battle! Hence you cannot control creeping adjustments to supporting artillery fire. And this is particularly so when the fire is directed to impact close about, <u>and eventually directly upon your own men</u>** At D Company requests for artillery support originate with the platoon commanders. These orders are passed to the company commander who, in the absence of an artillery officer, relays the order to Tactical HQ, where the Direct Support (DS) Battery Commander (BC) actions the request. The BC utilizes the telephone landline to D Company.

Conditions of the Night -
About midnight a brilliant half moon rises in the sky. From time to time darkness descends with passing clouds. From about 0330hrs onward the landscape is enveloped in darkness, the blackest two hours of the night are to come. The incessant artillery and mortar barrages ignite fires engulfing the area of D company's front line troops in a curtain of increasing smoke. The Chinese with their rubber shoes and rigid discipline of silence suddenly appear out of nowhere and are right in our faces. Everyone prays for an early dawn, which begins about 0530 hrs.

0200 hrs. - At 11 Platoon Pearson monitors the radio traffic between 12 east and company HQ. Sergeant Holligan at first somewhat jocular, reports to Mills that he is being hard pressed by the enemy. Pearson, on his own initiative, goes to company HQ and suggests taking 10 men and one light machine gun to reinforce 12 Platoon and relieve the pressure. Mills concurs. Pearson astutely assesses the flow of the battle at 12 Platoon. He considers taking control at 12 east, but rejects the idea as he is not familiar with the lay of the land, and the landscape at that moment is hidden by dark clouds. This done, he returns to his platoon. The strength of 12 Platoon now comprises four sections that include: soldiers 34+, four light machine guns, and one Vickers medium machine gun. Pearson is down to 15 men and two light machine guns. D Company always appears to be in the thick of the battle and thus is suffering from a greater shortage of reinforcements than the other companies.

D Company, 10 Platoon - The Chinese assaults continue without let up, pressing ever closer. Levy: "Via Company HQ I instruct the Vickers machine gun at 12 Platoon west, 50 meters east and about 20 meters forward of our position, to open fire." [2] Levy's message is passed to company HQ, then to Holligan to have the Vickers open fire. Holligan, recently reinforced, orders Private Neil Neufeld, to take his Bren machine gun and his number two Lessard, to accompany others to reinforce 12 west and to have the Vickers commence firing.

Levy continues: "The enfilading fire of the Vickers inflicts heavy casualties. There is a fleeting lull in the battle as the Chinese assault momentarily abates. I overhear the Chinese commander urging his troops on, ordering his men forward. The shrill screams of their wounded and dying haunt the night. The Chinese commander and I, speaking in Chinese, exchanged insults and shouts to surrender. This infuriates the Chinese officer, who orders his troops to **'Press harder! Press harder! Kill! Kill! Kill the Imperialist Pigs!'** I reply: "We are Canadian soldiers. Come to us, we have lots of food and medicine, and you will be well treated. The Chinese officer screams: 'Don't listen to that Son of a Turtle!'… a terrible insult in Chinese. The enemy officer urges his troops to press even harder. They assault the Patricias with ever increasing numbers laying down heavier small arms, machine gun and mortar fire. The firing becomes intense. After my continuing exchanges with the Chinese commander, one of my men shouts, "Tell the bloody platoon commander to Shut Up!" Each time our verbal exchange takes place the Chinese intensify their attacks." [2]

11 Platoon - Pearson: "A Chinese patrol climbs the hill approaching my northern most position and we drive them off by Bren gun fire and grenades. They wisely do not make another advance on our position." [3]

Mortar Platoon, Gray - "From our vantage point overlooking the valley we observe the Chinese perusing the 3RAR at a river crossing. We open fire on instructions from Tactical HQ, with 8 Browning's: 4 medium and 4 heavy machine guns. After firing a number of bursts I order the men to cease firing. Major Ben O'Dowd, Commanding A Coy 3RAR, believes we are firing on his withdrawing men. Two of O'Dowd's platoons cross at his designated point followed by the Chinese; the third choose a different location. O'Dowd cannot communicate directly with his Battalion HQ, but is in contact with our Tactical HQ. We participate in killing at least 71 enemy, a number, which is confirmed by actual count the next day. We do not know how many wounded and killed were removed from the field of battle by the enemy. It is Chinese policy to carry off as many of their dead and wounded as possible, so their casualties are no doubt much higher. Some suggest that when estimating enemy casualties a multiple of two or so times those left on the field of battle would be appropriate." [4]

0230 hrs. - The Chinese ease their pressure on 10 Platoon, to launch an attack on the detached section at 12 west. By 0300 they swarm over the Vickers machine gun killing both Privates Macdonald and Carr with a fusillade of fire from Burp guns. Neufeld manning his Bren kills the assailants, but his number two Lessard is killed. Lance Corporal Jimmy Wanniandy, remembers: "The charging Chinese make one hell of a lot of noise, banging bamboo sticks together, incessantly rattling noise makers and shouting. I think they are trying to scare us. As they come forward our booby traps are exploding. Our Vickers machine gun begins to fire but does not last long. Mortars rain down in front of us, and there is one hell of a lot of noise. I am scared. The Chinese are so persistent, they begin to infiltrate right into our position. I remember looking at Lessard, at the Bren gun, and he takes a direct hit in the head, his face is smashed to hell, disintegrating into contorted blood and mashed flesh - his head explodes close by in front of my face. Splattered with his blood and membrane I shudder uncontrollably. It is horrifying to see a man you know and rely upon positioned beside you, suddenly smashed to oblivion. This abrupt violation changes him from a warm and caring human being into an inert lump. It is terrifying. I can't remember anything after that." [5] Neufeld: "The enemy charges in continuous waves 20 to 30 meters apart. We are overrun." [6] Later at 10 Platoon voices shout from the gully below, "Don't shoot! We are coming up. We are coming up. Don't shoot!" [2] Soldiers from 12 west arise out of the gully. Four soldiers, including Wanniandy and Private Ken Barwise, plus two Korean porters withdraw to 10. Another 5 or so arrive at D Company HQ. The remainder scramble to the slit trenches of 12 east, 75 meters away, Neufield among them. Levy sends the Korean houseboys, who fought bravely in the action at 12 west, to his reserve section.

Barwise is responsible for the company's 60mm mortar and is initially posted to company HQ; however, prior to the battle Mills assigned him to form part of the protection force for the Vickers medium machine gun. Barwise: "I did not engage the mortar as the Chinese were suddenly in our face and I was afraid if I used it I might hit our own troops." [7]

Chinese Tactics: Stealth - Fire Power - Suicide Attacks
The Chinese concentrate their attacking forces on an extremely limited front. General P'eng's tactic, true to the Mao doctrine, is to destroy his enemy by the sheer weight of overpowering numbers; concentrated suicide attacks. The charging Chinese soldiers appear absolutely fearless of everything we throw at them. They all have automatic weapons,

and many are armed with the Burp gun, which releases a devastating rapid rate of fire.

The Government of Canada has armed us with the Lee-Enfield Rifle. It is a relic not basically altered since the First World War. It has a bolt action that requires cocking before each firing. A few Canucks acquired or "liberated" US carbines that could be bought for $30 or a bottle of booze, and on occasion for a bottle of Asahi beer. Our soldiers were allowed to have a quart of Asahi beer, purchase price .25 cents, about every two weeks or so, when things were quiet in the line. Alcohol is forbidden for Americans in Korea.

Stealth is a key element employed by the enemy. Utilizing rubber-soled footwear the Chinese are masters of absolutely silent movements of hundreds, and even thousands of men. We wear army issued leather boots; frequently the soles are covered in hobnails and a metal horse-shoe type heel, which are noisy on the rocks or gravel. Because of the silent movements of the Chinese we could, without warning, suddenly be facing overwhelming numbers of the enemy. They seem to be emerging out of nowhere. The shock of such a sudden attack can initially cause the pit of your stomach to plummet, and the taste of fear rise into your mouth. Immediately muscles and senses become tightly strung. Your first thought is, *I'm dead!* Survival demands, *Kill or be Killed!*

Fortunately their great element of surprise is blunted by their unique practice of signaling their troops to launch their attacks. To control their movements they blow their bugles, rattle noisemakers and make varied whistle calls. Due to a severe lack of wireless radio communications equipment at battalion, company and platoon level, the Chinese, in battle, are forced to employ crude movement control signals. Are these resounding calls also intended to fire their moral courage… and to skewer ours… but in fact, forewarns us of their attack.

0300 hrs. - Mills reports to Tactical HQ - **"12 Pl has withdrawn to D Company HQ, their position overrun."** [8]

Upon the withdrawal of elements of 12 Pl west to D Company HQ, Mills orders 10 Platoon to stand by to withdraw. Levy recalls: "On receiving the order to withdraw I am concerned. Has a part of the battalion been overrun? Has there been a further collapse at one of D Company positions, if so where? I am uninformed of the ongoing action of either the battalion or of our company, why am I not being informed of the situation? This frustrating lack of information fosters unnecessary confusion. What the hell is the order of withdrawal? Where are we to go? We are the western most platoon, and are we to be the last to leave, to fight our way out. Ammunition is low. Are we even capable of an effective rear guard action? I do not want unnecessary casualties; I must protect my men. We do not have a Medical Assistant with our platoon, how and when do I evacuate the wounded from the reserve section on the hilltop, where are they to go? We have not previously discussed contingency withdrawal plans. I must maintain control, but the lack of foresight and planning means I have more to contend with, the enemy is even now pressing hard upon my position. There are innumerable details requiring immediate action. I inform the company signaler that I require withdrawal instructions for I am not advised as to where company HQ is nor am I advised of contingency withdrawal plans. I am instructed to wait." [2] Mills then requests consent of Stone, for authorization to disengage the enemy and withdraw:

LCol Stone: Denied!

**"Mills wanted to pull out, I told him to stay there,
that nobody could pull out!
If we ever lose that hill, we lose it all!"** [9]

(I ask the reader to pause here to consider the conflicting evidence regarding the reported withdrawal of 12 Platoon, and the originating source of the later order for the artillery fire to descend upon 10 Platoon.

The War Diary entry April 25th reads: "By 0300 hrs 10 Platoon was cut off and 12 Platoon was completely over-run and had withdrawn to Company HQ. Lieut Levy asked for close in mortar and artillery support. The acting company commander Captain JGW Mills, realizing that his outnumbered company must have some relief called for the support requested by Lieut Levy, bringing fire to bear very close to his own positions. Most of this fire was concentrated on the most heavily engaged platoon of the company. This stratagem was successful in driving off the attacking Chinese....."

The fact that 12 Platoon east was successfully defending its position is not referenced in the War Diary of that date, nor is it subsequently noted. The Patricia's official history, VOL III of 1957, relates that 10 Platoon was completely overrun and that the enemy then went on to 12 Platoon. There are two significant points: -

1) Obviously the writer meant to say that 12 was overrun and the enemy then went on to 10 Platoon - 2) Once again there is no mention of only one section being run over.

An article in the "Patrician" four years later by Major G Henderson, states that Holligan advised Mills that 12 Platoon was completely overrun. Finally in 1966 in "Strange Battleground," Mills states a section of 12 Platoon was overrun; however, there is no mention of the situation at 12 east. Henderson, the Battle Adjutant at Tactical HQ who was in wireless contact with Mills at D Company, does not recollect being informed that 12 east were holding. We know that Mills was aware 12 Platoon east held fast, for Pearson records overhearing Holligan's communications to that effect with Company HQ on his Walkie Talkie. If Tactical HQ was unaware of 12's continuing battle this misconception may have played a critical part in the fact that Mills was awarded an MC.

Finally, consider the War Diary references of the order for close in fire support; which is attributed to Levy. The source of Stone's recollection appears to be a later magazine article stating that the order was only acted upon after Mills sought and received Stone's sanction. It was Levy who twice or more called for fire to descend upon his platoon. He also called for fire support to rain down upon the Chinese occupying the former 12 Platoon east abandoned position.)

Mills, having located his HQ out of sight of all his platoons, cannot read the battle, and is not familiar with the layout of his company. He is not in control of the fluid situation; his platoon commanders are controlling the fight at D Company.   In the magazine article Stone reveals he authorized Mills to fire directly upon "the company." The artillery fire is requested to DESCEND ONLY UPON 10 PLATOON, NOT THE ENTIRE COMPANY as so frequently quoted. It is entirely Levy's decision to bring artillery fire directly upon his own men!

A couple of minutes later the withdrawal order is rescinded. Had D Company withdrawn it would have opened the way for the Chinese to occupy the nearby high ridges immediately overlooking Tactical HQ, the Regimental Aid Post, the Anti-Tank, Mortar and Pioneer Platoons. A, B and C companies are each isolated 400 to 500 meters apart, and dug in on lower slopes. This would have potentially unleashed a fusillade of fire upon our soft underbelly, as well as cutting off each of the companies. Is it possible that we would have then suffered a fate similar to that of the Gloucesters at the Imjin? In the western sector, the

Gloucesters of 29th Brigade exhibited extraordinary courage opposing the Chinese 187 and 198 Divisions for 62 hours, only 42 plus members of the Gloucesters reached UN lines, 652 were captured, over 100 killed. Stone orders Mills to stand fast.

Had the company commander been in a position to observe and control the battle, he would have been aware that the majority of his company was still an effective fighting force. Had he been controlling the battle he probably would not have requested permission to withdraw, given that only part of 12 Platoon was overrun; 10, 11 and 12 east were successfully defending their locations.

Moreover, had Mills chosen a properly sighted fighting observation post, he may well have had elements of a reinforced 12 east launch a quick counterattack or at least kept the enemy engaged to preclude them from pouring fire into 10 Platoon. If Mills had possessed the foresight to scramble up the hill behind Levy's position he would have been aware of the pressure points and could have exercised effective control of the battle. All through the night members of 10 Platoon went up and down the hill in front of Mills. Levy, without artillery Forward Observation Officer, directs "pinpoint" artillery to fire within 7-10 meters of his men. The close proximity of the explosion is such that soldiers who do not get down as ordered are thrown up to be slammed around by concussion.

From time to time Levy calls for a **"Mike"** target (all 24 guns of the 16 RNZA to fire). Major Moore, New Zealand Battery Commander at 2PPCLI Tactical HQ, restructures many of Levy's calls into an **"Uncle"** order, (all available artillery, including American batteries, to fire). The American batteries have Variable Time fuses. The 16 RNZA do not have VT's, they are later supplied with them, and are instructed by the RCHA. American sources credit the Variable Time fuse, which bursts about 50 feet above the ground inflicting, casualties five times greater than ground burst artillery.

10 Platoon - Clouthier shares a trench along with privates Baxter and Simpson, who are manning a Bren gun. Because the enemy is in their faces they do not get down when ordered to do so by Levy. The artillery is going to impact their position. The concussion grabs Clouthier and Baxter as though by the scruff of their necks, tossing them up in the air, and then slamming them hard down. Clouthier falls under Baxter, the Bren crashing down on top of them. Baxter is up immediately shouting for Simpson, at the bottom of the trench to load more maga-

zines as he fires off continuing bursts. They were fortunate not to be wounded by flying shrapnel. The Chinese, running through the barrage, ignoring falling comrades, are but seven meters to their front.

The Chinese press attacks on the right flank. Levy calls for artillery and 2PPCLI mortar support "30 - 40 times" ,[2] over five and a half hours. This "pinpoint" fire inflicts heavy casualties on the Chinese, and is crucial to 10s successful defence. The line of descending fire from an artillery barrage is obviously uneven. The VT fire from the American batteries is placed forward of the 16 RNZA fire line to avoid unnecessary Patricia casualties. Levy states: "I cannot always get through on the Walkie Talkie to Company HQ. I have to be clear of the hill for the radio will not operate when I am centered in front of it. That means I have to move to either side of the hill to get through, then rush back to a given point to encourage the troops and to visually select the ongoing point of the supporting fire." [2] The 300 wireless radio at Tactical HQ is in communication with the various companies of the battalion. The landline from Tactical HQ to D Company HQ miraculously survives the battle; in this way Moore maintains contact with the signaler at D company, who in turn relays the instructions for supporting fire originated by Levy.

The American 155mm heavy Howitzers are firing on both 10 platoon and up the Kapyong Gorge slaughtering enemy reinforcements; the eight inch howitzers shells are slaughtering the enemy forces. Captain Porter, Adjutant 16 RNZA, reports the American 105s firing in support of D Company. In all that night the 16 RNZA alone fire some 10,000 rounds. [10]

The Chinese control the base of Hill 677 for about three km to the south. They occupy the high ground mounting the eastern and southern slopes above the road. At places they control the entire road. By midnight infiltrators are in the area of the New Zealand artillery gun line. All those not firing the guns are ordered into an all around defence. Occasionally shots are fired at moving figures. The gun line is not penetrated that night.

The supporting fire of the 16 RNZA, and American artillery plus our battalion's mortars played a crucial role in the success of our defence. Levy's calls for close-in support, at times directly upon his platoon, greatly reduce Patricia casualties. If the 3RAR had had more effective communications it would have facilitated "pinpoint" artillery fire, and they would have experienced far fewer casualties. If it had not been for the very effective artillery and mortar support, the Chinese would probably have brought about a very different ending for the Patricias and possibly the UN as a whole.

10 Platoon - Flying shrapnel wounds Private KJ Sheargold, he is cut about the head, bleeding profusely, and is hazy from his concussion. Levy escorts him up hill to his reserve section. Sheargold, out of it, with blood pouring down his face says to Levy, "I know I am going to die, please talk to my mother, tell her I love her." [2] Levy reassures the distraught man who survives to become a Company Sergeant Major.

11 Platoon - Pearson, lying on the open ground by his northern most Bren, is selecting targets with his binoculars to be able to direct fire upon the enemy as they show on the horizon at 12 Platoon east. Running low on ammo, he begins to crawl away to fetch more. Almost immediately a direct hit by a mortar shell inside the trench kills the two-man crew, twisting the Bren gun like a bent spoon. Pearson is down to only 13 men and one Bren. Pearson: "It was imperative the position be manned by a Bren machine gun. I have a difficult time dragging the inert bodies of my soldiers from the trench but they have to be replaced with the two men manning my last Bren. I order them to maintain their fire; keeping in mind we are running low on ammunition. Because of the steep slope I have difficulty preventing the bodies of the dead men from rolling down the 20-meter embankment. With difficulty I finally anchor them at the base of some shrubs. I return to my slit trench to monitor 12 Platoon radio transmissions. A mortar bomb lands nearby and sprays burning phosphorous into the other half of the trench. I leave with alacrity and find a safer trench." [3] Pearson via the Walkie Talkie communicates with Holligan (seconded from 11 Platoon) at 12 east and overhears their situation and reports to Company HQ. It is evident that Mills realizes 12 east is holding their own. Pearson goes to company HQ, three or four times, to ascertain how the overall battle is proceeding. Each time he finds Mills and Company Sergeant Major Ed Morris operating the 300 set to Tactical HQ, from their slit trench.

D Company HQ - Private George Nestor, runner, tells us: "The Walkie Talkie wireless sets are wonkie much of the time, and so I deliver messages myself to 11Platoon. Company HQ is about 200 meters south of the hill behind 10 Pl, which appears to rise about 20 meters from the valley floor. I have a Bren gun in a slit by myself. When it is light and enemy soldiers appear between the hills, I fire a burst. I do not fire a great deal. When 12's soldiers come to us, in their haste they are falling over each other in the dark. It is very confusing and I am nervous as hell. It's a wonder no one is shot. I am absolutely scared shitless. Morris tries to gather some ammo for 10 Platoon. Hardly anyone offers any as we all want to keep what we have." [11] (No one I contacted at 10 Platoon could remember ammo coming forward from company HQ).

Walkie Talkie (WT) - The battalion is initially equipped with British designed 88 wireless sets for company to platoon communications. They function very well but our supply of batteries is exhausted. The British inventory also runs out and they are taping flash light batteries together to run their 88s. Captain Coombe, signals officer, secures Stone's authorization to use American WT Sets. The US Army, the South Korean Army and the Chinese, who have captured an ample supply, use WTs. The WTs have interference problems when hills intervene and so they are used by 2PPCLI with only limited success. When Edwards became Quartermaster, he requisitioned new batteries for the 88s, from the British who had received fresh supplies. We were moving to a North American defence system. The Canadian authorities had altered the battery's terminal to fit with American installations. British batteries could not be utilized! American WTs continued to be employed. When 1st PPCLI, replaced the Second Battalion, they brought an adequate supply of Canadian batteries for their 88 sets.

10 Platoon - Private Vern Walker is in his slit trench right of Clouthier. Walker calls out, "Hughes is dead. He is lying at the bottom of the trench. There is no room." Clouthier: "Make sure he is dead, and if so throw the body out." [1] A few minutes later Walker cries out again and again complaining about the annoying dead body in his trench. Clouthier, exasperated and engaging the enemy, shouts for Walker to toss the f….ing body out of the trench. Hughes comes to life and screams, "I'm not dead. I'm wounded!" [1] Walker comments that he has never been so terribly frightened as at Kapyong. He credits Levy with being calm and reassuring while the battle rages. While his confidence is shaken, Levy's example lifts him from despair. Walker is under age being only 16 years old.

During the battle Levy and his batman, Allen, make a number of trips up the hill behind Platoon HQ, evacuating casualties and replenishing ammunition from their reserve section. Earlier in the night moonlight floods the area. Later the clouds provide cover and fires are ignited by the shelling. This creates increasing layers of smoke. When the moon is out they had to race some 40 meters around the flank before commencing their steep ascent. The wounded are escorted or pulled up hill, a tiring process. As the night darkens from the clouds and smoke Allen and Levy are able to approach the reserve from the front. These to-and-fro ventures invariably draw enemy fire; however, neither is hit.

0300 hrs. - Stone - orders a re-supply airdrop. The continuing Chinese attacks are exhausting the companies' supplies of ammunition, grenades etc. At D Company HQ - Grison moves around to observe the Chinese firing the captured machine gun at 10 Platoon. They are firing single rounds and are probably feeding the ammunition by hand.

0315 hrs. - B Company - Action is down to small groups of Chinese trying to infiltrate. They are repulsed. Major V Lilley MC, estimates they engage 1,000 enemy, kill 143 and wound 180(e) - total 323. This estimate is recreated 15 years after the battle from personal notes. [16]

0330 - 0345 hrs. - D Company, 12 Pl west - The enemy uses this abandoned position to repeatedly assault the right flank of 10. Levy, dodging intense enemy fire, is constantly on the move taking needed ammo forward and adjusting defensive supporting fire. The Chinese are mortaring 10 Platoon. Levy, facing the enemy now occupying 12 west trenches, has an American made Thompson Sub-machine gun he captured from the enemy April 14. He lies in the open to fire off four or five magazines. The Chinese simultaneously attack 10's front ranks. Levy: "I twice called for the 16 RNZA to fire on 12 west trenches controlled by the Chinese, then order a **Mike Target** (all 24 RNZA howitzers to fire) to impact within 10-15 meters of our position." [2] Major Moore converts the order to include the American 105s, and with the Variable Times fuses; and at times he includes the American 155s. Levy: "I direct the artillery up or down, left or right, depending on where I see the Chinese massing, and again upon their charging our position. We are being attacked on our right and the fire on our front continues unabated. We are cut off from the remainder of the company." [2] Concussion from the artillery again bashes about the soldiers who are engaging the Chinese at close quarters. At times a soldier takes the risk of not hunkering down in their slits. The enemy are in their face and you are fighting for survival.

Corporal Clouthier orders Baxter to fire his Bren on the captured Vickers MMG. Baxter, being a dead accurate shot, fires three short bursts. There is an explosion of blue flame erupting from the Vickers that permanently disables the gun. Ammo runs low - Levy organizes his reserve section to fill Bren Mags, then he, Allen or a man from the reserve section deliver them where required. Clouthier sends Simpson to pick up additional ammo at Platoon HQ. Simpson positioned at the bottom of the slit is reloading spent Bren gun magazines with 28 rounds of .303 ammunition. The magazine capacity is 30 rounds; however, thus loaded it sometimes jams.

0400 hrs. - Second Battalion PPCLI is surrounded by increasing numbers of the Chinese 60th Division. Signals officer Coombe reports Stone as sitting by the 300 radio set having a rifle across his knees, shaking with determination, *and growling as only Stone can GROWL*;

"Let the Bastards Come!" [12]

10 Platoon - With stealth and silence the Chinese move a formation to the left flank of 10, thus forming up their assaulting troops on all three fronts in an effort to take out the Patricias. The Chinese also quietly mass additional troops on the other two fronts that 10 Platoon is engaging. Levy does not realize the Chinese are forming up additional assault troops on his left flank. The Chinese having amassed much larger numbers blow their bloody bugles and scream as they charge.

The Chinese have launched a new assault on the 10s left flank while also pressing hard with increasing numbers on their existing front and right flank. Levy moves left and calls for the artillery to fire continuously. **At this time, on Levy's order the 16 RNZA launch a barrage that will last for 40 minutes. The New Zealand artillery alone delivers 2,300 shells to descend upon and around 10 Platoon.** [13] When the fire order reaches Moore, Battery Commander 16 RNZA, at Patricias Tactical HQ, he questions Levy's order: **"But that is your own position." The answer comes back immediately - "Yes, my Sunray wants it now!"** [13]   Levy contacts the signaler at D Company HQ via the Walkie Talkie. The signaler is also operating the landline in direct contact with the Battery Commander, at Tactical HQ. Mills, operating the 300 set, maintains contact with Coombe, the signals officer, and Major Gordon Henderson, Battle Adjutant, at Tactical HQ. Coombe, who operated the set throughout the night, advises that firing orders were not transmitted via the 300 set.

Lieut Richard Coote, 16 RNZA Forward Observation Office, advises: "At a distance of 7,000 yards the 24 guns cover a front as long as a football field and to a depth of 50 yards." [14] For Levy to bring the mean point of impact to within 15 - 20 yards of his position meant that he was ordering the fire to descend directly upon his men. This was a calculated and necessary risk that Levy took. To issue an order of this nature in the face of a charging enemy requires the cool nerve of an experienced, confident and gutsy officer... who has faith in the disciplined response of his men.

The Australian's Official History of their Army in Korea describes Levy's defensive fire order for continuous firing as **"...a rare and, possibly unique order... given to the New Zealand Field Regiment; the guns to engage at a designated rate of fire rather than as so many rounds. In an area 150 - 200 meters across. It was repeated on several occasions."** [15]

Captain Porter, Adjutant 16 RNZA, writing in 'Duty First,' **"In training they often referred to firing on one's own troops, but this was for real!"** Porter, after about 15 minutes, halved the rate of fire in support of 10 Platoon to conserve rapidly depleting ammunition. The Chinese, ignoring their increasing casualties, take advantage of the lessening artillery and are pouring through the slower rate of fire. Levy orders the fire to be doubled. The American Variable Time fuse inflicts heavy casualties. The noise is deafening.

The Chinese commander is determined to annihilate the Patricias. He pours in more troops. They come forth in masses and are slaughtered in the face of crushing artillery, mortars and intense small arms fire. This is the commander's obsessive attempt to force open his access to Seoul. The bloodied infantry advance upon Levy's position, stepping over and ignoring their dead and wounded, crying out for their comrades' help. Levy continues to direct artillery fire upon his position.

It is probable that 4,000 to 4,500+ rounds of 16 RNZA 25 pounder artillery shells, US Field Artillery Batteries air burst 105mm shells, along with 2PPCLI 81mm mortar shells rain down on and around 10 Platoon during that devastating 40-minute barrage. The American heavy howitzers mercilessly massacre Chinese reinforcements attempting to rush through the narrow Kapyong Gorge. How many hundreds or thousands of Chinese become casualties?

The Chinese Corps Commander has overwhelmingly smashed through 40 km of UN defences, and is flushed with anticipated victory. No doubt he is reflecting upon the triumph of his comrades when they overran the Gloucesters; threw back British 29 Brigade at the Imjin; and now have thrown the Australians back. If his troops could ascend the high ridges behind D Company and dominate all of the Patricia's positions, the commander no doubt believes he would effectively wipe out our entire battalion. He would then effectively control the high ground overlooking much of the Kapyong-Pukhan Valley. He can visualize himself leading the glorious march on to Seoul. The two Chinese divisions - the 60 and 118 - comprised 20,000 men in their assault of Kapyong. The Mao doctrine was to have 90% of their infantry forward in the fighting area.

Levy: "The Chinese are so aggressive they are taking heavy casualties. I do not have time to think, I am reacting to their attacking formations. I am proud of my men, although greatly out numbered and out gunned they are holding the enemy. The artillery support is awesome, without it we could not sustain ourselves." [2] Death pervades the battlefield greedily harvesting its youthful souls. The agonizing cries of the dying split the air as they cry out for their loved ones. It is impossible to accurately gauge enemy causalities as the ground in front of 10 Platoon falls away sharply. The Chinese dead and wounded descend into their start line. The continuing attacks involve hundreds or even thousands of brave Chinese solders seemingly exhibiting no fear of dying.

Levy, directing the defensive supporting fire, is continually moving from sector to sector, over open ground, to encourage his men. The reserve section is out of ammunition and 50% of his two forward sections are wounded. Casualties are evacuated to the reserve section and replacements are brought forward. One soldier, a recent reinforcement, refuses to go forward. Crying, he is curled up in the fetal position at the bottom of his slit and no amount of persuasion or orders can mobilize him. Levy has a dozen extra grenades and during the night he moves about distributing them sparingly, exhausting his supply.

The demands for artillery supporting fire are intense, and the ammunition supply is depleting. The howitzers cannot be allowed to run out of ammunition. The ammunition platoon, Royal New Zealand Army Service Corps, is running a continuous shuttle for the 25 pounder shells brought in from Changgong'ni. By the morning of April 24, the local supply of ammunition is exhausted and has to be flown in to Kimpo Airport from Kure in Japan, and by train from Pusan. The round trip from the gun line to Kimpo is in excess of 130 Km. Ammunition is also urgently needed by the 29th Commonwealth Infantry Brigade who are engaging the enemy at the battle of the Imjin. The road north is clogged with refugees, fleeing Korean troops and Chinese infiltrators. At times the drivers have to bulldoze their way through the fleeing masses regardless of the consequences. The British Army Service Corps vehicles are also hard pressed transporting the vital ammunition. The matter of supply is urgent if General P'eng is to be denied access to Seoul.

Some of the gunners are constantly firing, stripped to the waist, and surrounded by mountains of empty shells. Bielski of the 16 RNZA, noted, "We fired Mike and Uncle targets all night." (Mike - 24 howitzers firing, and Uncle - up to 78 howitzers firing.) [16] The gunners are working feverishly. The Patricias are holding, and the Chinese must break through to gain access to Seoul.

12 Platoon east are engaging the enemy and effectively defending their position. Clearly, D Company Commander **had not ascertained the disposition of any of his** platoons prior to requesting Stone's authority to pull out. It is obvious from Pearson's observations of communications between Company HQ-Holligan, that Mills is aware that 12east is successfully defending their position; there is no record of his revealing this to Stone.

As the enemy appears on the horizon at 12 east, 11 Platoon engages them in battle. The Chinese retaliate with mortar fire, light machine guns and small arms.

At 10 Platoon the Chinese twice advance to within seven meters. As the enemy press forward Levy continues to call for supporting fire to impact within his position, and abrasions occur.

0600 hrs. - The Chinese ease up on 10 Platoon. Eventually the enemy begins to abandon the captured 12 west position. Levy states that: "Through my field glasses I observe bandoleers of .303 ammo lying on the ground at 12. Some of the men are out of ammunition. I call for volunteers to run the gauntlet of enemy fire to retrieve them. Private Barwise, who was earlier at that position, dashes through enemy fire to retrieve 10 or so bandoleers. He returns again to retrieve a box of #36 grenades, but unfortunately there were no primers. Barwise has dashed through the gully separating the two positions to run a distance of about 50 meters. He is dodging enemy sniper fire." [2] **It is for this act of bravery in the face of the enemy that Levy recommends Barwise for the Military Medal (MM).**

Levy: - "From time to time we throw dud #36 grenades at the advancing enemy, it slows them down." [2] Clouthier: "The Chinese have an inexhaustible inventory of men; men they are willing to sacrifice at any cost to take our position. To me it seems to be one unrelenting assault over the entire night. I cannot believe they keep coming at us in the manner they do. Their losses must be horrendous." [1]

Pearson of 11 Platoon: "I knew that if the Chinese overran 12 platoon they would be in the centre of D Company's position above and behind me. Company HQ could then do little to stop them. I decide that if it appears that 12 is loosing ground I will move my men onto the crest between 12 and Company HQ to try and stop them irrespective of the cost. Failure will mean the destruction of our company. Sergeant Holligan and his valiant men hold their position throughout the night.

Pearson continues: "It is tactically unacceptable to allow an enemy to penetrate between the platoons since they can then be subjected to destruction in detail. It is obvious that if we survive the night, after first light, we will have to counter attack and re-establish the security of the company's outer perimeter. My unit is the obvious choice, however, I am now down to 12 riflemen and one Bren light machine gun. Our prospects do not look promising. I expect the Chinese will make one more determined effort during the very dark just prior to first light. That is a very long black hour of waiting, but when the dawn arrives the Chinese have withdrawn and D Company still controls their area of Hill 677. We are now virtually out of ammunition. I have often wondered if the Chinese commanders ever found out how close they came to destroying us?" [3]

Levy: "The artillery was so intense that my ears, and those of my troops, were constantly ringing for days after the battle." [2]

I would like to summarize the actions of Lieut Michael G Levy, (Major Retired):

Ten Platoon and D Company were fortunate to have had an officer of Levy's experience and calm manner. During WWII he fought the Japanese and later guerillas in 1945 in Malaya, where he was awarded a Mention in Dispatches (MiD). Levy is a very understated individual, with strong powers of observation. At times his 'silence' of observation unnerves those around him. At Kapyong, in a situation that can only be described as a frantic life or death battle, Levy demonstrated his capabilities under the most trying of conditions. He took the initiative to command the actions of the men of an adjoining platoon. In the heat of battle he called upon the artillery to impact on his own position. His accuracy was impeccable, "pin pointing" the impact so it would not annihilate his own badly outnumbered and beleaguered men.

With his strong presence of mind he gave a unique order to the artillery; not for so many rounds, but to fire on a continuous basis. This was necessitated by the unrelenting suicidal attacks of Chinese soldiers thrown at his position. Totally without regard for his own safety he moved continuously over open ground to where he could be most effective. Levy exposed himself to the fusillade of thrusting fire from enemy burp guns, machine guns and mortars. Private Walker attests to the impact Levy's equanimity had on his men in a time of high tension and shattering nerves.

Lieutenant Michael G. Levy, and the men of 10 and 12 Platoons, are deserving of official recognition by the Government of Canada for their actions at the Battle of Kapyong.

1. Clouthier: Statement June 1997, and on going interviews
2. Levy: Statement Oct 17, 1997
3. Pearson: Statement, April 1997
4. Gray - Authors experience
5. Wanniandy March 30, 1998, subsequent telephone call.
6. Neufeld: March 5, 1998
7. Barwise: 28 February 1997
8. 2PPCLI War Diary. An article in the "Patrician" of March 1961, page 145, by Major G Henderson quotes Holligan as advising Mills that his platoon is completely overrun - this is erroneous, 12 east held throughout the night.
9. Stone, 2PPCLI Archives, magazine article.
10. Porter: Personal notes, 10,000 rounds fired in support of the Brigade. O'Neill: page 160, cites 10,000 rounds being fired in support of 2PPCLI
11. Nestor: Letter, Feb 3 1998
12. Coombe: Feb 1997
13. McGibbon
14. Coote: Email March 2000
15. McGibbon, 159
16. Wood, page 77.

Chapter TEN

AFTERMATH AND WITHDRAWAL
APRIL 25TH and 26TH

The Chinese assault on the Patricias has abated. We are not aware of any enemy activity in front of D, C, and A companies. The Chinese are however patrolling the river valley on the east side of Hill 677. It appears they are concentrating their strength behind the Patricias. Do they intend to bypass Hill 677, to isolate the Patricias? Are they contemplating an attack to our rear? Or are they quietly assessing their causalities and their options? Sporadic sniper and mortar fire occurs at D Company commencing at about 1100 hrs. The men are exhausted from their night's battle. The morning stand-to is over, one quarter of the troops man their positions, while the remainder are resting and brewing breakfast. Soldiers are exchanging stories of their conflict, and boasting of their successes. Everyone is cleaning their equipment and the NCOs are taking inventory of casualties and available ammunition. Those on watch are ever mindful of the possibility of another attack.

0615 hrs. - Regimental Aid Post - During the night Private Copley falls asleep on a stretcher. Other stretchers containing those who have been killed are placed alongside him. Copley is awakened when he hears a voice asking, "When did Copley get killed?" [1]

0630 hrs, - 5 Platoon, B Company - Petrie, "We have by now been awake for a couple of days except for the odd short nap. The stunning quiet that develops with the dawn leaves us quite drawn. I remember during the height of the battle, looking at a few blades of grass and thinking I see the impression of the right side of a Chinese face, which is back lighted by flares during darkness. In my weary state, this vision gave me quite a fright. Now, once again, the blades of grass are just straws. There is no sign of movement, only a number of sprawling enemy bodies barely distinguishable in the early light, to my front. It has been a macabre experience of frenetic activity for the last seven hours overlain by the orange glow of explosions.

"I reconnoiter the abandoned 6 Platoon position I was to occupy. I find a number of Chinese dead lying throughout the trenches and then I spot the body of Private Hayes lying peacefully dead. One of my soldiers moving to report to Company HQ, decides to take a short cut behind my platoon position. Before anyone had seen him he trips a booby trap and is wounded. I'm afraid my severe scolding for disobedience further wounds him, for hazarding the others. There are the bodies of Corporal Evans and Private Tolver with their rifles; The name 'LYDIA' has been carved upon the left of its wooden stock." [2]

At 0700 at a slit trench that shall remain nameless two soldiers move forward of their position to a point where two wounded Chinese are groaning. Searching the bodies they find the usual pictures of loved ones and their families. The Patricias had been killing these bastards all night, why the hell stop now! Although the wounded Chinese are conscious and fearful, they are thrown over the nearby cliff and the Patricias are devoid of all emotions as they watch them screaming in their agony as they tumble down hill. Two less bastards to worry about. To this day that act gives the surviving member of this duo nightmares and surges of terrible recurring guilt!

Tactical HQ:

Major Gordon Henderson, Battalion Battle Adjutant, communicated with the companies during the battle to keep Stone updated. In assessing the events of their battle, Henderson cannot comprehend Mills' vague and very slow answers to his queries for situation reports at D Company.[3] All other company commanders were able to quickly summarize their situations, but Mills could not.

The PPCLI Mortar Platoon is down to four bombs. Private Neufeld at 12 Platoon east states: "Earlier in the morning we exchange fire with the Chinese, I knock out two of their positions. From our entire platoon I can only muster a limited number of rounds of .303 for my Bren gun." [4]

At 0730 hrs, Lance Corporal Smiley Douglas is an Acting Corporal, in number One Assault Section, Pioneer Platoon. On the night of April 24, some time after 2100 hours he installs five #36 grenade booby traps in the vicinity of B Company HQ. This area of scrub growth and small trees is not occupied by our troops. A booby trap is constructed by placing a #36 grenade in a tin can with the safety pin removed. The lever release handle is restrained by being placed within the tin can, which is then tied to the base of a tree. A string line is strung out for eight to ten feet at a height of about six inches above the ground. When the string is trampled or pulled the grenade is released from the can, the lever flies free to detonate the mechanism. The shrapnel from the grenade, depending on the ground and covering vegetation, sends fragmentation over a distance of 75 to 100 meters. Private Bill Beattie is laying similar traps in another area of B Company. On completing their mission they return to Pioneer Platoon, about 100 meters to the south. They remain on call throughout the night. Says Douglas: "It was the longest night of my entire life, with the incessant Chinese attacks, the never ending artillery, mortar, machine guns and rifle fire" [5]

B Company orders a patrol to locate the enemy, report on their movements and estimated strengths. When the patrol moves out they unfortunately pass through the booby-trapped area tripping a grenade. One man is killed and another seriously wounded in the throat. Sergeant Red Pennel, of the Pioneer Platoon recalls: "The sergeant patrol leader takes a pen out of his pocket, and breaks off the end and shoves it into the wounded man's throat allowing him to breathe. The remaining patrol is entangled in the booby-trapped field and Douglas, who laid out the traps, endeavours to extract the men. Upon Douglas' instruction the soldiers begin to move out but they misunderstood, and trip another booby-trap. I am at Platoon HQ, when I hear the second grenade detonate and I race to the position. The grenade is smoking, the fuse is lit, and Douglas bravely dives for it in an attempt to throw it out of harm's way. The detonator has completed its job and his right hand is torn off. His right leg absorbs much of the remainder of the blast, and his body is terribly mangled by the shrapnel. Having suffered multiple wounds Douglas's body is gushing torrents of blood. I do not believe he will survive the day but remove my bootlaces anyway to administer tourniquets. Douglas' heroic attempt to throw away the burning grenade is the most outstanding and selfless act of bravery I have ever witnessed." [6] Lance Corporal Smiley Douglas is awarded the Military Medal (MM).

Anti-Tank Platoon, 0800 hrs [7] - Commanded by Lieut Rick Constant, with second in command Sergeant Alex Sim - There are about 40 men in all, not including the halftrack drivers or gun fitters. They are ordered to deliver ammunition to D Company and to reinforce them. Constant spends the day with Mills at D Company HQ. Mills orders Sim forward to join 12 Platoon under Holligan. Sim distributes half of his Platoon's ammo amongst 12, assigning his men various jobs. Sim does not have his men dig in as there is no enemy activity and they remain on open ground. Sim ascends the hill immediately behind 12 Platoon, with one combined section and Holligan. They position the section on the reverse slope just clear of the crest so they have a clear view for miles to their front. Holligan and Sim take a position somewhat lower down the slope. Having such a commanding view to their front and rear, they can quickly react in either direction. With no sign of the enemy the day was undisturbed.

Lieut Rod Middleton, 2PPCLI Liaison Officer at 27 Brigade HQ, is assigned to guide two Bell Helicopters to the Patricias to evacuate the seriously wounded who cannot be taken out by jeep or ambulance. The available maps in Korea are old Japanese maps with English overprints. They are almost impossible to read, the gradient lines are indistinct and blurred. Middleton, who has not been to Hill 677, studies the maps and hopes for the best. He also has in hand a new set of map overlays (orders) for Stone. Though it is his first time in a chopper what concerns him is to find the proper location.

At 0800 hrs they arrive over Hill 677 and are greeted by columns of smoke from fires ignited by the heavy artillery and mortar bombardments. It is almost impossible to pick out any features. They are rudely informed that they have overshot their target when Rod turns to the pilot and asks, "What are those blinking white lights sparkling on the ground?" [13] The Chinese are trying to shoot the chopper down. The pilot curses, quickly taking evasive action, when an orange smoke grenade belches forth from ground level to signal the wind direction and landing point. They land safely nearby Tactical HQ. Middleton delivers the order for the withdrawal to Stone, and briefs him on the impending move. He re-enters the helicopter, already loaded with two casualties resting upon the pods. The chopper is overloaded, and the pilot tells Middleton to get out, "You are walking back buster!" [9] Leaving the Patricias, Middleton walks down the road track and counts 40 - 45 enemy, dead from the firefight of the previous night. He cannot see in the re-entrants. Middleton reports trees and shrubbery are cut as if by a mower. As he descends the hill, he proceeds cautiously for the enemy is moving in the open at the north-east base of 677. Middleton has to walk back to Brigade HQ.

Each evacuation chopper carries two body containers, which are attached atop the skids. The configuration of the containers, adhered to the very narrow skids, seem flimsy as hell and, they are coffin body shaped, and painted an ominous black. They have a small window about 8 inches by 5 inches. The wounded men locked firmly inside are apprehensive. The "flying coffins" vibrate heavily with the chopper's motors throbbing forcefully as they labour to gain altitude.

The 72nd tanks are ordered to move out and disrupt the enemy building up to the rear of the Patricias.

0900 hrs - Private Bob Menard B Company - "We are detailed to pick up our dead and put them into body bags, then take them to the Regimental Aid Post. We gather the bodies of those killed, and ensure their Dog Tags are in place so that their identification will be confirmed. Sergeant Ulmer takes note of the names and enters them in the platoon roll call book. We retain their rifles and ammunition." [10]

Corporal Swan, Medical Assistant, takes Richardson of 6 Platoon to the helicopter pad, from where he is flown to the 60th Indian Parachute Field Ambulance. Private Don Morrow is waiting his turn for evacuation and at the last moment he is bumped and taken to a truck, to be driven out. The Chinese hold the high ground overlooking the highway south and open fire on the convoy. Morrow turns to his driver, gritting painfully through his broken and bleeding jaw shouts, "Get me the hell out of here, I have been wounded twice. I don't want a third one." [11]

Corporal Bill Shuler, Medical Assistant - "Some of the wounded are evacuated by jeep ambulance. Stretcher carrying jeeps display a Red Cross on the top canvas. All ambulance jeeps are to fly a Red Cross flag on the left front fender, but at no time are we supplied them." [12] The Indian Field Ambulance is 27th Brigade's Field Hospital. The doctors are well trained in Britain: Cambridge, Oxford and Edinburgh. The Americans note the 60th has the lowest number of lost casualties in the theatre. They set up immediately behind our front lines and the wounded reinforcement shot on the truck at Kapyong was on the 60 Field Ambulance operating table within 15 minutes of being hit.

Lance Corporal Smiley Douglas lies alone on a stretcher awaiting the arrival of the last chopper. His right hand has been torn off from the exploding booby trap he dived to neutralize, and his legs are badly mangled. His dressing covers the stump where his wrist abruptly terminates. The skin of his missing fingers hangs pathetically in the wind. A lieutenant comes over to comfort him. Douglas speaks, "Sir I have lost my right hand, Sir… What am I going to do, Sir?… I did not want to lose my hand, Sir." Throughout the exchange Douglas constantly addresses the lieutenant as "Sir." [13] Douglas' strict attention to military etiquette seems incomprehensible to the young officer who is humbled by Douglas' bravery, and his sacrifice to save his comrades.

Douglas is evacuated to the Indian Field Ambulance, and recalls: "The Doctor at the 60th spoke with a very British accent. He told me that they had straightened out my leg and cleaned it up and also cleansed my arm. Then they said there was nothing further they could do for me, and that in a very few hours I would be in a first class hospital in Japan. I was flown to the British Commonwealth Occupation Forces Hospital in Kure, Japan, and placed on the Australian ward where I was extremely well treated. A cast was put on me that extended from my right foot to my waist, and I endured that for a month. They took off the cast and stated that as soon as I could walk I would be sent home. That was all the incentive I needed. I flew home by CP Air about the second week of June. I was hospitalized again and finally discharged in October 1951. The Army took very good care of me." [14]

Pearson at 11 Platoon receives the men he sent to reinforce 12 Platoon: "The base of the barrel of their Bren has been struck, ripping a hole and jamming the barrel so that it cannot be replaced. I go over to 12 to talk with Holligan and on the way pass two dead men, their upper bodies covered by a blanket. The boots of one of the men are very shiny, as though ready to march on to the parade square." [15]

1030 hrs - Flying boxcars from the US Fifth Air Force Combat Support Group pass low overhead parachuting ammo, medical supplies, rations and even water. Most of them land in our area. Lance Corporal Bill Lee at number one Platoon: "I don't know how low the planes are when they come over for their second run, but they appear to be thundering overhead at about 50 feet. The ammo comes tumbling out of the aircraft in free fall! When the containers hit soft ground they dig in up to two to three feet. We are informed this step is taken to assure greater accuracy. With parachutes the ammo may have drifted into enemy hands. It scares the hell out of the lot of us, some fellows actually have to run to dodge these missile like projectiles." [16]

Mortar Platoon - Czuboka: "We are re-supplied with ammunition from the air drop, they are mostly high explosives. Further attacks are antici-pated but we are pleased they do not materialize. Our halftracks are overloaded. I am always nervous traveling on the Korean tracks and roads. Once I saw a vehicle that was three or four in front of us blow up, it literally disintegrated. If we hit a mine I'm afraid our ammunition would be ignited creating one hell of an explosion, and kill our crew." [17]

Lieut Peter McKenzie, Intelligence Officer, sifting through the incom-ing reports of enemy movements, orders Corporal Rawlinson and Private Mel Canfield to A Echelon. McKenzie tells them he fears the enemy is massing to the rear of our position for another assault; he orders them out to form a new Intelligence nucleus should the 2PPCLI be overrun.

Corporals Bill Shuler and Anderson, Medical Assistants (Med A), deliver newly dropped ammunition and grenades to D Company HQ, Mills orders them to take it forward to 10 Platoon. In advancing to 10, Shuler and Anderson twice hit the ground as the Chinese try to pick them off. As the second round of fire ends Shuler rises, Anderson hugs the ground, Shuler orders him to move and they run forward. They find Lance Corporal Edmond lying on the hilltop where Levy evacuated him; there is not a Med A at 10 Platoon. Shuler releases the field dressing to check the wound. Edmond's kidney or liver is exposed due to shrapnel wound and Shuler applies a pressure bandage. Edmond is pale and unconscious having lost a lot of blood. Shuler fashions a stretcher from fallen trees. Levy removes his bootlaces to lash the stretcher together.

Shuler advises things at D Company HQ appear confused. The troops inform him that Levy was responsible for the firefight of the Company. That they are damn pleased and fortunate to have him in the front line.[18]

Corporal Clouthier 10 Platoon - "Today we are re-supplied: Lots of ammo from the US air drop, 24 Grenades, but no detonators. Two rockets for a launcher that we do not have, one quart of water per man, and a 24 hour C ration food pack." [18]

1400 hrs - 11 Platoon, Pearson: "We are unable to see what is taking place in the valley below because of the smoke from the fires. Mills orders me to take a patrol down into the valley to find out what the Chinese are doing. I take a few men and my only Bren gun and we move north down the ridge. About halfway down I stop to deploy my men in a defensive position as we are making too much noise and invite an ambush. (Compare this with the up to 500 Chinese noiselessly attacking us earlier). Moving as quietly as possible I go forward, leaving the men behind. At the bottom the smoke is so thick I cannot see more than 30-40 meters. I pass a small hut that I remember seeing on the way up, it is deserted. I go closer to the road but cannot see or hear anything. If there are Chinese in the area they must be asleep. I return to my men and we rejoin the platoon." [19]

Private Del Reaume, of C Company, is wounded by grenade shrapnel about 0900 hrs. He is evacuated from the Regimental Aid Post about 1400 hrs by jeep, along with two other jeeps loaded with wounded soldiers. "Beside me is a chap from Vernon, shot in the throat, and it missed his jugular vein by a hair. We descend Hill 677. While crossing the rice paddy leading to the main road, the lead driver is shot in the shoulder by the Chinese. Our convoy is forced to halt, remaining exposed in the paddy for 3 or 4 minutes while a substitute driver is located. It is frustrating to be wounded and perched like a sitting duck in a shooting gallery. All the while the Chinese firing is being stepped up. Thank heavens on the whole they appear to be using short range weapons and thanks to God they appear to be lousy shots." [23] Some distances farther on the wounded are transferred to waiting ambulances. About 2100 that night Reaume is in a tent near Seoul, the next day he is flown to the British Commonwealth Occupation Forces Hospital, Kure, Japan. B Company reports the valley access below is free of Chinese.

Brigader G "Fluff" Taylor, takes command of the Brigade and it is given a new designation: 28 BRITISH COMMONWEALTH INFANTRY BRIGADE.

1900 hrs - 2PPCLI receive 28 Brigade warning order to move, on the 26. The Chinese continue light patrolling without penetrating the Battalion perimeter.

April 26th

0600 hrs. - 28 Brigade Headquarters

The King's Own Scottish Borderers Battalion (KOSB) has just arrived from Hong Kong. The KOSBs are dug in on a low hill a short distance north of Brigade HQ. They are in their light tropical summer uniforms and it has rained during the night. They are cold and wet and are trying to start fires to warm breakfast. They are then loaded onto troop carrying vehicles ready to move off. Brigadier "Fluff" Taylor and Middleton are each in their own vehicles. Taylor, standing up holding onto the windshield, is driven along the column in a Montgomery like stance, within his left hand is a robust walking stick. As he passes each truck he strikes the side and announces, "Stand firm KOSBs, they (Chinese) are coming tonight." [13] The as yet untried, wet, hungry and miserable looking troops, become even more concerned. Rod following in his jeep stops and with a Canadian accent informs each vehicle that they are not going to the front, they are moving into reserve near Nongol. Some accept the information with relief and others question who is this bloody Canadian, seemingly overriding our British Brigadier's orders? The KOSB do go into reserve. The diverse Commonwealth integration of personnel leads to confusion from time to time, particularly with newly arriving British formations.

0700 hrs - Stone receives orders that the relief of 2PPCLI is to be completed by 1630 hrs. It does not begin until about 2000 hour, although the War Diary records an earlier time of withdrawal. Mills, after attending Stone's Order Group withdrawal instructions, calls his Orders Group. This is D Company's first meeting of officers during their entire time at Kapyong.

1200 - 28 Brigade Headquarters.
Middleton is ordered to proceed to a local airstrip, and to pick up the commanding officer of the US 24 Infantry Division. He arrives just in time to meet an L-19 aircraft and pick up Major General Blackshear "Babe" Bryan, (2 star General). Middleton cranks the engine to leave and is advised to sit tight for the Corps Commander will arrive momentarily, Lieut General William (Bill) M Hoge, (3 star General). Once again he is ready to depart when the Corps Commander advises they are to wait for the arrival of General Van Fleet, the 8th Army Commander in Chief (4 star General). As Middleton finally moves off a voice rises from the rear seat, "Son, you drive very carefully, you have got an awful lot of stars on board." [13] He drives extremely carefully, depositing them at the relocated 28 Brigade HQ and did not see them again.

1400 hrs - 5 Platoon - An American Forward Fire Officer (FFO) arrives to direct artillery fire. A little later the Commanding Officer of the 5 Regimental Combat (5RCT) Team joins the FFO. Two NCOs are left to provide a radio link overnight. Elements of the 5 RCT are briefly counter attacking in the area north of the 2PPCLI. A spectacular firefight! They break the Chinese hold on the Patricias.

1600 hrs - Middleton drives his jeep to 2PPCLI Tactical HQ from HQ 28 Brigade, delivering revised withdrawal orders and map overlays. "I return down the track, my jeep is loaded with parachutes from the airdrop, and a poncho wrapped body. I also have two wounded Chinese prisoners, one riding in the passenger seat and the other sitting on the hood. I pass through the long columns of Americans from the First Cavalry Division, Fifth Regimental Combat Team (equivalent to a British Infantry Brigade), coming up the track to relieve us. They are a dog-tired lot of soldiers who have just fought a difficult engagement, breaking through the Chinese encirclement surrounding 2PPCLI. With the looks of fear on their faces the prisoners must have wondered what they were getting into." [13]

Melnechuck of C Company: "It is an unforgettable feeling watching the

American 1st Calvary Division's 5 RCT troops making their courageous advance in open formation towards Hill 504. Mortar shells are
dropping amongst them, the men are hitting the ground then getting up
and continuing to fight and move forward. Viewing their hard fought
battle is like watching a Hollywood movie, but this is reality. I admire
their fighting spirit, it is inspiring." [24] The 5 RCT retook Hill 504 that
had been defended by the 3RAR.

Melnechick had an 8 millimeter movie camera with him and shot an
inspiring 15-minute colour film of the battle. He mailed the film to
Kodak in Canada, it was never returned. Five Platoon, Private Bob
Menard - "As the Yanks advance on the enemy to break our encirclement, I see them dropping like flies from enemy fire. Trucks evacuating
the wounded are piled high with stretchers, and they look as though
they are piled like cordwood. The poor bastards." [14]

Night fall

The entire front of the Eighth Army is withdrawing, thus preserving
their formations and stretching the enemy supply line. Middleton is
driving his jeep in a long line of vehicles that are moving south, bumper
to bumper. "Moving in defined bounds across a paddy field is a company of US Army tanks, periodically they fire their .50 caliber machine
guns and main armament at unknown targets, adding to the confusion
of the approaching darkness. What would the coming night hold? As
well as the Chinese wounded, I am carrying one dead body and the
light from the vehicle behind projects our shadow on the truck in front,
the lifeless limb stirring in a continuing evocative rhythm coincides
with the movements of my jeep. This haunting motion of a lifeless limb
will forever be my nightmare. We later arrive at 28th Brigade HQ, north
of the village of Nongol.

"I am again ordered out to deliver new movement orders for the next
night to the King's Own Scottish Borderers. They are still wet and cold
in their tropical uniforms. Their Commanding Officer refuses to accept
that I, a Canadian, should pass on a movement order to him. I am not
British I am a mere colonial. After a somewhat heated and uninspiring
'discussion' he orders his Lieut Intelligence Officer (IO) to follow me
to Brigade HQ to confirm the instructions. A mile short of HQ, I instruct the KOSB IO where to further proceed; I then deliver new orders
to the 16 RNZA. On returning I come across a British Land Rover
upside down, wheels spinning. I stop, dreading the unthinkable. The
KOSB IO lies on the ground in agony suffering a broken neck, his

driver is dead, pinned under the vehicle. He had been returning to his Tactical HQ, when his vehicle flipped. I advise him I will get help immediately. These are totally unnecessary casualties if only the commander of the KOSBs had not been such a self important and inexperienced commanding officer. In short order he was negating the very effective inter-unit trust within the diverse Commonwealth Forces fighting in Korea. This exemplary Division was an extremely successful force of arms." [13]

2100 hrs - 5 Regimental Combat Team, First Cavalry Division, US Army, relieve 2PPCLI. At D Company, a 5 RCT sergeant informs Levy, they have lost their officer and have suffered 50% casualties while penetrating the determined Chinese encirclement of 2 PPCLI. Having fought a bloody and hard battle the men are exhausted. Their sergeant is concerned that if they face another enemy attack they may not be able to hold them back.

Melnechuk, of C Company states: "Being transported south after Kapyong we come to a river crossing. We wait our turn to cross the bridge for it is plugged with refugees, ambulances and our withdrawing Army. Nearby is a large American supply depot. Everything is being torched. As the tent nearby goes up in flames we see it was loaded to the rooftop with unopened crates of Remington typewriters!" [24]

Munro, 2 Platoon, A Company - Leads their withdrawal from Kapyong. The vehicles are traveling without lights and it is a pitch-black night. Some miles down the road Munro barely makes out two shadowy figures standing by the roadside. Placing his loaded carbine on the spare tire, taking careful aim at the figures, Munro tells the driver to slow, but to be ready to hit the accelerator if he fires....

Out of the night, a very British voice calls out:

"I say, who are you?"

Munro: **"Patricias."** [25]

It is Brigadier G. (Fluff) Taylor Commanding 28 British Commonwealth Infantry Brigade and a Sergeant Military Policeman. Taylor waves his swagger stick in acknowledgment.

"Ah yes, Patricias."

"Would you mind climbing that hill over there and digging in?" "We will sort it all out in the morning." [24]

A cold rain begins descending on the exhausted Patricias. They begin the difficult ascent up another slippery muddy mountain slope. When they reach the top of the mountain they discard their packs and retrieve their trenching tools. Once again they force their way through the rain soaked mud and grime of Korea, and spend another miserable night in an all too familiar, abysmal slit trench.

Roland Batchelor of Reuters summed up this battle in an article, on the 26th of April 1951. The Department of National Defence released the article in Canada. I believe the reader will find the leading six paragraphs of his much longer article of interest.

"British Commonwealth troops turned back the clock 35 years to write the final and most glorious chapter in the history of the (27th) Brigade along the central front this week in an action, which has revived the epic phrase "They shall not pass" of the First World War.

"Three battalions - the 1st Battalion Middlesex Regiment, the 3rd Battalion the Royal Australian Regiment and the (2nd Battalion) Princess Patricia's Canadian Light Infantry - brought a new meaning to Marshal Foch's famous words in a 48-hour battle against two Chinese Divisions, which swept across the 38th parallel to break the United Nations' front wide open.

"This thin red line, supported by the (16th) New Zealand artillery regiment, took the full weight of the savage Chinese lunge along a 10 mile wide divisional front held by South Korean Troops who broke and fled a few hours after the Communist offensive began last Sunday night.

"It was an impossible task that was made impossibly true by the Empire troops who stood alone and hurled back wave after wave of attacking Chinese until the trenches and ridge lines where they fought a few miles north of the vital road junction town of KAPYONG, astride the main SEOUL- CHUNCHON highway, were piled high with the bodies of the Communist troops.

"This Brigade, thrown in the line on the eve of being relieved by the 28th Brigade from HONG KONG, inflicted more than 4,000 casualties in those 48 hours for the loss of 150 - nearly 30 to one - and yielded scarcely an inch of ground.

"It was a wall of guts and little else against which the Chinese flung themselves as they flooded south across the 3,000 foot hills and ridge lines which this Brigade battled for nearly three weeks to seize and which had been lost in a matter of hours by the collapse of a complete South Korean Division."

Over the next four days the Corps withdrew, to break contact with the enemy and to establish a firm base from which to commence further operations. 2PPCLI was assigned a defensive position on Line Golden. The withdrawal involved successive movements southward, boundary by boundary. And not everything could be withdrawn. The War Diary of 28 Brigade, in part, records: "On the 28 of April the Middlesex battalion was instructed to destroy 16,000 gallons of petrol left by the 5th Cavalry, RCT, due to the approach of the rearguard which precluded back loading. 16RNZA held 1,800 rounds of 25 pounder High Explosive ammunition, which they were unable to backload due to a lack of transport, this was fired prior to departure. The KOSB were forced to destroy all their Sea Kit Bags and certain Regimental stores - 10 good sets of pipes were saved but the kilts were burnt. The withdrawal was carried out without contact by the enemy. Rain and low clouds persisted most of the day which precluded air support."

We remained on Golden for 21 days, during which time many patrols were undertaken, and then once more commenced to move forward to push the enemy back. All the lost ground was subsequently retaken.

12 Platoon withdrawing from Kapyong.

1. Copley, Telephone interview Dec 14 1999

2. Petrie, Statement , 24 November, 1996

3. Henderson, Signed statement 3 June 1998, See Appendix "A", page 214.

4. Neufeld, letter, 1998

5. Douglas, Telephone Interview, 00 08 07.

6. Pennell, Letter and telephone, Aug 8, 2000

7. The Anti-Tank Platoon were equipped initially with long barreled 17 pounder guns, which could not be maneuvered over the hills and mountains. Stone had them assume the role of a reconnaissance force, nicknamed "Constant Force," after Lieut Rick Constant who commanded them. In late June of 1951, they were equipped with American Anti-Tank Recoilless Rifles to resume their anti-tank role.

8. Sim. Kamloops interview, 10 May 2000

9. Middleton: Interview October 1999.

10. Menard: Interview Dec ember 8th, 1999

11. Morrow: Interview November 1999.

12. Shuler: Telephone interview August 1999

13. Gray: Conversation April 25th, 1951

14. Douglas: Exchange of correspondence, September 2000.

15. Pearson: Memorandum April 1997

16. Lee: Telephone September 1999

17. Czuboka: Exchange of e/mails July 2001

18. Clouthier: Statement June 1997, Appendix "A", page 356.

19. Reaume: Telephone interview 1999

20. Melnechuck: Interview, Kamloops April 1999

21. Munro: Interview, Victoria, December 1996.

22. 27th Brigade War Diary, April 25.

Chapter ELEVEN

THE IMPROBABLE

A great deal of publicity has been given to Private Kenneth Barwise's recovery of a Vickers Medium Machine Gun (MMG) on April 25 at about 0900 hrs, at 12 Platoon west, Kapyong. The record of its capture by the Chinese at 0300 hrs that day, is not in doubt, but the details of its recovery are controversial. Unfortunately there are times when soldiers embellish their battle performance, but here is the real story according to five veterans I interviewed, who participated in the recovery patrol, as well as others who witnessed the event from nearby.

The 2PPCLI War Diary reports: " M800036, Private Barwise, risked his life leading Lieut's Whittaker's platoon from C Company in a successful attempt to recapture the MMG lost the previous night." [1] The Sun newspaper of July 9th 2000, relates an interview with Barwise in Seoul conducted by Peter Worthington, who also served in Korea in 3PPCLI as Intelligence Officer. In part his article reveals: "Barwise recalled... (he) picked up a Thompson Sub machine gun and began spraying the Chinese as he ran to the machine gun pit... with sniper fire all around him. He jumped into the pit, took over the Vickers and began firing at the Chinese who were advancing like ants." All of the above reports, including the War Diary entry, are inaccurate according to the eyewitnesses I interviewed. Barwise did perform a very brave act earlier that morning, as previously recorded, and was awarded an MM for his efforts, but in the case of the MMG his actions have been embroidered.

Sergeant Sim, and 40 members of the Anti-Tank Platoon reinforced 12 Platoon on the morning of the 25th. Sergeant Sim led 12 men to the top of the 15 meter high hill immediately behind 12 platoon's position. Sim recalls that Barwise that morning came up the hill behind 12 Platoon and discussed the need to recover the MMG lying unattended at the 12 Pl W deserted slits. Barwise complained to Sim that no one from D Company would go with him Sim observed, "If no one from D Company will go with you, neither will I." [2] Holligan's only laconic comment, "What the Bloody Hell, Barwise, bugger off!" [2] Sim, being at the top of the hill observes there is no enemy in sight at either of 12's positions, nor in the distance to their front. At the end of the day the anti-tank platoon leaving 12 Platoon ascends the hill. They leave all their percussion and smoke grenades with Holligan. Sim bids good bye and leads his men back to their location south of Tactical HQ. He does not address Barwise again. Cpl Sterling MacAuley, Anti-Tank, assigned to the main body of 12, recalls there was a bit of sporadic gun fire in the general area, but they remained undisturbed, and did not dig in during the entire time at 12 Platoon. [3]

At 10 Platoon, about 0630 hrs that morning Barwise was elated with his successful recovery of the bandoleers and grenades. It is a challenge to return once more to the point of the section's earlier defeat and liberate the captured MMG. He solicits assistance from a number of men, but 25% are on stand to, and the remainder are exhausted from their night's battles. Those "brewing up," are not interested, they are grateful to relax and eat.

Here's what really happened, according to those who were on patrol with him. At about 0900 hrs, Barwise arrives at C Company and convinces Major Del Harrison that D Company needs to retrieve the tantalizing MMG. It is obvious that Harrison would not authorize men of his company to go on such a patrol without the authorization of Tactical HQ.

Lieut Whittaker of 9 Platoon is assigned to proceed with two sections, about 18 men, and Acting Sergeant Major Melnechuk strengthens the numbers by assigning two additional soldiers: privates Don Worsfold and Fred Pickett. Barwise's story fires Whittaker's imagination. Being shut out of the prior night's battle Whittaker welcomes the opportunity to participate in a victorious firefight. During the 500-meter trek, as well as on their return, Whittaker's men sight no enemy. During Whittaker's agitated impatience, however, he repeatedly prods the back of the soldier marching in front of him carrying a Bren LMG. Finally Private Paul Sandor tells Whittaker to, " Shove off!" [4]

The patrol approaches from well below the crest of the steep hill to the front of 12 W. Reports of the recovery vary at this point. Herman Thorsen, Paul Sandor, Don Worsfold, and other survivors of 9Pl, think the Chinese occupy 12W slits, because Barwise has told them so. Nervous with anticipation the men believe they are about to face a determined enemy with a functioning medium machine gun. Below the crest they go to ground. Whittaker, percolating with anticipation and bravado, orders, "Fix Bayonets, prepare to charge!" [4] The troops' opinion of Whittaker is that he is brave but they do not trust his judgment. No one moves. No one fixes bayonets. No one stands up. This is not the first time that Whitaker issues such an order and his entire platoon reacts in defiance. (The troops have nicknamed Whitaker "JD," Juvenile Delinquent, for being overly "Gung Ho," this is according to Don Worsfold.[5]) Sandor cocks his Bren light machine gun, only to realize the mechanism had jammed.

Soldiers lying below the crest are not about to leap up and sacrifice themselves charging into the path of a death-spewing machine gun. Instead one man pulls the pin from a grenade and lets fly. Two others follow suit. (No one I interviewed peered over the crest. They relied on Barwise). It appears the grenades are thrown short and land on the descending hillside. The four-second fuse detonates the grenades. Almost immediately exploding shrapnel fragmentation wounds three men: Sandor, Parker and Perley, who are all prone and wounded in their buttocks. In the confusion, a third man throws his grenade and is horrified to see it rolling back toward him, but luckily he has failed to pull the pin. Sandor later informed me that a Chinese grenade caused his wound; others believe their own returning grenades inflicted theirs. "Barwise foolishly jumped up, ascended the crest, went to the trench and found the super human strength to retrieve the entire MMG, unopposed," said Thorsen. [6]

The only "assault" on 9 Platoon is two grenades. The soldiers <u>do not</u> experience any other incoming fire. The source of those two exploding grenades is a moot point. # 1 Section 10 Platoon, is 50 meters to the west across a gully and on ground about seven meters higher and overlooking 12W. Corporal Clouthier and his men are sitting on open ground preparing breakfast. They spot the patrol coming uphill close to their position and sling a number of jibes in the fashion attributed to competitive yet friendly soldiers. Clouthier observes their movements but remains unaware of their objective. He is unconcerned because both he and Levy realize the Chinese deserted the position at about 0600 hrs.

Worsfold reported: "Barwise grabs the MMG to join the rest of us below the crest of the slope. We remain below the entire time, and then move off with Barwise, who carried the MMG to the main body of 12 Pl. We returned to C Company." [7]

Barwise has been quoted as stating that he manned the MMG, and fired the gun. The men of 9 Platoon, who confirm the earlier observation by Clouthier that the gun was inoperable, deny this. Barwise is also quoted as saying enemy troops "were advancing like ants" and he sprayed them with a Thompson submachine; "Not so," say the men of 9 Platoon. In my research I was unable to locate anyone from the combined 9, 10, 12 platoons and the Anti-Tank grouping who reference any enemy fire of this nature on the 25th. If anyone had engaged an enemy force and fired a machine gun, surely the men of the patrol and the others - about 100 soldiers in total - would have dived for cover, manned their weapons. Levy would have been on the blower calling for supporting artillery and mortar fire. No Patricia fires a shot. A further point of interest is that later in the day, Pearson leads a patrol to the valley below searching for the enemy and finding none.

Barwise's determination to recover the MMG was a hollow victory. No one else witnessed the presence of any Chinese, or firing. No reports of enemy movement emanated from Sim or his men having a commanding view from the top of the hill, or from 10 Platoon. Rather than performing a heroic rescue, Barwise's action sadly inflicted wounds upon three fellow soldiers. The injured men are escorted to the Regimental Aid Post, wounds are dressed and they are placed in an ambulance. Their departure is delayed for a couple of hours as Chinese snipers are successfully picking off the drivers descending the hill.

The enemy from 1100 hrs on April 25 are taking the odd pot shot and launching an occasional mortar upon 10 Platoon. Subsequent events reveal that the enemy, reinforcing their elements south of Hill 667, is bypassing to the west of Patricia's 10 Platoon location. This was either to attack the 2PPCLI from the rear or to isolate them and re-launch their southward thrust to Seoul. The Chinese build-up south of the 2nd Battalion is evidenced by the tough battle waged by the American 5th Regimental Combat Team, (Brigade strength) of the 1st Calvary Division. Some formations experience 50% casualties.

The two Padres, Captain (Father) Joseph Valalee and Captain RG Cunningham (who later served as Chaplain General of the Canadian Army), are at Stone's headquarters during the night of the 24th. They go to D Company early the next morning, meet Mills and then proceed to meet with Levy and his men. Both Padres had worked in China, and were well known to Levy. Mills remains at his HQ. Levy relates the act of bravery undertaken by Barwise, twice retrieving the ammunition and grenades, and says that he is recommending him for a medal. On returning to D Company HQ, they advise Mills of Levy's intended award. Mills informs them he will not sanction Barwise being awarded. [3]

It was the retrieval of the bandoliers and the grenades that spurred Levy, over many months, to ensure that Barwise was LATER awarded the MM. His award was initiated only after Levy pursued the matter and became Intelligence Officer to be in daily contact with Stone, who finally agreed in October of 1951. Levy wrote the citation and handed it to Stone, who said it was not up to snuff. Levy was ordered to pass it along to Major Vince Lilley, MC, who would "beef it up." Levy did not see the citation again until I showed it to him in 1988.

Barwise performed a brave act earlier on the 25th. It is sad that embellished heroism has enjoyed such prominent publicity. Unhappily the exploitation of the MMG incident overshadows and diminishes true acts of heroism at Kapyong, such as: Barwise's earlier action, Private Wayne Mitchell DCM, Lance Corporal Smiley Douglas MM, and Lieut Michael Levy.

1. 2PPCLI War Diary, April 25, 1951.
2. Sim, interview Kamloops and Calgary 2001.
3. MacAuly, telephone interview, 2001.
4. Sandor, phone call 12-18 October 2001.
5. Worsfold, telephone call and interview Victoria, October 2001.
6. Thorsen telephone call October 2001.
7. Worsfold telephone interview Victoria, October 2001.

12 Pl, D Company (photo: Hub Gray)

Chapter TWELVE

A COMPLEX INDIVIDUAL

**Lieutenant Colonel James Riley Stone, DSO & 2 Bars, MC,
Commanding Officer, Second Battalion,
Princess Patricia's Canadian Light Infantry, Korea, 1950-1.
Born February 8,1908, England**

There are many factors that contribute to an Army's reputation: The political policies of the time, the commanding officer(s)' character, the decisions they make, the intention of the enemy, the battles fought, the individual acts of heroism, and last but not least, the vagaries of human failings. All of these combine to form a regiment's substance. These elements develop a greater focus of attention with time, which contributes to the ongoing scrutiny and assessment of a regiment's performance. Over time, retired soldiers write their accounts; appointed historians pursue army records, which have been withheld for a specified period of time ranging from 40 to 50 years, depending on the particular authority; and regimental archives have accumulated donated records. It's usually decades after an engagement that the greater accuracy of events emerges.

In August of 1950 the greater portion of 2PPCLI was thrown together in a hell of a hurry to satisfy the demands of a slow moving government. In order to quickly fill the required numbers, Ottawa specified that all applicants were to be accepted into the force. Unbelievably, it was literally the case that if a potential recruit could walk he was given a uniform. One recruit was subsequently found to have a wooden leg! Canada had delayed acting upon its commitment to a UN-US backed resolution to send troops to Korea. When the Federal Government finally reacted, under pressure from the United States, the recruiting of rank and file soldiers became a free-for-all. At the end of the Second World War Canada had half a million men serving in the Army. By 1949, there was an authorized establishment for 40,000 in all the services. The Regular Force Infantry consisted of three under strength battalions, the entire army numbered about 20,000 in all ranks.

Quite suddenly Canada was committed to sending a reinforced Infantry Brigade with supporting arms to Korea, comprising about 6,000 men. It was immediately necessary to recruit, equip and train at least an equal number of reinforcements - about 26,000 served in Korea. An additional Canadian Infantry Brigade and Air Force arm were soon to be required in Europe under the NATO banner. Thus the Second and Third Battalions, Princess Patricia's Canadian Light Infantry came into being. LCol James Riley Stone, DSO and Bar, MC, was appointed to Command the Second Battalion, Princess Patricia's Canadian Light Infantry.

Stone is one of only 22 officers in the history of the Canadian Army to be awarded three DSOs. It is virtually impossible to sum up this complex individual in a few words, however, I would describe him as: highly intelligent; exceedingly brave; fiercely determined; never one to suffer fools; decisive; opinionated; domineering; if he disliked you - you'd had it; and lastly - A Sphinx-like enigma.

Stone's battalion attracted a mixed bag of recruits ranging from raw kids (the greater part) looking for excitement, to experienced veterans from the Second World War. From the time the battalion arrived in Korea until it went into action raw recruits and battle weary veterans were weeded out for everything from alcoholism to battle fatigue stemming from WWII. Stone has been quoted as saying, "many were deadbeats, escapists from domestic and other troubles, cripples, neurotics and other useless types all of whom broke down under the rigorous training programme..." [1]

When the battalion arrived in Korea the enemy had pushed from the northern border with China to more than 40 Km south of Seoul. The Patricias, when dispatched from Seattle, were thought to be going to serve as occupation troops, for the war appeared all but over, and they were not fully trained. Upon debarking, Stone was ordered to commit his troops to battle within 72 hours, but he refused, an action which no doubt saved many Canadian lives. Canada did not want a repeat of the debacle at Hong Kong in 1941. Stone, invested with the authority of the Canadian Government, was to determine when his battalion was ready for battle - and not before. He demanded and was granted an additional six weeks.

A letter from Stone dated December 5, 1999, to Professor David Bercuson. "In Pusan a United States Staff Officer gave me an order to join the 29th British Brigade...I explained that we were not trained to combat standards and could not obey his order. His answer, "I have my orders– you have yours." I asked to see Gen Walker." Stone went to 8th

Army HQ. "… as a LCol I did not have immediate access to General Walker. I was expected and faced across a table several senior US Army Officers who, obviously had been briefed. My position was challenged by such statements as, "Your troops are trained as well as any of our reinforcements etc.", which I admitted but tried to explain that we were trained as formations; that we could function as sections but not as platoons, companies or as a battalion. I was made so uncomfortable that eventually, I produced my paper of authority which had the effect of stopping the inquisition." Stone met General Walker the next day, the meeting was courteous and 6 weeks of additional training was undertaken. Training of the battalion developed from platoon level to company and battalion exercises. All other nations' arriving forces, with the exception of the Patricias, and the New Zealand 16 Field Artillery Regiment, were thrown immediately into the fray.

During this phase an event occurred which left its imprint on the Battalion's historical lore. It began at Miryang where the battalion was undergoing its final training, in January 1951. The first beer ration was inaugurated and a few men were appointed guardians of the newly arrived and prized possession. The guards happily drank a portion of their charge, not anticipating their commanding officer's immediate and deservedly harsh response. It was a wintry January, and Stone had the offenders dig a hole in the frozen ground by the river and place barbed wire over the top. They each had one blanket, and for seven days they survived in this hole. Their morning ritual involved breaking through the ice to shave in freezing water and during the day, they moved constantly at the double with heavy packs upon their backs. [2]

Stone delivered a speech to his assembled battalion in which he developed two themes: First, he told his troops that if these soldiers would steal beer from their comrades they could not be relied upon to support their buddies in battle. Stone would not allow his troops to be at risk from shirkers and scruff. The harsh punishment sent a clear and necessary statement to a group of individuals who were quickly uniting into a cohesive fighting force. Over two months in Korea, about 200 men were rejected as unfit for battle. It is ironic that a number of those "shirkers" were once again to be sent back to Korea and eventually on to Europe, but that is another story.

Second, according to witnesses, Stone stated that they were all volunteers, well fed and well paid for their service and he would not be making any recommendations for individual recognition, regardless of what the future held. Once committed to battle he would not be awarding medals like the Americans! The statement was a shock for some of the assembled soldiers especially as this "Order of the Day" came from a commanding officer who had earned the reputation at Ortona, Italy, in WWII as, "The Epitome of the Fighting Human Leader." [3] As testament to his initiative and bravery Stone's chest displayed the DSO and Bar (twice awarded) as well as the MC - a unique combination. Edwards, initially posted to another regiment requested his transfer to the Patricias entirely based on Stone's outstanding reputation.

It is perfectly reasonable that a caring and responsible leader would want to caution his men not to be damn fools in battle. Each commander did it in his chosen way. Many of the senior officers in Korea had experienced horrendous actions against the Germans in both Italy and NW Europe. The fighting in Korea was different from the campaigns of WWII; the Chinese chose their own particular style of warfare. Did Stone have an aversion to recognizing heroics in battle?

Levy was appointed Intelligence Officer of the battalion on 24 July 1951. Levy reports that when he and Stone visited the positions of the front line troops, Stone would walk on the crest of a hill while Levy partially traversed the reverse slope to ensure a minimum of exposure to the enemy. Stone presented himself as a live target, defying the Chinese to strike him, and the enemy did retaliate by firing upon him whenever he was at the front. Stone let the troops know that he was with them in the front line and that he was unafraid of the Chinese. These actions made a lasting impression upon Levy, the men and officers. Whenever Stone went to the front lines the troops would gather around him asking questions, and obviously felt at ease with their Colonel.

"Stone came to this country as a young man and lived a very hard life," recalled Levy. "He worked on a farm in the Peace River district. He was so poor he could not afford shoes-laces, and used bailing wire instead. The Colonel possessed a photographic memory, and was a voracious reader. He poured over military books and could quote the actions of an extensive list of generals in an inventory of battles. He knew by heart many of the Gilbert and Sullivan operas and loved to sing them after mess dinners; and would corral his officers until well in to the early hours of the morning. I believe he was once or possibly twice thrown out of OCTU (Officer Cadet Training Unit, WW II), for being too domineering. General Chris Volkes phoned the Commandant, ordering him to pass Stone. He told me that when war broke out in 1939, he couldn't wait to get to Edmonton to join up. The recruiting officer looked at his size and physical strength and thought him well qualified for the role of a Regimental Policeman. In action, Stone was clearly decisive. When I was Intelligence Officer, I would accompany him to Brigadier Rockingham's Order Groups and Stone, though drinking coffee throughout absorbed every detail. When Rocky finished Stone would announce his appreciation on certain points. The other Colonels would frequently let out a collective sigh upon receiving "domineering" Stone's comments. I worked closely with Stone for a number of months and frequently, during conversation in the lulls in the evening, I found him to be a very humane human being. In my opinion Stone was born a soldier, waiting his opportunity to prove himself. I would gladly follow Colonel Stone anywhere, into any battle, at any time.

"Stone possessed an abundance of natural ability to analyze the advantages and disadvantages of terrain, both from his own and the enemy's point of view. He was a superb tactician." [4] Stone appeared to be a natural born infantry soldier's fighter, according to Edwards. Stone talked informally with newly arrived officers at Currie Barracks in August of '50 and exhibited the scars on his right arm received during a knife fight. Without doubt he was a brave individual who was capable of inspiring loyalty and inspiration, but he could also be arrogant and disdainful when it came to his fellow officers. This was painfully clear when it came to social gatherings, but first a short digression.

When the Patricias pulled out of the fighting line for a period of rest all the officers would assemble in the Battalion Officers' Mess. They would then celebrate together and compare experiences with the goal of improving their future performance and fighting cooperation in the line - and thereby their chance of survival. Not so in 2PPCLI. Stone issued another of his "Orders of the Day." It called for the Battalion Officers Mess to be reserved as the exclusive domain of James Riley and the officers of Battalion Headquarters. This decree raised a considerable amount of ongoing discussion amongst the officers. Why in hell did our leader declare us unacceptable? This ostracism by our Colonel did not pass unnoticed by the senior NCOs, all of whom were welcomed by the Regimental Sergeant Major into their mess.

One day I was so miffed by this discrimination that I went to the adjutant, Captain Gord Turnbull for an explanation. Turnbull gave currency to the story that Colonel Stone experienced such horrific casualties in the fighting at Ortona, that he did not choose to become close to those he would commit to battle, possibly sending them to their death. Well, that was the "heroic" version for the blackballing of company officers, who were then left to their own devices. The reader will appreciate that our resources for such enterprises were extremely limited, in fact virtually nonexistent. The truth for our exclusion may have been quite different. Stone evidently had the habit of unwinding through the intense action of a poker game. In the Battalion HQ mess Stone assembled a poker playing fraternity, the two Padres, Medical, Dental, Major Grant, Signals, Adjutant and others. Stone was not going to be "harassed" by the boisterous celebrations of his company officers unwinding from the intensities of their battles, celebrating well into the night at still being alive and well. The only occasion I remember ever being invited into the hallowed halls of Stone's Battalion Officers' Mess, was during the inaugural visit of Brigadier General Rockingham, Commanding the 25 Canadian Infantry Brigade (25CIB). Somewhat later, after being well integrated into the 25CIB, Stone relented, perhaps due to Rockingham's influence.

Our leader relegated us to what was clearly second-class status. Was it solely because of his poker fraternity or was it because Stone was comparing the fighting in Korea to the intensity of his experiences at Ortona, Italy? Was Korea a war of lesser intensity? I could not state where that contempt began or ended - or if it existed at all, but we all felt the sting of his rejection. In Italy, while Stone was a company commander of the Loyal Edmonton Regiment, he once berated a lieutenant under fire. Stone addressed him severely, in front of his platoon for failing in an attack upon German soldiers defending a strong point. The lieutenant, facing increasing casualties, had broken off the engagement to return to his own lines. Stone, shoving the officer aside, rallied and led the men to once more charge forth, only to be eventually beaten back having suffered further casualties. It is said that Major Stone subsequently made his apologies to the officer in the presence of the Brigadier. The officer in question, Captain Owen Browne, served with Second Patricias in Korea and later retired a LCol and has since passed on.

Stone occasionally commented on the underperformance of some of his officers in trying situations, Canfield reported after Hill 532. Three such incidents are reviewed in this book: First, Major Jack George was relieved of command of C Company just hours prior to the Battle at Kapyong. His replacement was a commander who was completely unfamiliar with the officers and men. Lieut Charles Petrie's assessment reveals the lack of preparedness in C Company. The second incident involved Captain Gordon Turnbull who commanded D Company at

Hill 532, but subsequently was posted to a non-combative administrative position. Research indicates his performance was lacking. And thirdly there is the case of Captain JG Wally Mills. While awarded a prestigious medal for an "outstanding performance under fire" - the Military Cross for bravery at Kapyong - he clearly under performed and did not follow the principles of leadership demanded of a company commander in battle. Most citations are very descriptive, Mills' is uniquely brief.

After the action at Hill 532, Stone retained Levy's command of 10 Platoon; but in retrospect Stone may have had second thoughts. At Kapyong, Levy originated the bold and highly unusual order for supporting artillery fire to impact upon his own platoon at least twice, and perhaps more; This order was not issued by Mills, as has so often been credited. Australian's official Korean History, Vol II, notes Levy issued a unique order for artillery fire to be continuous during a 40 minute barrage in the height of a battle that saw massed Chinese suicidal attacks on three fronts. Not for one moment during the battle did Levy ever consider withdrawing, despite the fact his men were greatly outnumbered; and due to his decisive action he and his men did not surrender a single inch of ground.

There were 33 Military Crosses awarded in Korea, and the 2PPCLI received one. I and many others, including those whose testimonials are in this book, believe that Levy should have been considered for an award for his actions far-outstripped the feats of many others who did receive accolades. Major Bob Swinton, MC (WWII), Commanding D Company was on five days R&R in Japan, during the battle. On returning, he immediately assessed the performance of his company at Kapyong, I attended one such evaluation. As a result of his review Swinton approached Stone with the intention of initiating an award for Levy but Stone had made an award to Mills and refused to hear Swinton out. Shortly after returning from leave Swinton and Levy were posted to B Echelon to establish training at a newly inaugurated 25 Brigade Junior NCOs School. Stone took compassionate leave in Canada because of a family matter concerning one of his very ill children. Other than Swinton, no one chose to evaluate the actions of D Company during our stand at Kapyong, even though we spent the next three weeks in a primarily static position, undisturbed by the enemy on Line Golden.

In 1973 during an informal reunion in Vancouver, Stone advised his former soldiers that Kapyong was not a great battle, as great battles go, but it was well planned and well fought. In an article written by Battle

Adjutant Major Gordon Henderson, concerning Kapyong and appearing in the "Patrician," of April 1961, 12 years earlier, Stone made this statement: "In the annals of history of the Korean War, it will be said that the Second Battalion PPCLI did not give an inch although attacked by overwhelming numbers with the front crumbling all around them. Cut off and with everything else pulling back, the Second Battalion PPCLI was the only battalion holding on the Eighth Army front. By their determination, steadfastness and courage above the normal devotion to duty, precious time was saved and an orderly withdrawal of IX Corps forces was possible."

Our Battalion did indeed fight a successful action, but Stone's enthusiasm concerning the extent of our involvement across the Eighth Army front, appears somewhat incongruous in light of Stone's previously noted remarks. In Vancouver Stone concluded his recorded address by stating flatly, "I have never served with a finer body of men." In a later written speech given in December 1973, to the officers of 3rd Battalion PPCLI, at Currie Barracks, Calgary, Stone in part stated: "…that Kapyong no doubt fulfilled the Chinese military objective, for had they chosen to, they could have defeated the Second Patricias at Kapyong." In fact the Chinese suffered such horrendous casualties at Kapyong that they fell far short of their goal. Clearly Stone is a complex man. If indeed he felt the men who fought with him in Korea were among the finest he ever served with, and that their actions showed, "determination, steadfastness and courage above the normal," then they were deserving of greater credit than he was willing to give in the form of medals, or in fact, in acceptance in his mess.

My research has been motivated by my deep desire to have Michael Levy, in particular, recognized for the tenacious stand that he directed at Kapyong along with the men of 10, 11 and 12 Platoons. Stone revealed the importance of Levy's actions, when he told Mills, "Nobody could pull out. If we lose that hill we lose it all." Had D Company withdrawn, the Chinese would have had clear access to the high ground dominating all of our positions. In my opinion, and that of many survivors of Kapyong, Levy saved us Patricias from a fate similar to the Gloucesters.

Highly successful military commanders tend to have a variety of complexities; yet their strongest feature is the swift decisiveness by which they obliterate all opposition. General Patton never hesitated to express his strong and on occasion eccentric opinions. Other well-known and highly successful egotists were Montgomery and MacArthur. Stone also possessed overbearing characteristics. His address at Miryang proclaims his distaste for recognizing heroics in battle, and his aggressive superiority was manifested in the way he excluded officers from his closed circle when out of the line.

I cannot believe that Stone, who was highly regarded for his ability to quickly and effectively sum up situations, did not consider available alternatives in the aftermath of dealing with Mills. No discernable attempt was made to investigate the questionable performance by Mills, or to recognize the Herculean efforts of Levy. Such an "oversight" is entirely out of character for Stone.

It is nearly impossible to effectively present a concise evaluation of this complex individual. Unquestionably, Stone is an able, brave and uniquely decorated soldier, who performed outstanding heroics in battle. When the Second Patricia's, post Korea, were once more stationed at Currie Barracks, Calgary, Stone basked in a considerable amount of publicity for his actions in Korea and most particularly for the defence at Kapyong. Clearly he was proud of his battalion and communicated more openly with his officers at mess dinners - we were then "his boys" - but there was always a clearly defined boundary to his openness.

Army discipline necessitates a barrier between officers and their Commanding Officer. One acknowledges the well-used axiom: "Familiarity Breeds Contempt." Levy recalls a side of our Colonel that I did not know. Yet there is a fine balance between inspiring loyalty, instilling discipline, being a charismatic leader and having an ability to relate to one's officers. I had the impression Stone, at times, was excessively distant and aloof.

After the battle of Kapyong, Stone appointed Levy as Intelligence Officer, a position of trust which fostered a developing closeness between the commanding officer and a junior officer. There may be two factors, diverse in their application, which motivated Stone's appointment. A battalion commander, of necessity, must sometimes direct his men into untenable positions in the field of battle. With the wisdom of Solomon, he must weigh the uneven balance of life and death. And because command is a lonely responsibility, there may be times when an officer wants to unload the tensions of command, or test his theories, through a sounding board. A commanding officer may yearn to confer with another officer who has a strong appreciation of battle tactics, who can offer reflected emotions, and maintain complete silence beyond their integrated harmony. Stone was a highly astute assessor of outstanding officers, and would no doubt have recognized the integrity and quick mind of Levy.

One may also consider the "Remorseful Conscience Theory." These are commanders who maintain an aura of de Gaulle-like Godhood, and earn a reputation among their men for "papal infallibility." These are the ones who maintain an aloof distance from their men, and constantly have a lot to live up to. They are one hell of a strain! Perhaps they instinctively select as their close confident, one who has integrity, discretion and is absolutely trustworthy - yet of lower station, so no material threat. In retrospect, this awarding of a personal plum in the field may have been the way Stone eased his conscience regarding Levy's lack of a medal.

When Stone was awarded his third DSO, in recognition of his valued service in Korea, he graciously accepted it alongside those he had been previously awarded. But for many of us, Korea was our only war and we were acutely aware of those who, in our experience and opinion, were deserving of recognition. I do not believe that Stone, who surely judged Korea in comparison to his intense battles of World War II, would intentionally have failed to recognize the deserving contributions of the citizen soldiers serving under his command in Korea, during 1951.

I cannot comprehend, nor can many of my fellows in arms, why Stone chose to ignore Levy's calm, decisive bravery at Kapyong. Was he not fully appraised? Stone had often been described as "a soldier's soldier." He demanded bravery and initiative. This is why it's so puzzling that in Korea Stone not only ignored Levy's bravery, but also devalued the lieutenant's superior performance under the most trying of battle conditions. That decision was totally out of character for a soldier like Stone; a Commander who never suffered incompetence! In light of the daring and stalwart bravery of Levy, one cannot help but wonder what deep recess of Stone's character motivated this contrary decision.

In this book I have attempted to present the facts in as accurate and precise a way as possible, to recreate a faithful record of this pivotal battle and the heroic men who fought it. After six years of exhaustive research, including five hours of videotaped assessment of these facts, the reader will come to his or her own conclusions about the performance of Lieut Michael G Levy, and the officer who commanded him.

I am hopeful my research and the significant memories of more than 70

Kapyong veterans of Second Patricia's, will reverse the long standing omission of the deserved recognition for Major Michael G Levy (Retired) at long last.

"Justice must not only be done,

but it must be seen to be done."

Advancing through a village. (photo: PPCLI)

1.Stone's speech, 18 Dec /73, to Officers 3 PPCLI.
2.Stone was authorized by a special Order in Council giving him Powers of Command, 90 days summary imprisonment subject to confirmation by Tokyo.
3.Article in the Ottawa Citizen, August 15, 1951.
4.Conversation with Levy 1998.
5.Transcript of 5 June 1951, with LCol GWL Nicholson, AHQ, Ottawa.

Moving to the Front

Refugee Family (photo: Hub Gray)

Chapter THIRTEEN

OBSERVATIONS

Stone, always cognizant of the changing enemy intentions, made four crucial decisions, prior to and during the battle:

1 Stone and his officers surveyed Hill 677 from the enemy's view-point and prior to sighting his battalion's positions, he assessed how he could both capture and defend the hill;

2 Because of the distances between the companies, Stone insisted that all platoons must be mutually supporting;

3 He relocated B Company to a location on the north eastern flank at exactly the point where the enemy launched their initial assault nine hours later;

4 Stone categorically refused Mills' request for D Company to withdraw at 0300 hrs, on April 25th.

Lieut Michael G. Levy, tenaciously and intelligently directed the Patricias main defence at D Company, on April 25, 1951.

Michael Levy, Sir.
The veterans named herein and I,
SALUTE YOU!

The individual Platoon Commanders were responsible for managing D Company's defence. The skillful defence, led by Lieut Michael G Levy along with the determined men of 10 Platoon; 11 Platoon, Lieut Pearson; 12 Platoon east, Sergeant BW Holligan, contained the Chinese aggressor. Had they not held the Chinese 60 and 118 Divisions, the Patricias may have become engaged in a horrific firefight or worse, according to LCol James Riley Stone, DSO 2 Bars, MC. During the battle the Patricias were surrounded and cut off from the remainder of the 27th Brigade. By 0700 the Mortar PI was down to four bombs. Many of the riflemen were virtually out of ammunition.

The resolute stand at Kapyong defeated the Central Sector Spring

Offensive of General P'eng Teh-huai, Commander In Chief, Communist Forces. Gen P'eng did not destroy the British 27th Brigade, nor the American 24 and 25 Divisions. The CCF offensive only gained 40 km at Kapyong, not the 160 km objective. This offensive lasted three days, not 10 - 20 as was his aim.

16 Field Regiment, Royal New Zealand Artillery

The 2PPCLI, 3RAR and Company A, US 72 Heavy Tank Battalion, were awarded the United States Presidential Unit Citation, for their resolute stand at Kapyong. The role of the 16 Field Regiment, Royal New Zealand Field Artillery and the American artillery was crucial to the success of our defence at Kapyong. Without the 16 RNZA the results could have been vastly different. For the previous 72 hours New Zealanders were heavily engaging the enemy, making fast moves, getting little sleep. In this writer's opinion: 16 Field Regiment, Royal New Zealand Artillery is every bit as deserving of recognition by the Americans.

The Government of The Republic of Korea recognized the Herculean 16 RNZA support and awarded them a Korean Presidential Unit Citation.

April 27th 1951 - Captain Wally Mills, D Company, gives withdrawal instructions to Lieut. John Pearson, Lieut. Hub Gray and Lieut. Mike Levy

Sergeant Alex Sims leads the Anti-tank Platoon in their withdrawal.

THE EVENING CITIZEN, OTTAWA
APRIL 18, 1951
PATRICIAS TAKE RIDGE

CP - West Central Sector. At least 12 Chinese were KIA and more wounded late Saturday when a platoon of Patricia's led by Lieut. Michael Levy of Vancouver mixed it up with the enemy atop a ridge about six miles north of the 38th parallel.

A company under Major Bob Swinton, of Vancouver, tangled with the enemy at dusk after a long afternoon climb up a 600 foot rock face through a spring mist thickened with smoke from Canadian fire.

The Patricias were assigned earlier in the day to help the Middlesex Regiment take a position which had been holding up the front for almost

two days.

Companies led by Swinton and Major Jack George, of Edmonton, advanced unopposed until right among the enemy positions.

There the fog and smoke cleared to reveal Levy's men in a relatively lightly held area although stronger than the opposition the Patricias have been meeting lately.

Rain of Grenades

The CCF let loose a rain of grenades, a defensive type resembling the Canadians' Mills grenade and not like the stick variety that cause concussion on which the CCF have been relying lately. The kind Levy's men got were made of good steel with higher fragmentation. Still, casualties were light.

Levy jumped into the fray with pistol and grenade, his men right behind him. After a spirited exchange, the CCF decamped and the position was secure in Canadian hands by nightfall.

Meanwhile, in the battalion's perimeter a "civilian" in blue coat and white trousers was the object of a flushing operation by a platoon under Lieut. Rick Constant of Calgary.

VANCOUVER SUN - APRIL 1951

CHINESE LOSE US WEAPON

The United States Army sub-machine gun caused trouble for Canadian troops before it's Chinese owner was killed. Chinese machine gun nests in Korea were cleaned out by Lieut Michael G. Levy of Vancouver and two other members of Princess Patricia's Canadian Light Infantry, Corporal James Watson of Kimberley, BC, left and Private Charles Baxter of Saint John, New Brunswick.

Department of National Defence Photo.

*Mike Levy, Hub Gray, at the dedication of the Second Battalion PPCLI Cairn,
The Battle of Kapyong, Korea, April 23/5 1951,
Radar Hill, Tofino, Vancouver Island, BC, April 1998*

The Veterans' Joyful Legacy

It is impossible for anyone who has not participated in the front lines of a war to fully appreciate the comradeship of veterans. The reunions bring back to life their wartime exploits in a manner that only those who suffered through them and survived, can actually enjoy and respect. At every gathering we tell the same old stories, listen once again to each other's exploits and applaud a tale well told. The sharing is uplifting because it is a heartfelt exchange of confidences and an appreciation for the sacrifices made so long ago. The exchange of confidences is only truly understood and appreciated in such surroundings, where everyone shares the moment, senses the agonies and the fears of death, the meaningful acts of bravery, sacrifices for a comrade, the joy of survival. It becomes a joyful release of sharing with those who have survived alongside you. When we veterans gather we remember the good times, the comradeship in its truest form, despite the fact, or perhaps because our numbers are fast fading into dust.

The Agonies of Remembering

There is a hidden element stored within, never forgotten, thrusting forward without introduction. Long hidden. Piercing suddenly. The unwanted intrusion. Only those who have experienced the battlefield can share in it. It is an evocative haunting that pursues one in the dark recesses of memory. Never to be spoken of. It is never shared, contained only within one's self. No one "outside" may intrude, not even a loving and caring wife.

The inhuman nightmares come and go. We try to forget them. Reliving a battle, listening to the haunting, agonizing screams of the wounded and dying, the bodies torn grotesquely apart and begging for your mercy, the crying out in vain for their loved ones. These apparitions move forward through time as we grow older, releasing their vengeance upon us, their assassins... a terrifying eruption of the human beings you sought to destroy...

These are...

The Recurring Screams of Agonies that Pierce the Soul.
The Infantry Veteran's Personal and Carefully Crafted...

Legacies of HELL !

A Korean feast.

*2 Pl. A Coy.
Bren
Gunners*

12 Pl. LINE GOLDEN - Back row: Shaver,............., Mcae, Dempsey,..............................
Front row: ...., Brown, Bjarnason.

Chapter FOURTEEN

K A P Y O N G

PATRICIA "OFFICIAL" CASUALTIES
PLUS THOSE NOT REPORTED

CHINESE CASUALTIES

The official Patricia's listing: Wounded - 23, Killed in Action - 10 [1]

The official listing of the wounded at Kapyong does not account for all the casualties that occurred during the entire time the Patricia's engaged the Chinese on Hill 677. The figure quoted appears to account from approximately 2130hrs on the 24 to about 0900hrs on the 25. Casualties were incurred either side of that reported time phase. As well, Chinese snipers were firing on the vehicles and ambulances descending Hill 677, conveying casualties and others.

Unreported examples:

Tactical Headquarters: - About 0630 hrs - 24th :
Lance Corporal HR Crocker at Tactical HQ is shot in the foot by a sniper thought to be lying south of his position. [2]

Moments later:

Two soldiers are injured when an American tank in the valley fires wiping out an enemy machine gun. Shrapnel wounds two soldiers who are evacuated, one later loses an arm. [1]

Private Del Reaume's Jeep Ambulance driver is shot in the shoulder descending Hill 677. A number of drivers are wounded descending the hill. [3]

I cannot confirm names in all cases; however, I am satisfied the total Patricias wounded may have totalled 35 or higher. Unfortunately the Patricias administrative records made in the field were dated upon being typed, not the day of the occurrence.

D Company Casualties

Reports are varied. Captain JGW Mills, MC, Commanding D Company, 15 years later from personal notes: Killed 7, Wounded 5. [4]

Author's Listing

D Coy HQ	No casualties
10 Platoon	8 wounded
11 Platoon	2 killed, none wounded
12 Platoon, west	2 killed, none wounded
12 Platoon, east	No casualties

B Company

6 Platoon	4 killed, 10 wounded
5 Platoon	1 killed, 3 wounded

C Company

9 Platoon	3 wounded

Support Company

1 wounded
drivers descending 677
1 unconfirmed, five others?

Pioneer Platoon

1 killed, 1 wounded

Reinforcement

1 wounded on a truck

HQ Company

3 wounded

The Low Patricia's Casualties

What accounts for the low casualties of the Patricias compared to the Australians losses? 2PPCLI supported more than four times the artillery that is normally assigned to a Brigade. They had; 78 artillery pieces: 16

RNZA 24 - 25 pounders; three American Field Batteries having 36 - 105s, and 17 - 155mm. In addition the 16RNZA called on a battery of 8 inch howitzers. The American artillery batteries fired Variable Time Fuses set to explode above ground inflicting heavy shrapnel casualties on the charging Chinese. The Patricias 80 mm mortars were in action throughout the night. American 4.2 inch mortars gave partial support.

By contrast, the previous night, the Australians had only the 24 field guns of the 16RNZA, and they were not equipped with VT fuses. Their batteries were out of action for a time as they withdrew to relocate; an artillery officer assigned to 3RAR was killed; and radio communications imperilled.

Assumed Chinese Causalities

B Company - Major Vince Lilley, MC, Commanding B Company, from personal notes, provided 15 years later: [5]

Estimated enemy strength	1,000
Enemy killed by actual count	143
Wounded, estimated	180
B Company Strength	110
Estimate: OGP Kapyong - 500 enemy casualties [6]	

Mortar Platoon - The result of mortar fire and machine gun fire:

Supporting the 3RAR at a river crossing, actual body count the next day: 71[7]

An attack essentially centred on our soft underbelly; Pioneers, Anti-Tank, Mortar Platoon; by count the next day: 100 +

D Company - The Chinese sacrifice men at absolutely any cost. They always carried off as many of their dead and wounded as possible. The sharply descending hill forward of D company, was responsible for Chinese casualties rolling back down the hill to the valley below.

Summary factors:

10 Platoon fought for 5.5 hours.
12 east was under continuous attack.
Levy and members of 10 and 12 Platoon, report the Chinese charged in waves, 30 to 50 men at a time, 30 metres apart.

Within ½ an hour of the battle the waves became a continuous flow.

Our 81 mm Mortars inventoried up to twice their normal allotment of bombs, a possible 2/3 of which were directed to supporting D Company.

The New Zealand gunners reported they fired Brigade and Divisional shoots all night, at times including 4 - 8in. howitzers. American Field Artillery Batteries fired Variable Time fuses.

During a 40 minute barrage the RNZA alone fired 2,300 rounds while 10 Platoon was being attacked on three fronts. Total estimated 4,000 - 4,500.

Levy, to save his men from annihilation, at least twice ordered the artillery to fire directly upon his own position.

The artillery was also engaged in defending other elements of the 27 Brigade, but the heavy Chinese concentration was now concentrated at one particular point, 10 Platoon. This was their final attempt to break through the 27 Brigade - and they threw everything they had into it. The supporting artillery fire was devastating. During the 40-minute barrage it is estimated 1.87 shells impacted every second. What a killing ground! Yet the Chinese continued to pour men into the hellish vortex of the battle, fully expecting to win. It is reasonable to assume that the seemingly unending Chinese suicide charges on all fronts resulted in the Patricias inflicting a possible 2,000 or more casualties. it is possible the Chinese lost in the order of 5,000 men combined with the 16 RNZA and Australian estimates,

At the battle of Kapyong 27 Brigade halted the Chinese onslaught that had smashed through 40 km in only 36 hours. During the eight days of their Spring Offensive, UN forces savaged the Chinese. **General Van Fleet reported the Chinese, haemorrhaging excessively, and they suffered 70,000 casualties; this was the equivalent of seven Chinese Divisions in the west and central sectors.** [8]

UN forces casualties are estimated at 7,000. Whatever the Chinese losses at Kapyong, their haemorrhaging resulted in General P'eng's, defeat. He elected not to commit his massive unscathed reserves. He terminated his Spring Offensive, in this sector.

In conclusion:

Kapyong may not have been a huge battle. The defeat of the over-whelming Chinese forces, by the soldiers of two under strength infantry battalions and supporting arms, was very significant for the Patricias who fought that battle, as well as for the IX Army Corps.

Kapyong was a Victorious Feat of Men and Arms.

2 P P C L I were a major contributor to the success of the Battle at Kapyong.

---

1. PPCLI Archives
2. Crocker telephone interview, May 2000
3. Reume telephone interview June 2000
4. Mills, 2PPCLI Archives
5. Lilley, 2PPCLI Archives
6. Petrie field notes
7. Wood page 77
8. Blair page 885

Korea - May - June 1951   2nd Bn. PPCLI, 25 Brigade   This is a photo of 12 Pl. "D" Coy. digging in during a Battalion fighting patrol, thrusting into the enemy lines. "D" Coy. were the reserve company this day. Armoured support is by A Coy. US 72nd Heavy Tank Brigade. (photo: Hub Gray).

Chapter FIFTEEN

P'ENG'S INJI OFFENSIVE,
MAY 16, 1951

Neither at Kapyong nor at the Imjin River did General P'eng commit his reserve troops. P'eng desperately sought to defeat the combined UN Forces, to take Seoul. Initially he had singled out the British Commonwealth 27th and 29th Infantry Brigades to be annihilated, for his battle experience revealed they were among the most dependable and aggressive of the UN Forces. P'eng urgently wanted a gateway into Seoul; however, his casualties were so heavy that he withdrew his reserves unscathed.

General Van Fleet was concerned the Chinese were preparing for another assault on Seoul. He was right, General P'eng was not yet finished, and he was maneuvering his Armies for another devastating offensive. Space does not allow me to do justice to these events; however, I will briefly summarize what occurred. Intelligence revealed P'eng had moved his forces to the east, in rugged mountain terrain, where the movement of vehicles would be somewhat restricted. P'eng had maintained four armies in reserve; for he was concerned the Americans would attempt an amphibious landing to his rear, as at Inchon. Convinced this threat no longer existed, he massed men in the eastern sector for another push south. In the middle of May the weather broke, rain and low cloud persisted. On the 16 May, the Chinese 27 Army's 81 Division smashed through between the ROK 5 and 7 Divisions. In all 20 divisions were assembled and 16 were now streaming south. Caught between the Chinese and North Korean V Corps, the ROK III Corps collapsed. During this assault 40,000 South Korean troops bugged out, abandoning artillery and masses of equipment. Since the beginning of the war the ROKs had abandoned enough equipment to arm 10 complete Divisions. While the intelligence was correct about the timing of the offensive, it was a surprise to Van Fleet that it took place so far to the east.

The situation for the UN forces was extremely grave. The X Corps were engaged in fierce firefights with the Chinese 12 and 15 Armies. LGen Almond asked for reinforcements Van Fleet was holding in reserve in the Seoul area in case the Chinese made a dash for it. After some deliberation Van Fleet concurred. It was against the principles of employment to engage paratroops as ground force infantry. Van Fleet, with Ridgeway's approval, confirmed the transfer of the 187th Airborne Combat Team (Brigade), the US 3 Division, less two Regimental Combat Teams, and the ROK 8 Division. Supporting artillery, 72 howitzers, were augmented by the inclusion of a Field Artillery Battery (18 guns) of 155mm howitzers of which one battery was eight-inch howitzers. The X Corps artillery ammunition allotment was increased five fold, and it was consuming 20 truckloads per hour, each gun firing 250 rounds per day. [1] Boyle reports, "On the 19 May X Corps and 2 Division artillery fired off 41,357 rounds." [2] and on the 20th 49,704." [3] Fighter aircraft and medium bombers were making continuous sorties that day, 165 close support missions. The UN forces were consolidating their lines. On the 20 of May aerial reconnaissance discovered four new enemy Divisions advancing along the eastern flank of their drive south. They were deemed a threat to the rail centre of Chech'on, because of the ability of the enemy to move, on foot in mountain terrain, 20 miles or more at night. There was an air of trepidation at Eighth Army headquarters.

The UN had won - P'eng had lost the battle. Making the best of it, P'eng ordered his armies to pull back reporting he faced "losses of men and equipment." [4] During these four days of intense fighting in May, Chinese losses were calculated at 36,000 killed and 31,800 wounded. [5] The UN forces took to the offensive with I, IX and X Corps commencing a broad advance across the entire front.

Combined with the earlier eight-day engagement, involving 70,000 casualties the **Chinese and North Korean losses, over the 12 days of their combined Spring Offensive, totaled a devastating 137,800 men.** And some stay-at-home armchair critics have contended the Korean conflict was not a war!

General Ridgeway ordered consolidation on Lines Kansas and Wyoming to the base of the "Iron Triangle" at Chorwon. **So ended The Chinese People's Volunteer's Army and The North Korean People's Volunteer's Army Spring Offensive of 1951.**

---

1 Blair page 880
2 Blair page 881
3 Blair page 888
4 Farrar-Hockley, page 257, Vol II, The British Part in the War
5 Blair page 890

Chapter SIXTEEN

A TIME TO FORGET

When the Patricias landed in Korea various messes were organized: Men's, Sergeants and Officers Messes. They were the gathering points for social relaxation and provided a venue for all to discuss operations and the progress of training. The messes also served to promote friend-ships. Stone and all of the officers patronized the Officers' Mess during the six weeks training phase at Miryang. Major Don Grant, a large, boisterous and fun loving individual who possessed the talents of a commercial artist, commanded HQ Company. Grant christened the Officers Mess, *Banglestein's Bar* and an appropriate song soon became famous in our theatre of war. It concerned the sexual appetite of that dirty old man and it was dubbed, *"Balls to Mr. Banglestein."* One enterprising soul acquired a piano under questionable circumstances and this enabled Captain Owen Browne to accompany not only the Padre's Sunday Service but also the Banglestein ditty. About the same time Grant decorated the canvas walls with a series of cartoons repre-senting Battalion and Brigade personalities and the mural covered an area of about eight feet by 12 feet. For contrast he drew two different subjects on two opposing panels: a British Military Policeman with his red cap and night stick in hand on one, and our Roman Catholic padre on the other. The latter, Captain Jim Valalee was depicted as an angel with a white shroud, wings and halo over his head and a bottle of Irish Whiskey attached to his toe by a string. Valalee had been an Irish priest in China for 17 years prior to Korea and he favoured Bushmills. The tent was struck during a move and when it was re-erected a The Brit MP possessed a halo over his head with white wings and a bottle attached to his toes, while Valalee was adorned with a red cap and a night stick.

After Kapyong we were released from the British 28th Brigade to join the Canadian 25th Brigade, but first we were to enjoy a few days out of the battle line; a time to forget the worries of the daily struggle for survival fighting our enemy. Major George Flint, selected the area to which the battalion retired from the front to rest. It turned out to be a quagmire. It was an area that consisted of a series of rice paddies. Unfortunately after the ground was selected and just prior to our entry, the spring rains descended. At the time of these floods the Imjin River would rise as much as 21 feet overnight. The paddy walls efficiently contained the deluge of water, a God given delight to the rice farmers but utter hell for us. The troops had to navigate the narrow pathways on the top of each pond dike. Being out of the line in the throes of celebration there was often a roaring drunk soldier seen in the prime of ecstasy. As the dyke pathways became a slippery slosh so they claimed their victims, to be slung into the mire of mud and water, to be serenaded by the everlasting rhythmic croaking frogs. Ah, the glories of a time of rest and relaxation. Thus the area became forever known to one and all as "Flint's Folly."

THE ALTERNATIVE OFFICERS' MESS

About this time we were given a new company commander, Major Don Grant, formerly commander of Headquarters Company, recalls Lieut Brian Munro, who adds it was Grant's first assignment with a rifle company.

"Just prior to being pulled out of the line, Grant called the officers together to inform us that LCol JR Stone had decreed that there would not be a Battalion Officers' Mess as such. Each company was to be left to their own devices. Frankly I have never before or since heard of such a decree during my 30 years of service in the Canadian Army. Access to a Battalion Officers' Mess was always the prerogative of every serving officer. When we were in the line, because of the amount of ground each platoon and company was responsible to defend, the only time that company officers would meet was on those occasions when the company commander called for an Orders Group. We were informed that Stone simply did not want the sanctity of his relaxation and nightly poker game to be invaded by celebratory (drunken) company officers. So we were frozen out!"

"Grant called together Captain Jock Campbell second in command, Lieutenants; Shammy Beauchamp, Jack Regan and myself. Grant suggested that if each officer anteed up $60, which was in the form of US Army military scrip, we would then have $300, sufficient to have a well stocked bar at A Company. The drinks would be served free and thus we would have the opportunity to commiserate with all our brother officers. Let's face it, most of our time was spent in the line and when we come out there was no place to spend our money since Korea was a desolate war-torn, Third World country. So why not, what the heck was 60 bucks? We all heartily agreed. Thus Stone would rule his domain free of his "interfering riffraff" and we would have a grand time without being concerned that he was peering over our shoulders. A stand off!

"Grant, having been in charge of Headquarters Company and the Officers' Battalion HQ Mess, was familiar with all the depots that our battalion requisitioned supplies from. One was the NAAFI, the Australian and British Army canteen service. The sergeant in charge of the NAAFI in Seoul had previously advised Grant that if he would supply him with a Canadian Battle Dress uniform, he would allow him to purchase all the booze he could pay for. The price of a bottle of hard liquor was something like 80 cents. Grant made a "quiet" arrangement for the use of a two and a half ton truck of the American 4.2 inch mortar company attached to the Patricias. The US officer was advised of the purpose of the mission and heartily approved. The only liquid refreshment allowed for the palate of officers and men in the US Army in Korea was Coca Cola. When the Yanks retook Seoul one of the first priorities was to build a Coca Cola plant and an ice cream factory. Ah, the priorities of the American Army to refresh their palate in a war zone.

"Lieutenants Shammy Beauchamp and Brian Munro were nominated to undertake the trip to Seoul. Beauchamp was a married man who had served in World War II, while I was about 22 and just a green kid. He was a fountain of knowledge concerning the ways of the world, as you will see. A coloured American soldier was in charge of the truck. So off we went to Seoul. It was a nice day and it was great to have a change of scene. The town, having been fought over a number of times, was virtually flattened. We consulted with the American MP checkpoints to locate the NAAFI and were fortunate that the named sergeant was on duty so we were able to successfully conclude our transaction. He was tickled pink to have a better quality Canadian uniform and of course our 300 bucks. We literally loaded the truck to the gills with a variety of hard liquor, a choice selection of wines and some beer. We did not go heavy on the beer because the men received a quart of Japanese Ashai beer from time to time, for which they had to pay something like 25 cents a bottle. I think it was at Chorwon, that our troops would trade with American soldiers stationed nearby; a quart bottle of Asahi beer for one bottle of Coke. By now it was late in the afternoon and having consummated our deal we set off back to the battalion.

"We were just nicely out of Seoul when the driver noticed there was a vibration developing somewhere and he thought he could smell something burning. We pulled over onto the side of the road, he looked under the hood and it was all in order. He went to the back of the truck to discover a rear axle was overheating and belching smoke. The driver advised there was a major supply depot, The American Sabre Ordnance, about 20 minutes further ahead and he felt certain that he could make it there. We did. This was the largest ordnance depot I have ever seen. It looked as though they could have completely re-equipped the entire Eighth Army in Korea on a moments notice. It was massive; they had everything but the RMS Queen Mary! A couple of guys looked the truck over and said that a wheel bearing was shot. They advised it would require about two hours to requisition the part and install it. Well, with a cargo like that what else was there to do but enjoy ourselves. Beauchamp and I broke out a bottle of wine and relaxed. It was a very warm day and in time we offered a bottle of beer to each of the mechanics putting our truck into running order. Soon they consumed another. After a while we noticed there were four or five extra guys all looking at this wheel, so we opened another case of beer, spreading the joy.

"Eventually an officer came by and asked, "Have you boys eaten yet?" We said no we had not. He advised the mess had closed down for the night and the cook who had to be up early in the morning had gone to bed. "I'll get the cook up and have him rustle up a steak dinner, how would that be?" We said that would be fabulous, could we bring a couple of bottles of wine along? Our newfound sponsor said that would be just great. We went over to the mess hall with two bottles of red wine and a bottle of whisky. We of course offered the benefactor of our incredible meal a drink. We had lived on nothing but C rations. About halfway through dinner our host inquired as to what was the content of our truck. On being informed of our precious cargo all he could muster was, "Jesus Christ, you're kidding me!" We assured him we were not. He said, "Do you think it might be possible that we could buy a bottle off of you?" Beauchamp looked at him, then at me, paused and said, "You will understand this is Battalion inventory, would you excuse us, I have to consult with my fellow officer." We went outside the tent. Beauchamp proposed we offer to sell them a case for $300, allowing us to recapture the money we had laid out for the entire load. I readily agreed. So we went back in and Beauchamp said, "How would it be if we gave you guys a mixed case of hard booze for $300?" "You'd sell us a whole case?" We said yes. Our host said, "My God, this is like deliverance from heaven! I'll immediately go and round up the money." In about ten minutes he had solicited his buddies and returned with $300 cash and a grin that extended from ear to ear. Again a deal was done.

By now it was about 10 pm and my experienced warrior buddy had a further inspiration. We were only an hour or so from Seoul, and with our vehicle now repaired Beauchamp suggested there must be pleasing entertainment somewhere in that city. We should seize the opportunity to avail ourselves of it. Well, after living for weeks in a hole in the ground, fighting the Chinese and feeding upon C rations the thought of further relaxation and the possible delights of Seoul was too much to turn down. I agreed. Off we went. Seoul was blacked out and full of roving American and Korean MPs. As we trundled down the road I asked Beauchamp how we would go about finding a place to land, the whole city was a wreck, destroyed; "Brian my boy, there is a very simple way of locating the best of times. We will go to police head-quarters, they know the city inside out and will be able to satisfy our needs." All the entrances to Seoul were guarded either by American MPs or Korean police. Some posts had both forces present. We came upon Korean police at the first checkpoint and made them aware we were trying to locate the police headquarters for Seoul. The fellow had a hand held radio, so he passed a message along and then informed us to go straight ahead to the next post and they would guide us on our way. By this method we went past various posts and eventually reached police headquarters. Beauchamp piled into the back of the truck to retrieve a quart of gin, put it in his blouse, and informed me that this was our passport to information. Most of the buildings in Seoul were flat or fire gutted, but this two-storey affair was intact. The driver parked the vehicle, and the men on guard directed us to a rickety eleva-tor that actually worked, maybe the only one in Seoul. Gaining the second floor we entered an office which was fully equipped. The Chief happened to be in, along with a half dozen assembled officers. None of the para military uniformed cops we spoke with were able to muster more than a few words in English. To our relief the Chief was fully fluent in English. Beauchamp explained that we had been in the line for many months, were poor infantry soldiers, we had a few hours and could he direct us to a place of entertainment. Then Beauchamp said "Presento" and deposited the bottle of gin on his desk. The chief, a portly fellow dressed in civilian clothes, smiled broadly announcing that he really liked gin. After a few minutes of polite discussion he addressed a nearby police captain in Korean and then informed us he had arranged guides to escort us to our destination.

"The city was pitch black and it was a moonless night. We had two police in effect riding shotgun on the running boards either side of the truck. For some time we weaved in and out of various streets. We came to a halt where there was a minor structure about the size of an out-house. All else was a pile of rubble. Our guards dismounted and had the truck backed into a wrecked building. They indicated we should go in what appeared to be the first cousin of a root cellar, one cop would oversee the truck and the other one was to escort us. If you walked by this place you would never have given it a second glance, absolutely nondescript. There were two policemen quietly standing guard over the entrance. Frankly I was not quite sure how we should evaluate our situation, after all this was wartime and the area was not very reassur-ing. Communication with our escort was exceptionally limited, we were quite literally at their mercy for we didn't have a clue where we were other than somewhere in a bombed out town in a war zone on a dark night with a truck loaded with prized booze. We ordered the driver to remain with the vehicle, not to touch any of the cargo for we would look after him when we got back to camp. Well, just in case we didn't come back the driver may represent some form of insurance? But worldly Beauchamp exuded confidence, the Chief was on the up and up and oh yeah, with that comment I felt very reassured?

"We entered the small and insignificant portal to discover we were on a stairway leading down to a basement. Music of a big band drifted upward. We descended into the largest and possibly the smartest night-club I have ever seen. In the middle of war torn Seoul, I could not believe my eyes. It was superb. The majority of those in attendance were Seoul police, some American MPs. As far as I was concerned *this was the best-kept secret of the whole darn Korean war!* Table cloths, fine silver, china, a variety of bars, food galore, Wurlitzers, a dance floor and smartly attired waiters. And Girls, Girls and still more Girls all in super skimpy dresses and high heels. The females were really attired in gorgeous outfits and after months in the trenches of Korea I could only feast my happy hungry eyes upon them. Here we were with dust on our boots in an Alice in Wonderland setting. We had a great time in unbelievable surroundings. The police knew how to fight a war with a vengeance. We could not pay for a drink, we were evidently guests of the Chief, and I couldn't even pronounce his name. After two to three hours, it now being well into the next day, we decided we'd better split and head for the battalion.

"On surfacing the Korean cop was still with the truck and not a drop of booze had gone astray. We woke the driver and headed out, our escorts once again guiding us through the city. We had to drive back to the battalion with caution as blackout lights were the order of the night and there was a considerable amount of traffic on the road. It was the last few minutes of darkness when finally we arrived back at A Company.

"Now Major Grant was a fun loving individual, always very approachable. Not this time. He exploded all over us! His face was beet red and his body language expressed anger and confrontation at every turn. Grant had been a lineman with the Toronto Argonauts Football Team, he was a big man, large hands and arms as long as an elephant's tusk, not one to mess around with.

"Where the hell have you bastards been," demanded Grant. "You were due back here fucking hours ago. Not only did you disappear but you took with you an American soldier and a truck on a trip that was not officially authorized. I just got dressed to go and wake Colonel Stone and tell him that I had lost a truck, two officers and a driver. How the hell would he react when I said that I sent you on a slippery mission to buy booze in Seoul? A Court Martial staring me in the face! I ought to break your bloody necks!" Eventually his anger ran its course and we had the opportunity to explain our case. When he heard we had the booze, the truck and the driver all in good order as well as our original investment of $300 dollars, a smile began to emerge. Congratulations all around. Both Beauchamp and I were very relieved.

"We went about setting up our proxy Battalion Officers' Mess. We each ordered our batman to become bar stewards. The other officers naturally flocked to our stable of free drinks. The newly appointed "bar stewards" had a great time contributing to their own welfare by both drinking from our supply and selling stock freely out the back door to all and sundry who needed a drink. We were so busy indulging ourselves that we did not have the time to check up on the stewards. What the hell, why not share our loot with everyone? I think our supply lasted about three days.

"My enterprising batman, Ron Bourgon, from this session and other enterprises had sent home $6,800 US by the time he returned to Canada; some war, some organizer. After bar stewarding in the A Company Officers Mess, Bourgon made a note of the NAFFI sources. He offered a premium price to the NAFFI vendor and was able to purchase booze at 60 cents per bottle (plus pay off) and "retail" it for $50 to $100 per bottle. He was even offered a brand new Sherman tank fully armed and ready for action, for a case of Scotch, by a thirsty US Army Ordnance Sergeant! He was able to access US Army uniforms, prized rubber soled US Paratrooper boots, plus any sort of weapon, all in exchange for booze. When he returned home he went on 60 days leave, bought a 1948 Monarch for $1,300 and spent the remainder while on leave. Terminating his military career and ever an organizer, he became a lawyer. When he tired of that he managed his own debt collection agency and today farms 1,000 acres in Quebec.

"War is hell, but occasionally there are compensations for those who have the will and creativity to find a way. Things don't always attain the final end envisioned in the beginning, as is obvious from the following story.

"Some individuals are natural born entrepreneurs and Bourgon was one of them, always thinking how events could be turned into an advantage, a personal advantage. At times this functioned in his favour but on occasion overseeing forces thought otherwise. In January 1951 Bourgon embarked upon his first enterprise in Korea and his resourcefulness was laudable, although some may say it backfired upon him. His dialogue follows.[1]

"We are departing our luxurious tents to move to Miryang for the final phase of training prior to going into the line. We were to develop our hidden talents of infiltration of enemy positions without getting lost or killed and taking advanced training in digging ditches, fox holes and of course the inevitable latrines.

"Our Sergeant asked if anyone would like to volunteer to drive jeeps to Pusan instead of going on another long training patrol. Of course DeFalco and I jumped at the opportunity to be the first to go. Sergeant: "OK, do you two have drivers; licences?" Yes we replied. "Good, we have a few jobs to do before the vehicles get here. You two, pick up these jerry cans and haul up water from the river, dump it into these six 45-gallon drums and make sure the water is good and hot. Keep it hot with these immersion heaters." The company would thus have hot water for all to shave and wash.

"While dragging the water buckets up from the river below I got the bright idea that this situation could, with a bit of ingenuity, be turned from a laborious chore into a profitable enterprise. A short distance from our sleeping quarters, tents with bunks and a stove, there was a gentle slope leading to the river. Now, if I could get some used tents and a few little extras I could turn all of this into a small and profitable gold mine. The plan was to secure as many 45-gallon drums as I could scrounge, army jargon for "liberating," a few damaged tents and a line of ¾ inch pipe from the engineers. I would construct showers. I told the sergeant the drums were full of water and the lines of men were moving slowly. I said I knew someone in the engineers who would give me what I required to erect a tent and showers for the platoon. For a moment he looked intelligent, then told me to be back in an hour.

"Finding the material was the easy part, getting it away from the Engineers was another matter. A Corporal was having a smoke and I approached him stating that I had been sent by our Platoon Commander to pick up six 45-gallon drums, six lengths of ¾ inch pipe eight inches long and a number of one-gallon paint cans. Immediately he balked telling me I must produce a written requisition. I informed him my officer sent me here to bring the stuff back and he is on his way to Battalion Headquarters and will arrive shortly with the order. With that he told me to have my men load it on the truck and it would be delivered as required. A darn good bluff will always work. In the Army it is 'Bullshit will always baffle Brains.' Our friendly engineer proved he was no exception to the rule. Within 40 minutes everything was on the truck and on its way to our assigned destination.

"The truck arrived with me directing the unloading of our newly 'liberated' gear. That done, my buddy DeFalco wanted to know what all this crap was for. I told him that we were going to build a shower and that we would charge everyone for having a go. DeFalco, "Who are you trying to kid? No one is going to take a shower in that freezing river water." Lighten up I said. We'll set up one tent, lay the other over the ground for flooring, the water will flow down hill into the ditch below. DeFalco, "And who the hell is going to break their backs hauling the tons of water up the bloody hill, not me that's for sure." They will, you moron. Every guy who wants a shower must haul up the jerry cans to establish a sufficient supply. Look, they have no place to spend their money, we will charge them a buck, they will gladly fork it over for the delights of our Spa. My not so smart ass DeFalco wanted to know how long we would allow them to enjoy the shower. I tested the cans, to see how long it took for ten gallons of water to drip through the hole I punctured at the bottom of the paint cans. If we kept the pipe taps half open three minutes would be the duration.

"Naturally we experimented by giving each other the treatment. Out in the wilds of rough and ready Korea it worked like a charm. With your eyes closed it was as though we were transported into a magnificent hotel. We decided to economize for the others by making fewer holes in the can dispensing the water.

"But all did not go according to my plan. I made a tragic mistake. I invited the NCOs to have a go first, giving them a freebie. I was immediately denied my eagerly anticipated entrepreneurial harvest! Not only were we denied our revenue; we were made responsible for the operation of the shower, the maintenance and cleaning of the equipment. A few days later a United Press correspondent brought along a photographer and took a photograph of Private Ron Bourgon, of Ottawa, who erected the first mobile shower in Korea. It made the national newspapers back home. My Mother was very proud of me!

"Ah yes, that age-old army sucker game strung out by the NCOs, we never did get to become drivers. We had to train all day with the soldiers of the battalion and spend additional time administering the cotton pickin' showers".

Chow line - Flint's Folly.

---

1. Burgon: statement, author's files.

Chapter SEVENTEEN

DESERTION AND THEFT

CORPORAL WILLIAM (BILL) SHULER. Medical Assistant
2nd PPCLI, KOREA, MAY 1951, "FLINT'S FOLLY" REST AREA

CHARGED WITH: DESERTION IN A WAR ZONE
                      THEFT OF AN ARMY VEHICLE

Corporal Shuler was a Medical Assistant (Med A or MA) serving under the command of the Medical Officer (MO). Med A's serving in the front lines were assigned to rifle companies to provide immediate medical assistance to those wounded during battle. The first MO within the Battalion was Captain "Doc" Karpetz, who was succeeded by Captain Keith Fitzgerald.

Karpetz, a WWII veteran, was a competent doctor and a relaxed individual, who got along well with the Med A's. Once in a while Karpetz would secure a supply of fruit juice which he then mixed with medical alcohol to share with his Med A's. While deeply concerned about medicine and the care of the men, he was relaxed about regimental protocol. Fitzgerald, who was also a good physician and later became head of the Canadian Army Medical Corps, was younger and "gung-ho" when it came to regimental spit and polish. The Med A's were to be well dressed, saluting, boots polished, uniforms spiffy etc. The MA's of Second Patricias had yet to familiarize Fitzgerald with conditions in a war zone, especially as they had come to appreciate them under Doc Karpetz.

After the battle at Kapyong, during a battalion's rest period out of the line at a place christened "Flint's Folly," everyone was in a mood to celebrate. Major George Flint, was also know as "GAF or Cough-Cough," since when checking the alertness of his troops in the line at night in their slit trenches his nasal cough altered them well in advance. He picked an unfortunate rest area. It consisted of a series of rice paddies separated by narrow topped, walled dikes. It had recently poured rain so that the fields were soaked in water and the place became an unremitting quagmire. The troops had to walk along the slender dikes separating the ponds and as their celebrations developed many were catapulted into the slimly mud.

A couple of soldiers at different locations sat on the dike walls and each put up a foot. They then took up their rifles, aimed and shot off a toe or two, and then yelled, "MA, MA!" They were then evacuated, hospitalized and sent to serve time in a military prison for committing an SIW, (Self Inflicted Wound). After that they were dishonourably discharged. The preceding was preferable to once more going into battle, hiking up hills in 80 to 90 degree heat loaded with equipment, digging slit trench after slit trench to fight a very determined and aggressive enemy.

At night the rest area appeared to be owned by millions of resident frogs that sung their croaking choruses unendingly. Company Sergeant Major Trenter, then Transport Sergeant, dumped a 45-gallon drum of petrol into one pond at about two in the morning. It created a hell of a fireball but failed to deter the masses of happily frigging frogs.

As the Colonel would not allow company officers to intrude into his Battalion Headquarters Mess, we had to formulate our own recreation and one particular night it got out of hand. The next day Colonel Stone selected certain personnel to be reprimanded as examples. I was singled out to be the officer sacrificial lamb. Captain Gord Turnbell, adjutant, nicknamed "Bugs Bunny" because of protruding teeth and a droopy moustache that literally strained his soup, called Lieut Hub Gray to the orderly room. In front of half a dozen sniggering clerks I was severely admonished for being insensibly drunk and disorderly, a totally unacceptable performance in front of the men of the battalion. It goes against the grain of military etiquette to dress down an officer in front of NCOs or private soldiers. So when Bugs finished his overly self-righteous harangue and asked if I had anything to say prior to being disciplined I was eager to respond. With vigour and pleasure, I informed Bugs that he had made a really bloody stupid mistake since I was the only officer in the battalion who had never had a drop of liquor in his entire life! I turned on my heel to leave and, pleasingly, the snickers grew even louder.

But back to our Med A's. Corporal DG Kostis received a parcel from his mother that contained a loaf of bread. But the bread conveyed a particular indulgence, for concealed inside was a bottle of scotch. The Med A's, fed up with recently arrived Fitzgerald and browned off by the slimly mud bowl we were living in, happily shared their new found "bread." As the party wore on they became gently pissed. Drinking away their sorrows were Corporals Bill Shuler, Danny Kostis, Anderson, another soldier and their Korean interpreter. The more they drank the more vocal they became about the unhappy offensiveness of Fitzgerald and the deplorable local conditions. Suddenly they agreed that it was time to get away from it all to celebrate their moment in time. Currently they were some miles from the variety of entertainment they sought; destination, Seoul. Transportation? Easily done, they agreed as they liberated a box ambulance so they could head out in relative comfort seeking the enchantments of the ladies. On their way they decided to change their destination to Inchon, for Seoul was bristling with Military Police check points and they figured they would get picked up for sure. But they had to go through the outskirts of Seoul to reach Inchon. Seoul was a blacked out area and they navigated through the night as unobtrusively as possible, but their luck ran out when American MPs flagged them down.

Thinking quickly, Shuler told Corporal Anderson to lie on a stretcher and to commence shaking. Anderson immediately complied. The MPs opened the rear doors of the ambulance and peered in with flashlights probing, demanding to know what was going on. Shuler reported that the battalion's Medical Officer had ordered them to the American 121 Evacuation Hospital at Kimpo Airport, near Inchon. While the MO thought it was probably malaria he was uncertain, and he was therefore concerned that it might be one of the unknown and "very contagious" Korean diseases. On being informed of the suspected condition of the Patricia's patient the MPs did not enter the ambulance, but preferred to evaluate the situation from a safe distance. Without lights the MPs provided a military escort for Shuler et al, delivering them past numerous MP check points, depositing them at the entrance of the parking area in front of 121 Evacuation Hospital. Being a large building, Shuler simply drove in and around the other side of the hospital and then continued to their destination: a well-known house of ill repute!

For the first time in weeks they enjoyed showers, "conducted" bathing, hair cuts and availed themselves of the spectrum of available "facilities." Meanwhile the interpreter spent the night in the ambulance, to ensure its safety.

Later the next day, fully invigorated after a very late breakfast and a round of Pom Pom, the Med A's happily headed back to their assigned duties at the battalion. Once again they had to navigate through Seoul, but with an ambulance in daylight they proceeded unattended. Driving through the city Shuler spotted Major "Snuffy" Harrison, and told the chaps that he was his company commander, so they stopped to pick him up. Harrison immediately dumped all over them. "Where the hell have you bastards been? What do you think you are doing? Everyone in the Battalion is looking for you." They drove directly back to camp where they were all placed under close arrest, charged with desertion in a war zone and theft of a Department of National Defence Army vehicle. These are very serious charges in a War Zone.

Shuler and Anderson had worked together for some time. During Kapyong, serving in the thick of the battle, they were shot at a number of times. Shuler, a tall and powerful physical specimen, killed two of the enemy in hand-to-hand combat on the night of April 24, while tending to the wounded at B Company commanded by "The Black Prince," Major Vince Lilley, MC. On the morning of the 25, they were assigned to care for the wounded at D Company. Captain Mills ordered them first to take needed ammunition to Lieut Mike Levy's besieged 10 Platoon. Over a distance of some 200 yards Shuler and Anderson hit the ground twice with Chinese snipers endeavouring to pick them off. Anderson clung to the ground and Shuler had to drag him up to keep moving. After Kapyong, Anderson became a little "weird," and insisted on always packing a loaded .45 on his right hip. During the prior evening when they began to get a little tipsy, Shuler had quietly unloaded the .45, Anderson evidently being none the wiser.

Placed on charge at the Patricias' orderly room, Regimental Sergeant-Major Les "Daddy" Grimes ordered Anderson to surrender his .45 to the senior Med A, Sergeant GH Pay. Pay who was of slight build and about 5'6", looked up at Anderson who was over 6' tall. Anderson snarled, challenging Pay to, "Come and get it." Shuler and the others presuming the pistol to be still empty began to chuckle, which really got to RSM Grimes. Pay hesitated, and then made a move toward Anderson who, placing his hand on his right hip, growled; "I am not giving it to you." Anderson was very visibly agitated so Sergeant Pay moved hesitantly and then came to a halt. RSM Grimes barked out, "Sergeant, stand back! Corporal Anderson! You are on charge and under close arrest! Take off your hat and belt!" Under such circumstances this was a standard military disciplinary procedure. Anderson, being a good soldier, automatically obeyed the RSMs' harshly delivered order, dropping his belt and gun, smartly removing his hat, and standing rigidly to attention. Grimes picked up the belt, gun and hat, and then proceeded to chew out the unfortunate Sergeant Pay. Corporal Anderson was detained under guard overnight. Major Harrison, in attendance, vouched for Shuler who was allowed to attend to his quarters.

The next morning at 1000 hours, the accused were duly marched into the Colonel's office, under the glare of the RSM and their charges were read formally out.

Colonel Stone to Shuler: "How do you plead, guilty, not guilty?"

Shuler: "Guilty to desertion.
                 Not guilty to theft of a DND vehicle, Sir."

Stone: "Where the hell do you get off pleading not guilty!"

Shuler: "That ambulance belongs to us, Sir."

Stone: "What the bloody hell do you mean that ambulance belongs to you?"

Shuler: "There is no ¾ ton box ambulance on establishment to begin with. We bought it in December in Pusan from an American desperate for a drink, it cost us a bottle of Gin. Sir!"

Col Stone telephoned Harry the Horse, the Patricias transport officer, and recited the numbers of the vehicle entered on the charge sheet. Lieut Harry Inglis confirmed the ambulance was not on charge to 2PPCLI.

Shuler: "I was found guilty of desertion, given an automatic fine of one day's pay and a reprimand, the latter being removed from my charge sheet after six months. I was found not guilty of theft.

"Colonel Stone called me back as the RSM was marching us out… with a half smile and a chuckle, Stone expressed his thanks for our generosity in loaning our ambulance to the Patricias.

"Corporal Anderson was evacuated, a casualty of battle fatigue."

In the mid 1950s, Shuler is arrested for assaulting a General!

Major General Chris Vokes, in his biography, "My Story," copyright 1985, by John P MacLean, relates the incident.

"I was pleased when in the 50s the peacetime regular army finally got back to a size where inter-Command boxing tournaments were possible. I am more pleased that Western command won most of them. We emphasized boxing and had good instructors.

"One of my instructors was an ex-Kraut, a former Hitler Youth boy, who'd come to Canada and fought on our side in Korea. He was then Lieutenant WW Shuler. One evening in the bar, as we stood around having a pre-dinner drink or several, my chief of staff Lt. Col. JB Clements, Lt Col. Tony Bailey from the artillery, and a few airmen, for we shared the Tactical Air Command watering hole, I mentioned an opinion of mine to Shuler.

"Shuler," I said, "there's one thing about these boxers of ours, they're pretty good, but I don't think a single one of them knows how to do a straight left." "Oh?" he said. "Yeah," I said. "Would you like me to demonstrate? I'll demonstrate on you, if you like." Shuler said, "O.K., Sir."

"So he assumed the position. I assumed the position. I did a straight left and dotted young Shuler on the chin. His knees buckled a bit. His reaction was a great looping left hand. It hit me in the eye. I thought, as it started to land, "Gee this is great fun!" That's all I remember for a minute or two.

"Next day at noon I looked around and missed Shuler. "Where's Shuler?" Could I possibly have hurt him?

"What had happened next was some silly buggers standing around the previous evening had put Shuler under open arrest for knocking me out. Could he, an officer, be in the clanger, of all places? "Don't be ridiculous," I said to the small breakfast group. "One of you go and get him out. I want him over here. I want to buy him an eye-opener."

"I did and I complimented him on his quick reflexes."

Note: Shuler retired from the army in 1973, with the rank of Major.

180

Chapter EIGHTEEN

UNFINISHED BUSINESS
MASS MURDER

Those of us who fought in Korea witnessed horrific methodologies of killing. Napalm, a deadly agent of death, administered unbearable suffering through an intense heat that could melt the flesh off a living body, wasting it away in a slow and torturous drip, drip, drip. It has been estimated that the UN Forces used 70,000 pounds of Napalm (jellied gasoline) upon the enemy each day.[1] What has not been revealed prior to these writings is the horrific agent of instantaneous mass annihilation employed by our enemies. In war, Man's inhumanity to Man knows no bounds. Let me tell you about a personal experience that occurred on May 15, 1951.

We are standing to from 0500 to 0600 hours. It is the morning ritual, the time of day when armies commonly launched an attack so we are in our slit trenches, weapons at the ready. After an hour passes we prepare to have our C rations for the 24th consecutive day. Tinned C rations were necessary in the mountainous country, as transport could not deliver hot meals. But now A Echelon was nearby, the connecting gravel road was of a good quality, and the enemy was about 34 Km north of our static position. For whatever reason we continued to consume C rations, and after a time they become monotonous. As well, one has to contend with the system of distribution. For many weeks, Captain Andy Foulds, of the Medium Machine Gun Platoon, thought there were only beans and wieners, until he discovered that his batman, Private Jimmy Wanniandy, was exclusively consuming the beef and chicken. Wanniandy, by default, won a transfer to a rifle company and Foulds began to enjoy a broader selection of victuals. We endeavoured to enhance our reparative diet by scouring farmers' fields for onions and other delights and while the added flavour was immediately rewarding it occasionally proved to be disastrous as the fields are cultivated with human waste and the product inflicted havoc upon our limited western digestive systems. We are fortunate this day though, there are no intestinal causalities.

D Company is in Battalion reserve, about half a mile or more behind the Main Line of Resistance. We have occupied this position since the first of May, soon after defeating the Chinese 60 and 118 Divisions at

Kapyong. Our position is about 25km south of Kapyong, 3-4km NEE of Seoul. Battalion Headquarters is a km or so to our rear, adjacent to Tokso-ri. The Eighth Army has withdrawn, breaking contact with the enemy to consolidate our forces in a strong defensible position. The Chinese have taken such a brutal beating they have broken contact to collect casualties and regroup. Refugees are coming along the adjacent road everyday. We are cautioned not to fraternize with them as they may be Chinese soldiers in disguise; however, the troops ignored the rule and passed along many an unused C ration. Most of these bedraggled groups possessed few belongings and included several young children, hapless victims of this war. Many children were orphaned and wondering aimlessly on their own, begging for food. The Patricias were sympathetic to the pathetic plight of the Koreans and our battalion "adopted" a number of "Korean House Boys" who ran errands and were fed and clothed. I wrote to a former teacher in Canada who sent over a number of school text books for the kids and Andy Foulds sponsored one of them bringing him to Canada. He is now a producer with CTV in Winnipeg. I found the Patricias to be most sympathetic to the pathetic plight of the Koreans.

On the 14th of May Lieut Hugh Cleveland, of Montreal, was leading an early morning patrol out of A Company when he unfortunately misread the map of the minefield and detonated a "Bouncing Betty" anti-personnel mine, and suffered severe wounds to his legs and groin. Hugh was bleeding terribly and in tremendous pain but amazingly rational and able to speak He asked Lieut Brian Munro to ensure that the photo of his father in his kit not go astray. Though he was quickly evacuated by helicopter he passed away from loss of blood. Hugh had a great sense of humour and was nicknamed "Foo-Foo" by the troops, for his interpretation of the noise made by the two-man operated rocket launcher.

From Line Golden, our Brigade, the British Commonwealth 28th Infantry Brigade, is mounting patrols each day to search out enemy formations and strengths, prior to launching an offensive. Patrols vary in size from a single platoon to a battalion, the latter usually having air and armoured support. Sometimes we engage the enemy, though frequently we do not. Today my platoon, 12, is to be transported by tanks to the rail stop at Gumcochyi, on the main rail line east of Seoul. We are to proceed north on foot until 1300 hours or until engaging the enemy.

We do not realize it but we are about to embark upon one of the most

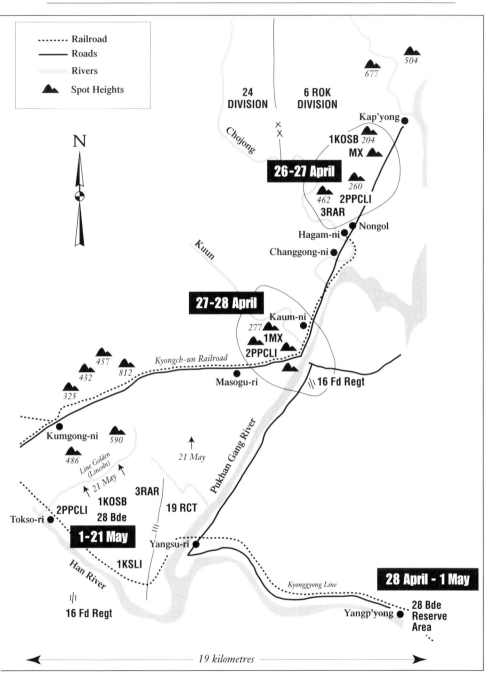

Brigade Operations

81 mm Mortar pit.

Vickers Machine Gun (photo: Hub Gray)

bizarre patrols of our lives. We are about to witness a scene of mass murder committed by an uncaring government - but whose?

A squadron of Patton tanks of the United States Army 73 Heavy Tank Battalion arrives at 0730 hrs. The approach road is of gravel and delivers a cloud of dust as they come to a halt. We have received reinforcements after Kapyong and at 34 men I now have the greatest number of soldiers under my command during my entire time in Korea. As usual we are undermanned, still six men short of establishment number; my average number was about 28 or so. Stone thought our low numbers were adequate. [2] We mount the tanks, I confer with the American officer, checking maps, destination and timings. The tankers give our boys a set of instructions, which mainly consist of where not to stand and to get off the tanks immediately if we are attacked, and of course some bright soul immediately placed his foot on the exhaust and in second half the sole of his boot vaporizes! His indignant scream alerts all of us.

After we disembark at the rail station of Gumcochyi, the tanks draw up under the shade of trees and park, while I brief the men on our instructions once again. We are to locate the enemy, take a prisoner if possible and return to base. Formed up in single file we move north on foot and by the time we are underway it is about 0900hrs. Unfortunately we are told the tanks do not have communication equipment that will enable us to contact them by wireless. An oversight?

Each soldier is equipped with: a Lee-Enfield bolt action .303 rifle; 100 rounds of ammunition carried in two bandoliers slung about his neck; two #36 Grenades attached to chest webbing, a water bottle, two sandwiches and an apple - a delightful break from the inevitable C rations. There is the usual establishment of one Bren Light Machine Gun in each of the three sections. It is a blisteringly hot day, about 85 degrees. The warm weather has come on suddenly, commencing about the 20 April. We are still attired in our winter battle dress uniforms; namely, heavy trousers anchored by putties at boot level. Everyone wears rolled shirtsleeves. We are saved from one US infliction: instead of wearing heavy steel helmets we are equipped with soft berets, a few have British army balaclavas. American soldiers incur a $15 fine if caught without their steel helmets positioned upon their heads. As the Chinese are largely without medium and heavy artillery, our Brigade Commander does not foresee the necessity of wearing heavy steel helmets for protection against fragmentation bursts.

As we move off we are confined in a narrow valley about 400 meters across. Soon the valley broadens to become about a mile wide. It is treeless, although the hills to our right are spotted with sparsely spaced trees that become relatively dense higher up. To our left the coverage is limited on the lower, almost bare hills. The rail line continues on its eastern axis while we move north. Making our way along a rough track we feel exposed. Our uneventful patrol continues for almost three hours when we sight an enemy formation about half a mile ahead. Sergeant Major, platoon sergeant, and I bring the men to a halt and into a defensive formation. I examine the enemy through my binoculars. I can hardly believe what I see. The enemy does not move, the soldiers maintain an almost parade square formation, steadfastly in column of route. We are totally exposed in the middle of a broad treeless valley. Are we walking into an enemy trap, to be ambushed from our right flank or from the rear? For some time I carefully observe our front and flanks. Everything is so still. We are in an inverted "V" formation: two sections forward one in reserve, everyone at the ready in case we are ambushed.

We advance unopposed towards our enemy. It is so quiet our nerves are on edge, anticipating that at any moment a sudden burst of fire will engulf us. The silence becomes deafening. The heat of the day under a cloudless sky is increasingly oppressive. After a cautious and tense 10-minute advance we come full upon the enemy formation, comprising two officers, three NCOs and 51 soldiers - 56 in all. They are lined up in four ranks in column of route, a captain at their head and a lieutenant and sergeant to the rear. There are a number of features that I had never encountered before in my Korean experience and I cannot believe what lies in front of me.

First - these men are armed to the teeth. Never have I seen the enemy with so much weaponry and such generous allotments of a variety of ammunition. The officers have high-powered binoculars, much better than ours. There are burp guns, two medium machine guns, grenades and a light mortar. The enemy we had previously faced was always short of weapons. Prisoners taken at Kapyong were instructed to acquire additional arms, ammunition and food from us!

Second - these troops are not dressed in the standard issue green "Mao type" uniforms. They are attired in a summer drill formal kaki dress and the tunics have dull brass buttons.

Third - they are all sitting on their haunches, torso bolt upright, uniformly at attention. It is as though they were seated in formation resting between photographic shoots.

They are all dead. Stone dead. A concentrated examination does not reveal a point of penetration on even a single body.

Once again I pause to examine both our flanks and rear for any sign of movement. None. We are strangely alone, exposed in the middle of a plain about a mile or more wide with 56 dead enemy soldiers, positioned like statues about five or six miles forward of our armoured support. Where is our living enemy? And how the hell did these men die? What and who snuffed out their lives, and why are they positioned here, appearing like chessmen?

My thoughts are interrupted when one of my troops asks permission to accumulate souvenirs from the enemy, a not unusual request in action. I readily concur. The soldier immediately makes for the officer positioned at the head of the column on whose chest rests a pair of high magnification binoculars. The soldier gives a tug, the glasses hold fast to the body. Determined to liberate his prize he pulls harder. The glasses finally break free, but adhered to them are first the officer's shirt, then his skin and then his ribs, leaving a gaping circular hole about 10 inches across. Our soldier falls back, engulfed by a black mass, which storms out of the body. Some of us laugh nervously as the vermin migrate to a newly found deliciously warm Canadian body. The mirth, which has broken the tension, is short lived as others retrieve photographs of loved ones, wives and children from the 56 statue-like corpses. Suddenly we are also reminded they were human beings who had a terrible injustice inflicted upon them.

I move to inspect the body exhibiting the gaping chest hole. Inside is an empty shell, the innards have been totally consumed. No amount of training or months of warfare have prepared me or anyone for this bizarre horror. Some of my soldiers continue inspecting the bodies while others are highly disturbed and move off from this grim scene. Lance Corporal JC Wanniandy, a Canadian Indian, finds the retching stench of this unnatural death so nauseating he will not stand anywhere near the formation. Here are 56 soldiers, having no innards, no point of penetration, unvaryingly positioned rigidly upright on their haunches, dead.

Although I had taken the ABC course (Atomic, Bacteriological and Chemical Warfare) at The School of Infantry, Camp Borden, I cannot reconcile this situation. I first consider Nerve Gas, which kills in seconds, but that would have sent the men into convulsions. Had these men been drugged? It is a bazaar scene, totally unreal and its implications terribly disturbing. It is as though the assembled enemy may have been on their knees praying for forgiveness to an unseen, all knowing and all-powerful deity. They may have been pleading for their lives, but if so they pleaded in vain.

It is time to return to Gumcochyi, to have the tanks transport us back to the Patricias. We are three to four hours away from our armoured allies. Once again I am concerned that we might engage an unseen enemy force, but our return is uneventful. On reaching my slit trench, I write my report and deliver it to my Acting Company Commander, Captain JWG Mills. Meanwhile the troops are abuzz informing everyone of the devastating sight they have just witnessed. The word quickly circulates D Company. Soldiers wonder if they will be next. How did these men die? What agent killed them? How would our men protect themselves from a similar attack? Is it even possible to defend oneself? The soldiers of D Company soon have variations of this incident flying in all directions as only a body of troops can. I expect to lead a formation back to the site the following day but I hear nothing more of the matter. There are other patrols to be undertaken and on 21 May UN Forces advance forward from Line Golden.

Forty-five years after witnessing this dreadful sight, I examined the Second Patricia's War Diary, for May 1951 at the Museum of the Regiments in Calgary, where the PPCLI archives are held. Incredibly there was no mention of this incident. I could not believe it! I decided to reference all available records. Finding nothing I widened my search. During three years of enquiry no consulted authority has admitted to having any knowledge of this incident. Each of the many United States authorities I contacted recommended an alternative source. Amongst others I wrote the following:

> National Archive at College Park, MD
> Department of the Army, The Center for Military History
> US Army Intelligence and Security Command
> US Army Chemical Corps Museum   (Twice, no reply)
> US Army Chemical School   (Twice, no reply)
> US Air Force, Classification & Review team, SAF AAZD
> Maxwell Air Force Base, Alabama
> Republic of Korea, Military Attaché, Ottawa
> Director of the War Museum, Institute of Military Affairs,

Seoul (Twice, no reply)
Canadian Military Attaché, Seoul, Korea

All the above correspondence included photographs of my platoon on the armour, the bombed out rail station and one including the name of the station - but sadly I never took a picture of the ranks of dead men, because I had run out of film.

Once I did have a near favourable reaction, but that was short lived. I telephoned the US Army Intelligence and Security Command, IACSF-FI, Fort George G. Meade, MD. I gave a description of the event and a chap assured me he would inform me, but that I should first submit my evidence in a written report and he would subsequently telephone me. I did so. After a wait of three months I telephoned again requesting to speak to the individual I had previously talked with. His receptionist informed me I must first explain myself. I did so. I was advised she was aware of my earlier enquiry but, regrettably, their filing system was such that unless I could provide the name of the individual filing the report within their archives they could not be of assistance!!!

I also forwarded a copy of my reconstructed report to Colonel Stone. His return letter of March 16, 1996 in part said: *"To say that your cor-respondence surprised me is an understatement. I fought in Italy, NW Europe as well as Korea and never heard of an incident such as you describe. I was not in Korea in May 1951, being with my family on compassionate leave. However I should think such a story would have been impossible to keep from the press."*

Stone did me a great favour, because I realized that to be believed I had to obtain corroborating signed statements. So more than four decades later I commenced my search for the men of D Company who were associated with that patrol. It took me three years and a great deal of searching. Amazingly two of them were nearby in Edmonton. I now have three signed statements from those who witnessed this incident. (See Appendix "E" page 247).

In July 1999, I traveled to London, England, and I met with an excep-tional soldier, General Sir Anthony Ferrar-Hockley, who served with the Gloucester's in Korea. Captured at "Gloucester Hill" he escaped enemy POW camps five times only to be caught on each occasion. He also wrote the two-volume 2,000 page official history of the British Army in Korea. Sir Anthony informed me that he had thoroughly searched US and UK Korean historical records and found no documentation relative to such an incident. He suggested if I wrote to the Chinese Military Museum, in Beijing, I might chance upon something. (I did this and received no reply.)

Through Colonel Jeffrey Williams (Retired), who served in the First Patricias in Korea and a former Canadian Intelligence Officer, I was advised that neither the Chinese, nor the North nor South Koreans at that time possessed an agent capable of instantly killing 56 men. A bone-chilling alternative was developed as a strong possibility.

How did these men suffer the indignity of an instantaneous massacre? I was advised that only two nations had the capability of instant execution resulting in a body being frozen in position: The United States of America and The Soviet Union. I was informed it was no doubt the Russians, who were known to have committed this type of annihilation previously in experiments upon their own people.

About this time I consulted a pathologist friend and described the conditions of the bodies and the temperatures at that time in Korea. I was informed they had probably been in place for three weeks to a month. This raises one vitally important question: which side in this war controlled the land at the assumed time of this murderous action? The reader can consult the map on page 189, which reveals the land in question was in both UN and Chinese hands during this time frame.

The 56 died as a result of Biological Warfare.

Is this threat to be unleashed by some future world dictator, or mad man? We had been on Line Golden for 21 days, and I have often wondered what would have happened if we had come upon these contaminated bodies much earlier? Would I be here to relate this macabre story? What might have taken place in Korea had this weapon been unleashed upon us has haunted me, mostly in my nightmares, but they meld into my living days. It took me years to work through the horrors of this incident, and I thought I had. But I was hospitalized in 1999 with a herniated disk and morphine was administered to relieve the intense pain. The drug combined with my recent research brought forth the nightmares with a far greater harshness than in the past. Over and over I relived the cursed hell that forever permeates the soul. The nightmares are an experience that I never, ever share with anyone, not even a loving wife. The agonies of so many deaths in such varied and horrific circumstances, the stench of decaying bodies, the screams and agonies of the dying, both your comrades and the enemy that you were determined to destroy, are ingrained upon the psyche, never to be erased.

So many questions persist. Why would an experiment of this nature be conducted so close to the front lines? One would think it would have been undertaken in the greatest of secrecy, miles from the front. The required equipment was at the front. Had the enemy determined this devastating biological weapon would allow them to regenerate their failed Spring Offensive? If so, what stopped them? They could have made a disastrous and gapping hole in the UN line. Yet retaliation no doubt would have been swift and far more appalling, possibly engulfing the world.

Why were the exterminated troops left there? Was it because of lingering contamination, or as a message? If so, to whom? The Americans openly discussed the possibility of using an Atom Bomb to turn the tide of events in Korea. Was this supposed to be a deterrent? Use an atom bomb and here is how we will retaliate?

Assuming the bodies were in place for 21 days or longer, it is incomprehensible to think that no one else stumbled across our grisly discovery. During this time, across the central front, UN forces were mounting daily patrols. What other patrols penetrated this area and what other intelligence was gleaned? What aerial photography captured the landscape? What of the daily aerial flights of a variety of spotter aircraft flying over no-mans-land at relatively low altitudes? It is an irrefutable fact that on May 21, 1951, UN forces took the offensive, ultimately retaking not only this area but all the lands given up to the enemy and more. I can find no explanation. Who disposed of the bodies? Why, 50 years on, would an innocent nation refuse to reveal acts of enemy aggression? Assuming the Russians were experimenting with this type of genocide, had democratic forces deemed it necessary to demonstrate conclusively that others were not above retaliation? This incident is a double-edged sword that both confounds and menaces the intellect. Yet somewhere, the answer lies in some secret archive.

Was it a coincidence that the only means of communication I had on that patrol was an American Walkie Talkie? We were too distant to make contact with our company headquarters. The American tanks, three hours to the south, were too far away and unfortunately did not have the equipment to receive our wireless communications. Were we to carry casualties out on our backs? There were no means of periodic situation reports. Were we operating under an enforced silence? Did some experimental intelligence group, knowing full well what we would discover, want to find out if the contaminates were still active? Perhaps we were truly earning our nickname of being labeled the "PBI," The Poor Bloody Infantry.

Thank God, we are fortunate enough to live in a civilized nation where one questions how men could possibly commit such horrific crimes. At Los Alamos, the atomic bomb experiments inflicted cancer from radiation upon the American and Canadian troops who volunteered, despite the fact they were reassured that they were perfectly safe. The final incident involved placing the troops within a mile of the detonation point where they were ordered to advance to prepared slit trenches. There were none. The men were radiated while lying on top of the open ground and it was years before the two governments finally admitted their responsibility. Similar experiments were conducted injecting LSD, at the direction of governments. For years they were denied their unfortunate "guinea-pigs" status. For some, compensation came decades later. During the Second World War, Canada subjected soldiers to live Mustard Gas experiments at Suffield Military Establishment. One cannot but wonder what other undisclosed and irresponsible actions may have been committed, or are being committed, in the name of the defence of a nation.

The United Kingdom Korean War Veterans newsletter, The Morning Calm, published my report of our 1951 patrol in April of 1999. The magazine later received a letter from a UK Korean veteran, Derek Bennett, formerly a Field Linesman, Royal Corps of Signals, with the 27th Brigade. Bennett and a chap named Price reported finding 25 to 30 North Korean troops, lying down as if resting in a field about 100 yards from a road. They were attired in the usual white winter parkas, having a red star on their headgear. They were all dead and they could not find a point of penetration on any of the bodies. The book, "Rangers in Korea," by Robert Black, on page 190 cites a similar incident. They found an entire village with people in positions reflecting their carrying out a variety of chores - all unexplainably dead. "Men hardened by the many faces of death wiped tears from their eyes and hastened from the valley." [3]

This lingering threat begs haunting questions:

The following map illustrates that both the Chinese and American forces held the ground at the time of this incident. It would be convenient for a government, intent upon implying it was the other antagonist, to indifferently annihilate their own, or prisoners of war, in the midst of no-mans-land. Why was this "incident" undertaken? Who possessed the

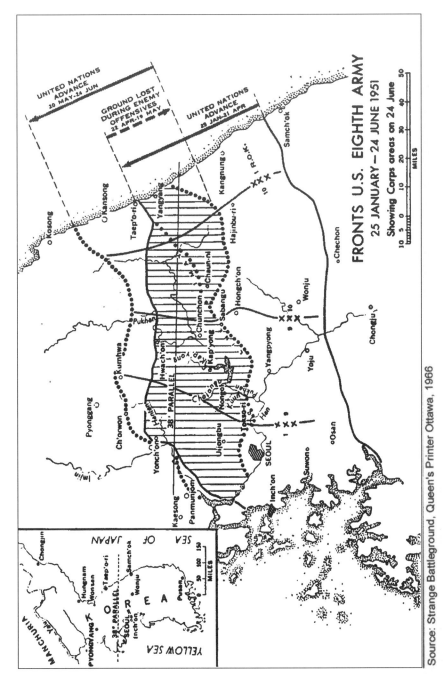

FRONTS U.S. EIGHTH ARMY
25 JANUARY – 24 JUNE 1951
Showing Corps areas on 24 June

Source: Strange Battleground, Queen's Printer Ottawa, 1966

"creative" know how?

For what future purpose?
and
Why was my written report suppressed?

Relaxing on a Korean Grave (photo: Hub Gray)

B Company, Kapyong (photo: PPCLI Archives)

1. Edicott & Hagerman, page 63.   Also see: MBC -South Korean Documentary, "The US Biological Warfare in Korea," http:/www.imbc.com.sisa - and - doc/nowtell/htm/vod/vod_000702.htm
2. Stone in an interview with LCol GWLNicholson, D. History, Army Headquarters, 1630 hrs, 5 June 1951, stated that he was receiving sufficient reinforcements in Korea. I find this curious for in my experience we were always well short of establishment numbers for soldiers.
3. Black: Ballantine Publishing Company, (Random House) 1989

Lieut. Mike Levy - Line Golden. Asahi beer & Vancouver Province.

*Korea, May 1951, 12 Pl. D Coy. 2PPCLI. We mount US Patton tanks,
move forward to bombed out rail station Cumcochyi, Korea. Platoon fighting patrol.
(photo: Hub Gray).*

Korea, May 15, 1951.
Gumcochyi
Patrol, burned out rail station, US tanks under the trees.
(photo: Hub Gray).

Korea, May 8, 1951.
The burned out rail station of Gumcochyi,
(photo: Hub Gray).

196

Chapter NINETEEN

THOSE DAMN MOSQUITOS

A Canadian soldier recalls three months of high anxiety while serving with the US Air Force. An enemy soldier under interrogation was asked what was the most annoying thing about fighting the UN Forces in Korea. He replied, **"Those mosquitos; the aggravating and incessant buzzing of the deadly accurate silver mosquitos that buzz, buzz, buzz overhead every day, all day long."** [1]

NOTE: To distinguish their unique character, the executive of the Mosquito Association, have terminated the "e,"... at the end of the word.

Lieut Bud MacLeod - It was on Line Kansas, just after daylight on May 23rd, 1951, I was sitting in a Chinese dug foxhole when the battalion runner sauntered up and said, "Lieut MacLeod, you are to report to Battalion Headquarters (BHQ) ASAP. Take all you gear with you." [1] He didn't have much gear to scoop up - a 9mm pistol, a webb belt and his small pack. But MacLeod grabbed what he had and headed toward what was to become the greatest adventure of his life, and the highlight of his Korean war service.

At Battalion Headquarters the bewildered MacLeod, was informed he had just been seconded to the United States Air Force for 90 days and was to report immediately to airfield K-6. The remainder of his worldly possessions had already been packed and tossed into a jeep that stood idling outside. "Yes Sir," said the young Lieutenant, "But where is K-6?" "How the hell do I know, get out of here, we have a war to fight."

"Where to Sir?" Asked the driver once MacLeod had hopped into the jeep. "Well soldier I was hoping you would know," it didn't appear wise to head North, recalls MacLeod. There were no lateral roads East or West, so I directed the driver to head South, and look for an airport where we could go into the Operations building and get further directions. We arrived at Kimpo airfield (K-14), which was abuzz with transport and fighter aircraft. Proceeding to the Air Movements Unit, I asked the NCO in charge, if he had a Lieut MacLeod on the manifest for Japan. After going through a series of manifests, he replied there was nothing and asked where I was destined to go. I informed him K-6. He replied, "The K stand for Korea, I don't know where it is but K-5, is 40 miles down the pike at Suwon. Enquire there." At Suwon the road ran down the entire length of the runway where F 84 Thunderjets were taking off. Proceeding into the Operations Centre, I asked the Captain on duty where K-6 was. With this, he said, "K-6!" and broke into gales of laughter citing something along the lines of "you poor bastard" and a collection of similar epitaphs! Certainly not the most reassuring of answers! I will never forget that guy. He told me to follow the road south. It was now dusk, I reported into the HQ, where Sgt Bill Cleveland advised I was expected and was billeted in tent 24.

Arriving at the tent I knocked on the flap and heard "Enter." I beheld a dark, smoke filled interior with a central table under one dim light bulb. A Halicrafter portable radio was belting out "So Long, its been good to know you," and five guys were sitting around the table playing poker. I introduced myself advising I was from the 2PPCLI. McAllister, the tent captain replied, "Pats eh, a fucking, good outfit, I hear. Throw you gear under that bed," pointing to a cot in the corner. I noted there was someone else's gear there. "Oh, George won't be needing it anymore, he was shot down today. Pete, (pointing to another officer) grab George's gear and put it by the door, Graves Registration will pick it up in the morning." Turning to MacLeod, "Welcome aboard, Canuck. Pull up a stool. Got any Money?"

Thus began the Canadian Army's association with the 6147th, Tactical Control Group (Mosquito) United States Air Force, formed at the start of the Korean War to control all air strikes between the United Nations Forces front line and the Bomb Line. The latter was an arbitrary line drawn across the Korean peninsula, approximately 10 KM to the north of our Army's Main Line of Resistance. An important function of the Group was to prevent casualties to the United Nations' troops from what is now euphemistically designated "Friendly Fire." Tasks included locating target areas with smoke rockets to identify them to fighter/bombers, directing strikes, assessing damage, and estimating casualties upon the completion of the strike by low passes over the target area, often just 25 feet off the ground.

When I flew with the Mosquitos we were located at K6, 150 miles behind the front so on each mission we had to fly not only up to the front but across the peninsula as well. This took one hour, plus two hours on station and one hour back. Four hours twice a day. In 1952 the Mosquitos were moved up to K47, the flight area being 10 minutes off the end of the runway. While memories of sheer terror and constant airsickness have faded, the memory of sitting on those #%@&+ parachutes for eight hours a day - has NOT.

We flew the USAF TEXAN, known in Canada as the HARVARD, armed only with 12 smoke rockets. The airborne team consisted of a USAF pilot and a combat arms observer in the rear seat. The combat arms participant, a soldier seconded from the front line infantry, was to use his intimate knowledge of the probable targets to identify the positions of friendly forces. That was my new job. The next few days were spent in drawing specific kit and indoctrination. The pilots, over time, ensured the observer had at least a rudimentarily knowledge of flying the aircraft; an insurance against pilot failure. This aspect did prove to be a lifesaver, as will be seen later on. Soon Capt Harry Hihn of 2 Battalion The Royal Canadian Regiment arrived. The British Commonwealth contingent consisted of two Canadians and two British officers from the 8th King's Own Irish Hussars, who had been attached for several weeks.

The kit consisted of a flight suit, a leather-flying jacket, a belt mounted survival kit and what they termed a "blood chit." This was a piece of silk-like cloth, upon which were printed the flags of South Korea, the United States, and United Nations. Inscribed were statements in Korean, Chinese and English, that the holder was a UN Flyer and that if he were assisted the UN would pay the assistor a cash reward.

The most significant part of my indoctrination was on my first day on a Mosquito Snowflake. This aircraft - a C-47 Skytrain/Dakota/ Gooneybird whatever, was the key player in our Air Support Operations during the Korean War. Along the sides of the cargo compartment were ten to twelve radio consoles and operators, one each for the number of front line infantry divisions. Flying a racecourse pattern over the Korean peninsula from dawn to dusk, these crews had control of all aircraft operating between the front lines and the Bomb Line. The only exception being the artillery spotter L-19s, and the Austers flown by the artillery regiments. Attack aircraft flying in from Japan, off aircraft carriers in the surrounding seas, or off local airfields would first report to these MS Controllers, who would parcel them out to specific Mosquito sectors. We would then meet them on a common radio frequency and direct them to their targets.

My first flight was launched at 0430 hrs, 29 May 1951, and it was to be the most action packed flight I made during my entire tour with the

Mosquitos, and I wish I had a better recollection of this first example of the effectiveness of air strikes. At the time I was quite frankly terrified. It wasn't until later that I became "just scared." Upon reaching the front line I was startled to see red flashes streaking by the canopy. I instantly took them to be tracer bullets from a high-powered machine-gun and thought, "My God, we are under attack by MIGs. Should I bail out?" Luckily I didn't jump because I soon learned the smoking pilot flicking the ash out of his canopy caused the red streaks.

There was an intense action on the Eastern Front and the Battle of the Injie was full blown. We arrived as the enemy was in full retreat on a road that led through a narrow defile north of the town of Injie. Hundreds of soldiers could be seen marching through the defile, and there was nothing left to do but to put the fighter/bombers on them. I vividly recall the US Navy/Marine Corps F4U Corsairs and the AD Skyraiders repeatedly making attack runs on that defile. From our altitude the retreating troops looked like a line of Army ants, moving along the road between the mountains and the streams. During an attack the pilots always dropped their load of napalm first because they were not eager to have 50 gallons of jellied gasoline on each wing during low flying attacks. As each napalm bomb fell on a line of "ants" the tiny figures were either killed outright or ran into a stream or up the hill to escape the flames. Next came the 500-pound bombs and finally the rockets and the 50 caliber machine guns, with the pilots flying up stream to finish the terrified soldiers off. As I recall, we called in at least five flights of four aircraft each, during those two hours stay on station, and as an infantry soldier I could appreciate the horrifying agonies that those ground troops, enemy or not, must have gone through. Perhaps it's better that my memory fades.

We learned later that a flight of three C119s Flying Boxcars on a re-supply mission during the battle was shot down by "Friendly fire." They had flown through an artillery barrage using Variable Time or proximity fuses. These projectiles are designed to explode about 50 feet above ground to enhance their devastating shrapnel effect over a distance of 100 meters or so. They would also explode if they passed in close proximity to an aircraft. This was a graphic example of a serious failure in the support system. In our operation we had no control or knowledge of the targets the artillery units were engaging. The infantry Divisional Forward Controllers (FACs) were supposed to monitor this, but in the compression of activity that did not always happen. You would think that this obvious failure would have been corrected, but in every subsequent war there have been casualties from friendly fire because the left hand does not know what the right hand is doing.

I don't know how many enemy casualties we reported due to these strikes, but it did introduce me to the term body count, which later became a common accurieum in the accounting practices of the war in Vietnam, and a means whereby the United States Government appropriating funds for various of their armed forces. Here is an oversimplified example of how it might work in a theoretical attack on a Korean hill. In preparation for an infantry attack Mosquitos were called in to direct air strikes, and afterwards we were required to make a post-strike low fly over to estimate casualties, which was bloody difficult under the best of circumstances. Let's assume our estimate was 100 killed or wounded. The next phase of the attack was for the artillery to fire softening-up barrages prior to the infantry assault on the hill. Assuming success, the actual bodies were tabulated - let's say 500: 400 for the artillery and 100 for the air strike. Bizarre as it would seem, there are minions representing each of the Army, Navy, Air force and Marines in the cellars of the Pentagon, who would then trot out these comparative figures in an attempt to justify increased appropriations for their own service. During my tour with the Mosquitos I can't recall being encouraged to inflate the casualty figures, but we weren't encouraged to low-ball them either.

By and large the Mosquito pilots were a very competent group. They were brought in from all occupations within the Air Force to fly the T6 for 100 missions and then transfer out. My principle pilot had been a manager of an officers' club in Japan. He had previously flown F51 Mustangs. As the jet age was relatively new, few were jet jockos, but they had all flown high performance aircraft; Mustangs, Thunderbolts et al prior to becoming Mosquito pilots. They had all flown the T6 during Advanced Flight Training, but initially they tended to forget that the T6 was underpowered in relation to the high performance fighters. In one instance that was more my fault than the pilot's, we wanted to switch over to another valley near the Iron Triangle. I was reading the map and the pilot asked me to advise him of what re-entrant to turn up, which I did. Unfortunately It was one entrant too early, I misread the map. Not only was it much narrower than the one intended, it had a higher pass. We struggled up the re-entrant, the pilot poured on the power and the sides of the mountains loomed closer and closer. At this point I suggested we should turn around but I was curtly advised that the mountain walls were too close and the aircraft's turning radius too wide. I pulled up on my seat in the hopes of making the aircraft lighter. As we approached the pass we could see two soldiers cooking breakfast right in the saddle. We cleared the mountain pass by about ten feet and the enemy dived for cover. There were four of us who required a change of laundry that day.

Some pilots played the game and others thought they could win the war by aggressively attacking the enemy with relatively inoffensive smoke rockets. I had only one pilot like that, and I shuddered when he showed up on the flight line with an M1 carbine and a bag of grenades. When we found a target and no fighter/bombers were available, he circled the target and shot at them with the carbine and dropped the grenades, while I cowered in the back seat. Under normal circumstance the enemy would not fire at us because they knew that if located, we would return with Corsairs, Skyraiders, Mustangs or whatever. At the end of the flight I thought, "God forbid that I be assigned to that pilot again." Several days later I had to return to the Patricias because I was out of money and being a foreigner there was no mechanism for the squadron to pay me. For some reason I was delayed returning, possibly because of a hangover incurred at our infamous Banglestein's Bar! Upon entering the Squadron Operations, I was advised I had been scheduled to fly the first mission with our aggressive pilot but they had to replace me with an artillery sergeant. The aircraft had been shot down. After some searching the squadron located the plane well north of the Bomb Line; however, they were unable to get a close look because the enemy had set up a flack trap on the hills surrounding the site. To this day we do not know what happened to that aircrew. The bodies have never been recovered and diplomacy has not advanced to the point where the Yanks can go in and search for the remains.

Do I regret being late that day? For obvious reasons I don't. What I do regret is that I did not have the guts to report that pilot for his dangerous and inappropriate flying. He was in his thirties and I was a novice of 21. I particularly regret the loss of the artillery sergeant. I subsequently learned the pilot was undergoing some serious marital problems, but to take another life with him was unforgivable.

I have often been asked what we did when we were not flying. Immediately after returning from a mission, and after a mission whisky (Bourbon - yuck!) we would write up each other for medals/decorations or write fallacious stories for the Far East edition of the Stars and Stripes. Perhaps we would pen an article about us landing behind enemy lines.

On 1 July 1951, the word came down that peace talks were to

commence. I don't know what the operational ceiling is for the T6 Texan/Harvard, but I can assure you that we exceeded it for the next few days. Nobody wanted to become a casualty on the last day of the war, or at any other time for that matter. After several days of anoxia, we learned it was a false alarm and we were back down on the deck, business as usual.

The Air Medal is normally granted for a number of missions flown - 30. The Distinguished Flying Cross for 75, or for a specific incident. I was the first Canadian to fly with the Mosquitos, but my medal was not awarded to me and it wasn't until 1954 that I read in a newspaper about Ward, Bull and Robertson being so recognized. Some say Korea was not a war, but it was the only war I got to, so I wasn't going to let this pass. I immediately wrote Army Headquarters and the award came back so fast it was obvious that it was held at AHQ, but never processed. The Chief of the General Staff, General Guy Simmonds, during WW II, had been a Corps Commander under Montgomery and had disliked Patton and the US Forces generally. In fact it was not until the day he retired in 1956, that the Canadian Government approved of the Second Battalion Princess Patricia's Canadian Light Infantry, accepting the award of the American Presidential Unit Citation for its action at Kapyong, 23-5 April 1951. Finally the Patricias were allowed to wear the Distinguishing Unit Emblem.

In August of 1951, I was attending my last pre-mission briefing prior to returning to my unit and being immediately posted back to Canada. At the briefing the general situation along the front, weather and various intelligence developments were discussed. One item raised my concern when the Intelligence Officer reported that our spies behind the enemy lines advised that the enemy were re-supplying their forward troops at night, using beasts of burden, which they let graze on the hills during the daylight hours. Consequently we were told to be on the lookout for these animals during our mission, and to "Shoot on sight All Quadrupeds." On the truck on the way to the flight line, I recall musing, "Well that's just great. My last mission and they are asking me to shoot a bunch of cows!" Arriving on station, we conducted our normal reconnaissance of the entire sector and lo and behold we encountered a herd of oxen grazing on a hillside just below the Bomb Line.

We proceeded to terminate this means of re-supply with "extreme prejudice." The Radio Transmission went something like this:

"Hello Mosquito Snowflake. This is Mosquito Burden Five. We have a herd of 15 oxen at Grid reference 856544. Advise ETA of inbound aircraft. OVER."

"Hello MBS 5. This is MS. All our resources are tied up on the Western Front, however naval gunfire may be within range. Contact Turkey on radio frequency 182.2. OVER."

"ROGER MS - OUT. Hello Turkey, this is MB5. We have a herd at GR 856544. Can you range?"

"Mosquito. This is Turkey. We can range."

"ROGER - Turkey. Give us a William Peter (a white phosphorous ranging round) at GR 856544 and we will adjust."

"Mosquito. Turkey. We have not WP."

"Turkey. Mosquito. No WP. Do you have coloured smoke or any other kind of ranging round?"

"Mosquito. Turkey. Negative."

What to do? There is a large sandbar at the confluence of two streams just South of the target. We thought that if we could get a high explosive (HE) round onto that sandbar we would be able to observe it and adjust the fire from there.

"Hello Turkey. Give us an HE at GR 856544 and we will adjust."

"ROGER - Mosquito. SHOT now! Time of flight 45 seconds."

After waiting the prescribed time, we search in vain for any sign of an explosion. It must be appreciated that the lush green foliage on the east coast of Korea made it impossible to detect the fall of a shot of High Explosive, because the impact threw up small clouds of green foliage, hence the need to use WP, which is readily seen. Well, long story short, we spent two hours trying to get an observation from that cruiser, but to no avail. During that time the navy must have fired 15 or more five-inch shells.

Note: Since retiring Bud has received the Ed Daminco Memorial Award trophy for his work and dedication on behalf of the Mosquitos Association.

Eighteen Canadians flew as observers with the Group during its activation, 1950 - 1956. There were three casualties: Lieut Neil Anderson, 2 Battalion Queen's Own Rifles of Canada, was killed during an airborne training exercise in 1954, and Capt Roland Yelle of R22eR and Lt Albert Bull, PPCLI, were wounded-in-action, prior to the Cease Fire, 27th July 1953. Four Distinguished Flying Crosses and five Air Medals were awarded to Canadians. Captain Pat Trembly, 2R22eR, was awarded the Military Cross for heroism. On his first flight, Pat's pilot was hit and rendered unconscious. Pat was a trained parachutist but rather than bailing out and leaving the pilot to a certain death, he stayed with the aircraft and managed to manoeuver it back over friendly lines to crash land at Kimpo Airport. Up to that time he had never piloted an aircraft.

Seoul, Old City Gate (photo: Hub Gray)

1. MacLeod, his written statement in author's files

R. S. M. Les Grimes - 2 PPCLI & Cpl. Roy Rushton 10 Pl. having a party with the men.

Major Don Grant and Fred Kaye enjoy a beer with the men.

Chapter TWENTY

IRONIES OF WAR.

"Justice For All"

This story is about a Royal Military Policeman, Criminal Investigation Division, who was serving in Korea in 1951. It relates his run-ins with the Patricias and the unique ending that terminated his military career. But before I begin to relate this sorry adventure it is important to understand that in wartime, when killing is the only way to advance across the battlefield to defeat the enemy, personal feelings undergo hard conversions; to survive, you have to become cold hearted about killing your fellow men. The horrors of war tend to numb one's feelings, thus individuals undertake actions they would otherwise never contemplate.

This story may rival the tales, though not the writing, of renowned English author, Jeffery Archer, and the many twists he skilfully weaves into his spell binding fiction. But these incidents were real. To protect the family of the central figure, a British Military Policeman, I have named him Sergeant-Major Bloggins. I refer to the Canadian, described in part two of these related and unfortunate incidents simply as Company Sergeant Major (CSM) Jones. Both instances coincidentally relate to another Patricias officer, Lieut Brian Munro.

Camp Wainwright, Alberta, September 1950.

A divergent group of individuals was being trained to become an integrated fighting force, to be shipped to Korea with the Second Patricias. It was a Saturday night and the Men's Canteen had just closed. Lieut Brian Munro, Orderly Officer, and Orderly Sergeant Gerald J Goldsworthy, a regular force soldier seconded from 1PPCLI, were making their rounds of the camp. Emerging from the Men's Canteen they spotted a soldier who was having trouble making his way. He had his beret in hand, and looked decidedly dishevelled and obviously drunk. Goldsworthy, who was always immaculately dressed, was a relatively small man but possessed a penetrating gravel voice. He shouted out: "Soldier! You there! What is your name?" The soldier stumbled to a halt and replied, "Blank, Sergeant." Goldsworthy, thinking the man was a smart ass barked, "I did not ask you for the state of your bloody mind, I asked for your fucking name." It was in fact Private Blank, who is featured in the first part of this story.

Korea - 17 March 1951.

This was the first time the Patricias came out of the line since being committed on the 17 of February. It was the birthday of the Colonel-in-Chief of the Regiment, Lady Patricia Ramsay, and there was to be a Brigade sports day and an issue of beer for the troops, a celebration.

Lieut Brian Munro recalled, "I was sitting in the company tent with Lieut Jack Regan and in front of us there was a volleyball game in progress. One of the players caught my attention for he had taken his shirt off, it was the middle of March and still relatively cold. He was also wearing a beret with two cap badges on it, a Patricia's and one of the Middlesex Regiment. Appearing somewhat in the form of the notorious and legendary Field Marshall Montgomery, who invariably wore two cap badges. I chuckled at the man's gall. He looked familiar to me but his face did not register."

A day or two later a terrible incident occurred. Three of our men went down to a local police post or something of that nature, where there were Korean soldiers and some girls. The Canadians wanted to jolly up the girls and the Koreans would have none of it. Being told to bugger off in no uncertain terms they, in their drunken stupor, decided to teach the Koreans a lesson, throwing a #36 grenade into the room and regrettably killing one of the soldiers inside. The following day, a Royal Military Policeman, Criminal Investigation Division (CID), Sergeant-Major Bloggins, arrived at our Battalion. He informed our Adjutant that he wanted to interview all the Patricia officers. He found A Company and talked with our five officers, explaining the terrible incident we had no prior knowledge of. A witness to the murder stated that he thought one of the assassins was a Canadian, and that the man displayed two cap badges on his beret. When Bloggins said that I replied, "That's a coincidence because the other day I noticed one of our men was wearing a beret having two cap badges on it. One thing I do know he is not from my platoon and I don't know if he is from A Company, I don't know all of the men." Off went detective Bloggins who eventually traced down Private Blank along with his cohorts.

Blank was court-martialed and sentenced to life in prison - Private Davis to 18 months, Private Gibson to 18 months - and all three were returned to Canada to serve their time. A year earlier the Canadian Army had established an Appeal Board, granting servicemen the same privilege of appeal to a higher court, as that available to civilians. Composed of a Judge of the Exchequer Court and two lawyers, the appeal court heard the three soldiers' cases. It was considered that a new trial was unfeasible because it would be almost impossible to round up all the South Koreans and Canadians who testified at the original trial. Blank was offered full reinstatement in the army, but chose to retire. Davis was sentenced to time served, four months and released. It is believed Gibson was similarly dealt with. So ended Bloggins first encounter with Canadian soldiers in war torn Korea.

Many weeks later.

Munro: "Captain Gord Turnbull, Adjutant, went off on R&R to Japan. I was given his job and thus was to have five days Left Out of Battle (LOB), a pleasant change from running up and down the hills fighting the Chinese. One day early in the evening I was in the Battalion HQ Mess tent when field telephone call came from the Battalion Orderly Room (BOR) van, advising that a British Army CID policeman wanted to meet with the adjutant. So off I went. I entered the BOR van and lo and behold there was our Sergeant-Major Bloggins of the Royal Military Police, accompanied by an MP Staff Sergeant. "Oh Sergeant-Major Bloggins, we meet again, my name is Munro."

Bloggins; "I'd like to speak with you about a bit of sticky business, Sir." Bloggins turned to his Staff and issued an order, "Ensure we are not interrupted." The Staff slammed his feet to attention, gave a crashing sharp salute, "Yes Sir," about turned, smashed his feet together again and stomped loudly out to secure the door. Bloggins, in a mystifying fashion, furtively moved to each window, studied the area outside for a moment to ensure no one was nearby, and then he drew the window shades closed.

Now Bloggins was the type of policeman whose cold and piercing stare penetrated your very soul surveying all that you are. I thought, "My God what does he know about me, I almost felt guilty just looking at the man." "You know Sir, it is a strange thing, but every time I find a murdered corpse in Korea, it leads me to a ruddy Canadian," said Bloggins. I thought oh hell, what is it this time? Bloggins picked up a manila folder and proceeded to extract a number of large and gruesome photographs of a dead Korean, an older man with a beard. The man's body had been dug up and it was evident that it had been in the ground for some time for his body was in a state of advanced decomposition. A revolting sight despite the fact that we had become largely immune to the sight of death, and the horrors of war.

It turned out that the Korean Military Police reported this incident advising that the old man had been killed and buried by Canadians. It related back to a time when we had come out of the line, and Major Don Grant was the company commander. He told us that he was going to have the men issued a ration of beer and let them have a party, to work off some tension. There was a house just outside the company area with some girls in it and Grant did not want any problems to develop. So he called in Company Sergeant Major Jones and told him to find four or five men who did not drink. We issued them with baseball bats, and ordered them to become roving pickets to keep our boys away from the Korean girls and out of trouble. The party got underway, the troops were having a good time, the pickets were patrolling, doing their job. One picket checked the house and found two Lance Corporals inside just about to engage in some sort of activity with the young ladies. The picket entered the dwelling saying, "Hey boys come on out of here, you know about Company Commander's orders." So they withdrew and the picket continued on his rounds.

Shortly thereafter, while carrying out his responsibilities, the picket heard a noise. He turned and suddenly found himself faced with a Korean man threatening him with a machete. Evidently the man had been stalking the picket, awaiting his return. At times the Koreans were "selling their women" to our troops for sexual pleasures in exchange for money, C rations or whatever. The people were very poor and frequently suffering from hunger and/or disease. Had the picket interrupted a family or a business transaction? The picket defended himself by hitting the man on the head with the baseball bat. The man crumpled to his knees, holding his head and remaining there while the picket moved on.

Later, while still covering his beat, the picket once again came across the same man but this time his head was immersed in the local stream, blood oozing forth. He was obviously dead. A couple of distraught girls were present and they were crying with grief. The soldier was flustered at seeing the poor man and because of language barriers was unable to convey to the girls what had earlier transpired. The picket immediately reported the incident to the Company Sergeant-Major, turning himself in and explaining the circumstances. Company Sergeant-Major Jones, also celebrating and being a typical hard-nosed warrant officer, in a theatre of war, where killing is the object of every day life, responded with indignation: "What! A dead body in Company lines, a civilian! Get a squad of men and go out and bury the piece of garbage!" A sergeant formed a detail and they buried the body. So much for that.

However, the girls reported the man's untimely death to the Korean Military Police, who in turn informed the British Military Police.

Bloggins, in his analysis, determined that CSM Jones was involved in a murder cover up and he continued for some months to stalk the Patricias, doggedly pursuing his case against Jones.

October 1951

Bloggins finally succeeded in securing a warrant for Jones to be detained and interrogated. It was a dark, cold and rainy night in October, and the battalion was in the front lines engaged in fighting the enemy. Bloggins was making his way along a one-lane track between the hills, just behind the front lines, searching for the 2PPCLI position. He was forced to stop when he came upon another jeep blocking his path. In the other vehicle were Lieut Mike Levy, Intelligence Officer, and LCol JR Stone, commander of the Patricias. Bloggins had been pursuing the matter with Stone for some time without success so he proceeded to Stone's vehicle, saluted and issued his warrant of apprehension for Jones. Stone replied: "Mr Bloggins, you may go forward to the base of the hill behind me and await the presence of CSM Jones, he is descending the hill and will be with you in about 20 minutes. Now get that jeep out of my way, I have a war to fight." Bloggins snapped his usual smart salute but proceeded to his jeep at a slow and defiant pace. Stone drove on and Bloggins, satisfied at last, smiled as he awaited his prey. When Jones finally appeared he was on a stretcher, having been killed in action an hour previously. A defeated Bloggins, seething with anger at having his prey denied him, was doubly humiliated at being royally stone-walled by a very cool and imperious Stone.

In time Bloggins had a birthday to celebrate. The boys of the British MP force stationed at their headquarters in Seoul decided to give their highly respected boss a humdinger of a party. Bloggins proceeded to get drunk, very drunk. Like most senior administrative officers in Korea he had a Korean houseboy to do his every bidding. Evidently Bloggins, in his drunken desire for affection, settled upon his unfortunate houseboy, who wanted none of it. So Bloggins, a tireless disciplinarian never to be defeated or refused by anyone, reached for his pistol to discipline the lad. He shot the boy and wounded him. Arrested by his dismayed underlings, Bloggins was handcuffed and placed in cells. Meanwhile a vehicle was commandeered to rush the lad to a military hospital. Seoul was a starless, moonless night as the vehicle moved hastily through a honeycomb of deserted and rubble strewn streets.

Suddenly the emergency vehicle struck a man and his wife, killing one of them. The MPs left one man with the corpse, called another MP unit to care for them, and continued their race against time to save the lives of the boy and the now smashed up adult.

Totally disgraced and thoroughly humiliated in the eyes of his peers, Bloggins was charged and secured in cells. The formidable bloodhound and guardian of justice for all, now himself faced the harsh course of justice he had tirelessly administered to his many "victims." He was transferred to Japan to face a court martial and sentencing but on entering his cell one morning his guards found Bloggins had elected to terminate himself. He had committed suicide.

And so the dedicated master of the chase, by his own hand, became a victim of violence. It is one of the ironies of the Korean War that Bloggins true to all that he had stood for during his committed career as a military policeman ensured by his final act that there would be justice for all.

Refugee Line Golden (photo: Hub Gray)

APPENDIX "A"

TESTIMONIALS

To the actions of

Lieutenant Michael G Levy,

Commanding 10 Platoon at Kapyong.

April 23 to 25, 1951

The following individuals, all of whom served at Kapyong,

attest to Levy's actions.

Name	Kapyong	
Major Gordon Henderson, CD	Battle Adjutant	Tactical HQ
Lieutenant John Pearson	Commander 11 Platoon	D Company
Corporal LeRoy Clouthier	Sec Comd 10 Platoon	D Company
Private George Nestor	Runner	D Company
Pte Vern Walker	Rifleman 10 Platoon	D Company
Corporal WJ Shuler	Medical Assistant	B & D Companies
Captain Murray Edwards	Quartermaster	Tactical HQ
Lieutenant Charles Petrie	Commander 5 Platoon	B Company
Lieutenant Brian M Munro	Commander 2 Platoon	A Company

Lieutenant MG Levy Certification

Major Gordon Henderson
BATTLE ADJUTANT
2nd Bn PPCLI, at the Battle of Kapyong, April 23/5, 1951

There is one aspect of the battle that I have never understood. It has bothered me for some time. Now that I have read your report I understand.

Being Battle Adjutant I was in continuing communication with Captain Mills. I passed the information to the CO, who was commanding the battle. I could not understand why, when I would ask for a situation report, there were often long pauses. Frequently the answers were vague.

Now I understand, because of the topography, Mills could not see any of the battle taking place at his platoons.

Captain Mills had to check with Lt. Mike Levy and other Platoon Commanders to be updated. They in turn were busy controlling their fight with the Chinese.

We, at Tactical HQ, were not fully aware of the situation at D Company. We did not know which of the battle decisions were initiated by the Platoon Commanders; i.e., Levy's decision to call for the Artillery and Mortar fire to virtually rain down on his 10 Pl.

Having studied this report, I am of the opinion that, Lt. Michael Levy (Major Retired) is deserving of Official Military Recognition, for his actions at Kapyong, Commanding 10 Pl.

Major Gordon Henderson (Retired)
14411 - 29th Avenue
White Rock, BC, V4P 1P5

John Pearson
7272 Adera Street
Vancouver, B. C.
V6P 5C3

Kapyong - D Company - Commanding 11 Platoon

April, 1997

Dear Hub,
You have asked me to provide my recollections of the battle at Kapyong in April of 1951, and my conclusions as to who, if anyone, of "D" Company, was worthy of decoration for valour for his actions during the battle.

Prior to and during the battle I was the Lieut. in command of 11 Platoon, "D" Company 2 Battalion PPCLI. Lt Michael Levy for sometime had been and was the OC of 10 Platoon and my Sergeant., the late B. Holligan, was acting OC of 12 Platoon. The CO of "D" Company was the late Captain W. Mills. I have already provided you with my involvement in the action and will not refer to it here.

There is no doubt the main massive thrust of the Chinese Army attack was against the defensive positions occupied by 10 and 12 Platoons which were located to deny the enemy any further advance along the ridge overlooking the Kapyong valley and therefore access to the valley leading to Seoul. Had they got past us I believe they might have succeeded in capturing Seoul.

During the night I could hear and talk to Sergeant Holligan on the "walkie talkie" radios we were using. Because we were on opposite side of and below the crest of the ridge I could not hear or speak with Lieut Levy. I could however hear the sounds of the battle which at times became quite intense accompanied by artillery and mortar shell explosions which came close to our positions and, as I found out later, were being aimed at us. I visited Company HQ several times that night and spoke with Captain Mills. We did not have any artillery officer from the New Zealand Artillery Regiment with us and so far as I am aware, and one never visited our position. Sergeant Holligan was forced back from some of his positions and I had to reinforce his platoon by transferring one of my sections to his platoon. It was only because of the leadership and bravery of the commanders of 10 and 12 Platoon and the bravery of the men of these platoons that the Chinese attack failed.

In the morning (25th) I spoke with Sergeant. Holligan and some of my men who fought with him. Holligan said the while he survived a heavy attack the main thrust of the Chinese appeared to have been against 10 Platoon. Had it succeeded the road to Seoul would have been open.

Based on what I know, there were two men who deserved a medal for valour:

1. Levy for his selection of his positions, siting his weapons, control of his men and ultimately calling down artillery and mortar fire onto his positions rather than allow the Chinese Army to pass.

2. Sergeant Holligan was 11 Platoon's Sergeant. But he had been given temporary command of 12 Platoon. He was an excellent soldier and had fought with the British 51 Highland Division in Europe.

   Sergeant. B. Holligan, (deceased) for his bravery and leadership of 12 Platoon which prevented the Chinese from securing the highest point of land from which they could probably have destroyed Company H.Q. and my platoon which was on a lower part of the hill.

Following the battle no one ever asked me who, I thought, should receive a decoration and I don't know who made the recommendations in that regard.

Best wishes, Hub!

Kapyong - D Company - Commanding #1 Section, 10 Platoon

LeRoy Clouthier
332 – 2911 – 109 Street
Edmonton, Alberta
T6J 5C9

7TH June, 2000

Dear Hub,

After speaking with you on Tuesday the 6th of June, I thought, My God, I do not recall anyone in 2nd Battalion PPCLI, being recommended for a decoration until we joined the 25th Canadian Infantry Brigade in May 1950, when they started handing out medals.

When I think back to those times they missed one platoon commander who was my leader at the battle of Kapyong. If not for Lieutenant Mike Levy ten platoon would have been overrun and the enemy could then have easily beaten the battalion from the high ground.

To Mike Levy I say, "Sir, you deserve a commendation."

L. L. Clouthier
S/Sergeant (Retired)

Kapyong - D Company - Runner Company Headquarters

January 3rd, 1999

<u>To Whom It May Concern</u>

At the battle of Kapyong, Korea April 23/5 1951, I was a member of D Coy, stationed at Company Headquarters throughout the battle. I was the company runner and manned a Bren Light Machine Gun. Company Headquarters was out of sight of the company platoons. I could not observe the battle at any of our platoons.

It is my firm belief that Major Michael G. Levy (Retired), then a Lieutenant Commanding 10 platoon, should have received the Military Cross, for his bravery and coolness under fire.

Mr. Levy was in the front line of the battle and I believe he virtually directed the successful defence in the battle at D Company.

I hope by some chance that he may receive this honour at this later date.

George Nestor

APPENDIX "A"

Kapyong - D Company - Rifleman #1 Section

Telephone Conversation with Vern Walker, Pte. (CSM Ret'd)

Cpl Clouthier's Section, 10 Pl, at Kapyong.   Dated: 98 06 13

Levy was a very good man. I could never understand why he was not recognized for his actions at Kapyong. Levy kept things cool and calm during our battle, I will never forget him.

Vern Walker
1626 Alexander Avenue
Winnipeg, Man, R3C 1L1

Kapyong - B & D Company - Stretcher Bearer

Statement by Major (Ret'd) W. J. Shuler
2 PPCLI at Kapyong: Cpl Shuler, Medical Assistant (MedA)
My Observations at D Coy, 25 April 1951.

D Company, leading up to Kapyong, sustained more casualties than any other unit and the men must have thought "here we go again!"

After the parachute drop by the US Air Force, 1030hr/25, (ammo, medical supplies. Rations, and even water) Lt Rick Constance led a supply party to Charlie and Dog Companies. Corporal Anderson and I were sent to D Company HQ, with grenades and ammunition. Captain Wally Mills ordered Anderson and me to take a case of grenades and ammo to Lieut Levy's platoon. 10 Platoon were out of grenades entirely and had very little ammunition. We were to evacuate whatever wounded.

We drew fire on the way across but reached 10 Platoon HQ, expecting confusion somewhat like Company HQ; however, Levy appeared to be in full command after a very hectic night. Everything seemed as organized as it could be expected under the circumstances.

One casualty, Lance Corporal Edmonds, had to be evacuated by stretcher but none was available. Edmonds' kidneys or liver were hanging out. I had to improvise and asked for some wire or laces or rope. One man volunteered, however, Mike Levy said, "No, take my laces," which I did. We proceeded to make a stretcher and evacuate Edmonds.

219

I asked some of the men how things went during the night and they stated that Levy practically ran the whole company. They thought they were fortunate that they had him. Lieut Levy gave positive leadership under extreme duress, adverse and hectic circumstances. Apparently he didn't get too much help from Company HQ.

I feel very strongly that Levy's performance should be recognized.

W. W. J. Shuler
11 June 1998.

Kapyong - Tactical HQ - Quartermaster

Apartment 409
1575 Begbie Street
Victoria, BC, V8R 1L2
7th December, 1996

Dear Hub,

I make reference to our recent discussion on the matter of recognition by our military of the actions taken by Lieut (later Major) Mike Levy, on the night of 24/5 April 1951, at what became known as the "Battle of Kapyong." I, with many others, have felt strongly the injustice of the absence of official recognition for Lieut Levy's action.

To put the matter in perspective I detail an incident that bears strongly on my feelings:

Shortly after our arrival in Korea, in late 1950, we carried out our final Company-Battalion training at a location outside the Korean town of Miryang. While there our Commanding Officer, LCol JR Stone, paraded the battalion wearing his DSO and Bar, MC, proceeded to tell us that, since we were all volunteers and all being paid for our services, he would not be making any recommendations for individual recognition regardless of what the future held once we were committed to action.

To a newly formed unit, made up of experienced officers, warrants and NCOs plus many fresh recruits, who had been looking up to their Commanding Officer, as a brave and decorated soldier whom they were prepared to follow into battle with a confidence that he had inspired, this was a morale shaking shock!

To put this on a personal plane: when I was accepted for the Special Force my orders were to join the RCR. Because I wanted JR Stone, as my leader I arranged, through 6 Personnel Depot, Toronto, to have my orders amended to the Patricias. To a degree I might have accepted the Colonel's "No Recognition" policy if he had abided by his own criteria. But Col Stone failed to do so in accepting a second bar to his DSO, for his own "Volunteer" service in Korea.

Now - as to my own witness to Lieut Levy's actions. I was Battalion Quartermaster, present at Battalion Tactical HQ on the night of April 24/5, 1951, and thus conversant with all the actions during the battle.

Following Kapyong and our successful withdrawal all the battalion were aware of Lieut Levy's actions. I take nothing away from Captain W. Mills, Lieut Levy's commander, who eventually received the Military Cross, for this action. It was a surprise to all when Lieut Levy, who initiated all requests for close-in artillery support at 10 Platoon, received no recognition. Captain Mills' award was understandable, he made the decision to back up Lieut Levy's request. It was Captain Mills who had to relay the request and so he was the officer recognized in the action by Brigade HQ.

It was 25 Canadian Infantry Brigade HQ, who actioned the award - not LCol Stone. Brigade did not know of Lieut. Levy's role in the overall action.

I trust that we can see a deserving officer receive this due recognition, however belated.

M. C. Edwards

MC Edwards, Major (Ret'd)
ZB 4108 (707 973 129)

Kapyong - B Company - Commanding 5 Platoon

1206-1035 Belmont Avenue
VICTORIA, British Columbia
V8S 3T5

Statement concerning Lieutenant M G Levy, No 10 Platoon, 2PPCLI at Kapyong 1951

I am Charles Alexander Petrie Platoon Commander No 5 Platoon 2PPCLI at Kapyong in the period 23 to 26 April 1951.

On the morning of 24 April 1951, I was required to withdraw up the mountain's North side, between 'C' Company and 'D' Company, while protecting a section of Vickers machine guns, when 'B' Company was relocated to the Eastern flank of the mountain. As we reached the crest, the Chinese forces could be clearly seen following us up its Northern slopes in considerable numbers, I would estimate a two company force followed by one considerably larger. I had watched this development from about 0630 to 1100 hours as we made our way up the North slope to the crest. The thrust of the enemy movement seemed to be west toward 'D' Company.

During the night of 24/25 April 'B' Company had been quite busy, but at Orders Groups we were kept informed of action within as well as around the battalion. I note that it was No 10 Platoon that was mentioned as having been overrun and that it had required 16 NZ Field Regiment to lay down neutralizing fire on its position. In this I refer to a 1952 account of the battle based upon my notes from the Orders Groups which I still had when writing. Major CV Lilley, MC, CD "B" Company Commander at Kapyong, validated the written account.

While those of us in this battle had no knowledge of its implications; we had immediate accounts, in part garnered by listening to the wireless, that were explained by the Information given at orders groups. Before we were relieved in the line, it had become very clear that it was Lieutenant Levy who had held forth and effectively directed his defence while having to seek support weapons fire by wireless or runner communications with 'D' Company headquarters.

I know that I felt, and still do, that Lieut MG Levy should certainly have been decorated in recognition of his courage, ingenuity and tenacity in the face of a much larger enemy force than it would be expected that he could deter.

I heartily support the recommendation that the Government of Canada, right this error of omission by accepting that Major MG Levy (Retired) CD, should as a special case, now be decorated.

C. A. Petrie
24 November 1996
Victoria, BC.

Commanding 2 Platoon - A Company

4066 Cavallin Court
Victoria, B.C.
V8N 5P9
5 December 1996

Statement by Brian M. Munro regarding an award to Michael G Levy for his actions during the Batttle of Kapyong, April1951,

1. On 22 Nov. 96 in Victoria, B.C. I met with Hubert A. Gray, Charles A. Petrie, and Murry C. Edwards, all former officers of 2PPCLI and veterans of the Battle of Kapyong, to discuss a suggestion put forth by Hub Gray regarding a belated award being made to Mike Levy for his actions during that battle.

2. Hub Gray showed us the proposed outline of a letter he would send to MGen C.W. Hewson, Colonel of the Regiment, if we three supported it, in hopes that Bill Hewson too might be favourable to our recommendations and lend his support regardless of what administration obstacles might be involved.

3. 1 joined 2PPCLI as a re-enforcement lieutenant when they were in the line and commanded 2 Platoon of "A" Company. This was just after the Battalion training period at Miryang therefore I cannot comment on any of the alleged statements made by LCol James R. Stone regarding awards and/or decorations.

4. As perhaps was common throughout the action, most platoon and company commanders were totally absorbed with enemy activities in their own immediate areas of responsibility. I cannot comment on what specific actions occurred during the battle in other company areas, as the situation was very confusing what with the mingling of Korean DPs, retreating ROK soldiers and possible infiltration by the Chinese through our position which caused us considerable concern.

5. It was not until some days later when the Battalion was in reserve to re-organize, re-supply, rest, and clean-up that we had an opportunity to discuss the events at Kapyong with other company personnel. As a result there was no doubt in my mind who had initiated the call for supporting fire to be brought down on 10 platoon/ "D" company and who had subsequently relayed the request to Battalion HQ.

6. It was, I believe, largely because of these specific actions that the enemy forces were unable to break through the Battalion position thereby bringing a singular honour to 2PPCLI in the form of the United States Presidential Unit Citation.

7. Notwithstanding the individual awards that were made for actions at Kapyong, I sincerely believe that the initiative and actions taken by Mike Levy should be recognized, however belatedly. In this regard I fully support the letter put forth by Hub Gray.

Brian M. Munro

INCORRECT STATEMENT

CR Stevens, Official Historian of the PPCLI , 1919-1957, page 302 reported that:
"At 0130 hrs an enemy force ...dashed against 10 Platoon, Lieut Levy and his men disappeared in a swarm of enemies."

Levy: 10 Platoon was not overrun at Kapyong, they held their assigned position throughout the battle. Various details of 10 Platoon's fight, in a variety of writings, have been misrepresented.

I Certify that:

I was not requested to file a report of my actions at Kapyong after the battle. Nor did my Company Commander choose to discuss it with me.

I have not at any time thereafter, been consulted by a Military Authority, writer or historian. **This is the only occasion that I have been requested to provide a statement of my actions, written or verbal, at Kapyong.**

M.G. Levy

Michael G. Levy, CD
(Major Retired)

APPENDIX "B"

CITATIONS

An Appreciation of Prerequisites for Awarding The Military Cross

Degree of personal danger faced

Demonstrated courage within the "danger setting."
> Physical courage by way of risking death or injury to himself.
> Moral courage by way of decisions taken and consequence.

Leadership
> Exercising command and control in the circumstances.
> Inspiring performance in subordinates.
> Maintaining group morale.
> Personal example in action and deed

Professional competence

Success in accomplishing his unit's mission

Impact of his unit's success on:
      His Company mission
      His Battalion's mission
      Other organizational/elements

Consequence of his unit failing
      On his Company mission
      On his Battalion's mission
      On other organizations/elements

Circumstances "outside" his organization that impacted negatively on accomplishing his mission; namely, immediate and higher headquarters through their actions or inactions.

APPENDIX "B"

Lieuteant M.G. Levy, awarded an MiD, Malaya 1945.
Also a Confidential Report

SUPPLEMENT TO THE LONDON GAZETTE, 25 SEPTEMBER, 1947

Infantry.

E. Surrey R.
3336305 Pte. A. H. CROWHURST.
6102861 Pte. W. SLADE.
S. Staff. R.
Maj. (temp.) ~ A. B. ALLAN (224636).
4921952 Pte. E. J. HARPER (posthumous).
R.W.K.
6387010 Sgt. (actg.) A. A. ORR.
Manch. R.
Capt. R. S. DAVIES (285393).
Gordons.
2889999 Pte. D. A. FLETT.

Royal Army Ordnance Corps.
10571614 Sgt. L. C. HILLS.

General List.
Maj. (temp.) A. S. OLSEN (221509).
➤ Capt. (temp.) M.G. LEVY (343923).
Capt. (temp.) A. RABINOVITCH (234268) (post-humous).
Lt. T. C. COFFIN (231091) (posthumous).
Lt. G. HAWKINS (363085).

INDIAN ARMY.
Indian Armoured Corps.
Ris-Maj. AULIYA KHAN, Sardar Babadur O.B.I. (IO.4974).

Infantry.
12 F.F.R.
Maj. (temp.) I. A. McDONALD (EC.6387)

Indian Army Postal Service.
P.1064 I.W.O.I. R. R. DAVE.

BURMA ARMY.
Burma Rifles.
Maj. D. C. HERRING, M.C. (ABRO.32).
Maj. (temp.) SHAN LONE, O.B.E., M.C. (ABRO.130).

Burma Army Service Corps.
A.146 Corp. POE WHATT LOW.

CIVILIAN.
Mrs. Evelyn Clodagh MACKENZIE.
The ranks shown above were those held at the time of recommendation.

India Office, 25th September, 1947.
The following awards have been made in recognition of gallant and distinguished services in Malaya prior to the fall of Singapore in 1942:—

Indian Order of Merit.
Jemadar BADLU RAM (12312.IO), 15th Punjab Regiment, Indian Army (posthumous).
Subadar FRAMURZ KHAN (6801.IO), 15th Punjab Regiment, Indian Army (posthumous).
No. 14483 Sepoy HASHAM KHAN, 2nd Punjab Regiment, Indian Army (posthumous).
Subadar KARTAR SINGH (6010.IO), 15th Punjab Regiment, Indian Army (posthumous).
No. 12099 Lance-Naik MAWAZ KHAN, 14th Punjab Regiment, Indian Army.
Subadar MOHD YUSUF, 6th Rajputana Rifles, Indian Army (posthumous).
No. 18985 Sepoy MUHABBAT KHAN, 14th Punjab Regiment, Indian Army (posthumous).

The Indian Distinguished Service Medal.
No. 8097 Havildar MOHD. KHAN, 14th Punjab Regiment, Indian Army.
No. 9732 Naik HARNAM SINGH, 15th Punjab Regiment, Indian Army (since deceased).
The ranks shown above were those held at the time of recommendation.

India Office, 25th September, 1947.
The following awards have been made in recognition of gallant and distinguished services whilst Prisoners of war in the Far East:

War Office, 25th September, 1947.
The KING has been pleased to grant unrestricted permission for the wearing of the following decorations which have been conferred on the under-mentioned personnel in recognition of distinguished services in the cause of the Allies:—

DECORATIONS CONFERRED BY THE PRESIDENT OF THE UNITED STATES OF AMERICA.

Silver Star Medal.
Major (temporary) James Hugh BROCK (172341), The Queen's Own Royal West Kent Regiment.

Legion of Merit degree of Officer.
Brigadier (temporary) Francis Smith REID, C.B.E. (6058), late Royal Regiment of Artillery.
Colonel (acting) Alfred Henry MUSSON (6094), Royal Regiment of Artillery.
Lieutenant-Colonel (temporary) Thomas CHILD, B.Sc., A.M.I.Mech.E. (58970). Corps of Royal Engineers.

Bronze Star Medal.
Lieutenant-Colonel (temporary) Alexander Paterson SCOTLAND, O.B.E. (127896), Intelligence Corps.
Major (temporary) Cecil Ernest BELLAMY (110655), Intelligence Corps.
Captain Frank Dennis WHEELER, Indian Army.

Medal of Freedom with Bronze Palm.
Major (temporary) Francis John STRATTON (52010), Royal Regiment of Artillery.

Medal of Freedom.
Colonel Lionel Denham HENDERSON, C.B.E., M.C., T.D. (36081), late The Gordon Highlanders.

DECORATIONS CONFERRED BY HIS ROYAL HIGHNESS THE PRINCE REGENT OF BELGIUM.

Commander of the Order of the Crown with Palm.
Croix de Guerre 1940 with Palm.
Major-General (temporary) Lashmer · Gordon WHISTLER, C.B., D.S.O. (13017), late The Royal Sussex Regiment.

Commander of the Order of the Crown.
Major-General George SURTEES, C.B., C.B.E., M.C. (631), late The Lancashire Fusiliers.

Commander of the Order of Leopold II with Palm,
Croix de Guerre 1940 with Palm.
Major-General Harry Leicester LONGDEN, C.B., C.B.E. (17955), late The Dorsetshire Regiment.
Brigadier (temporary) Charles Barnet Cameron HARVEY, D.S.O. (18516), 10th Royal Hussars (Prince of Wales's Own), Royal Armoured Corps.
Brigadier (temporary) George Frederick JOHNSON, D.S.O. (28480), Scots Guards.
Brigadier (temporary) Leslie Keith LOCKHART, M.B.E., M.C. (13407), late Royal Regiment of Artillery.
Colonel Richard Maurice Hull LEWIS, C.B.E., M.C., A.M.I.Mech.E., A.M.I.E.E. (11419), late Corps of Royal Engineers.
Colonel (temporary) John Alton BELL, C.B.E. (131953), Corps of Royal Engineers.

Commander of the Order of Leopold II with Palm.
Brigadier (temporary) Fergus Y. Carson KNOX, D.S.O. (20532), late The Royal Ulster Rifles.
Colonel (temporary) Adrian William Bay BECKER, C.B.E., M.C. (8850), The King's Own Yorkshire Light Infantry.

Officer of the Order of the Crown with Palm.
Croix de Guerre 1940 with Palm.
Brigadier (temporary) Frederick David MOORE (23670), Royal Regiment of Artillery.
Brigadier (temporary) James Newton Rodney MOORE, D.S.O. (32071), Grenadier Guards.
Brigadier (temporary) Robert Arthur PRAYER, D.S.O. (18173), Royal Regiment of Artillery.
Colonel (temporary) Guy Seaburne MAY (66631), Royal Regiment of Artillery.
Colonel (temporary) Peter STAMPE (130691), Intelli-

CONFIDENTIAL
==============

P.L.T. GALVANIC / GUITAR / BROWN
==

Confidential report on each member of my P.L.T. and those attached from GUITAR / SLATE.

Captain Mike Levy.

A young chap - with previous experience of Guerillas in a recent escape from internment in China. Full of guts and really at his happiest when Japs or Puppets were reported in the vacinity. Deserves full praise for his handling of the ugly situation at Salak South (reported fully in my Operational Report) - when he led his Guerilla. with flying colours. It is most disappointing to me, as well as him, that his well deserved promotion to Captain has been so negligently delayed by C.B.O. As it is he holds local rank only. He is very anxious to get leave to Shanghai to trace his family who were interned there.

TO: FORCE 136.

FROM: 3 Dec 45

COUNTRY SECTION: M.C.S.

OPERATION: Galvanic / Brown

I hand you herewith:-

---------Sovereigns.
---------British Malayan Dollars.
---------Japanese Malayan Dollars.

which I certify is the total of Operational Funds returned by me from the above Operation:-

I further certify that I have no Operational Funds in my possession.

Date 2 Dec 45

Received the above Funds:

Date 3 Dec 45

Finance Officer.

KOREAN WAR

DECORATIONS—C. A. S. F.

FILE No. 4H-4018

MILLS, JOHN GRAHAM WALLACE
MC CD

CAPT   RCIC

SURNAME (IN BLOCK LETTERS) CHRISTIAN NAMES				REG. NO	RANK	C.A.S.F. UNIT

AWARD	L. G. AUTHORITY	DATE	PAGE
MILITARY CROSS	CG 27	7-7-51	1885
CANADIAN FORCES DECORATION	CAO 107	25-6-56	

THE KING HAS BEEN GRACIOUSLY PLEASE
TO APPROVE THE FOLLOWING AWARD FOR
GALLANT AND DISTINGUISHED SERVICES
IN THE FIELD:

CITATION: FOR RECOMMENDATION FOR THE MILITARY CROSS

On April 24, 1951, 2Bn PPCLI was holding a position in the vicinity of SOCHANAMNI, Korea, (Mr 6893, Sheet CHUNCHON.) Capt. W. Mills was commander of "D" Company which held the west flank of the battalion and brigade area.

At approximately 0100 hrs, the enemy, switching his attack from the eas flank, struck hard at "D" Company on the west. A lenghtly battle ensued and the enemy succeeded in infiltrating in strength through the "D" Company area.

Capt. Mills disregarding his own safety called artillery fire from thre regiments right on top of his HQ and after two hours in this hazardous position broke off the attack killing over one hundred of the enemy with very few casualties to his own troups.

CAPT John Graham Wallace Mills

Award Of

The Distinguished Conduct Medal

To

M800148 Private Wayne Robert Mitchell

Royal Canadian Infantry Corps

PRIVATE MITCHELL TWICE WOUNDED ON THE 25TH OF APRIL 1951 AT KAPYONG, KOREA SHOWED EXTRAORDI-NARY COURAGE DURING AN ATTACK MADE BY A STRONG ENEMY FORCE ON HIS PLATOON POSITION. AT 2150 HOURS APPROXIMATELY ONE HUNDRED CHINESE ATTACKED A POSITION HELD BY NO. 9 SECTION, 6 PLA-TOON, PRINCESS PATRICIA'S CANADIAN LIGHT INFAN-TRY OF WHICH MITCHELL WAS THEN A BREN GUNNER. NOT WITHSTANDING THE OVERWHELMING ODDS, WITH MARKED DETERMINATION HE HELD HIS GROUND, SKILL-FULLY USING HIS BREN GUN TO INFLICT MAXIMUM CASUALTIES ON THE ENEMY. HE WAS LARGELY RESPONSIBLE FOR REPULSING THIS ATTACK AND WAS WOUNDED IN THE CHEST DURING THE COURSE OF THE BATTLE. ALTHOUGH WOUNDED HE REFUSED TO LEAVE HIS BREN GUN AND WAS AN INSPIRATION TO THE REMAINDER OF THE PLATOON. HE WAS ORDERED TO REPORT TO PLATOON HEADQUARTERS TO HAVE HIS WOUND DRESSED, HE VOLUNTARILY CARRIED A WOUNDED COMRADE BACK TO SAFETY. BY 2400 HOURS THE CHINESE HAD OVER-RUN TWO SECTIONS OF 6 PLATOON AND WERE ATTACKING PLATOON HEADQUAR-TERS. PRIVATE MITCHELL AGAIN SKILLFULLY BROUGHT HIS BREN GUN INTO ACTION TO REPULSE THIS ATTACK. AT ONE STAGE SEEING HIS PLATOON SERGEANT WITH SIX WOUNDED MEN PINNED DOWN BY ENEMY FIRE, VOLUNTARILY, WITHOUT REGARD FOR HIS SAFETY, HE RUSHED TOWARD THE ENEMY FIRING THE BREN GUN FROM HIS HIP, THUS ALLOWING THE WOUNDED TO BE MOVED SAFELY. IN THIS ACTION PRIVATE MITCHELL WAS WOUNDED FOR A SECOND TIME BY AN ENEMY GRENADE. AT 0100 HOURS ON 26 OF

APRIL 1951, PLATOON HEADQUARTERS AND ONE SEC-
TION WERE STILL HOLDING OUT BUT WERE NEARLY
OUT OF AMMUNITION. THE PLATOON COMMANDER
ORDERED HIS MEN TO WITHDRAW 100 YARDS TO THE
DEFENCES OF 5 PLATOON WHO WERE ALSO UNDER AT-
TACK. DURING THE WITHDRAWAL PRIVATE MITCHELL
EXPOSED HIMSELF TIME AND AGAIN, MOVING FROM
FIRE POSITION TO FIRE POSITION, WHERE HE COULD
BEST ENGAGE THE ENEMY TO COVER THE WITH-
DRAWAL. AT 0300 HOURS AFTER THE FOURTH ATTACK
HAS BEEN REPULSED, MITCHELL HAS HIS WOUNDS
DRESSED BY THE COMPANY MEDICAL ASSISTANT BUT
REFUSED TO BE EVACUATED AND STAYED AT HIS BREN
GUN POST FOR THE REMAINDER OF THE NIGHT. PRIVATE
MITCHELL'S COURAGE, DETERMINATION AND SKILL
WERE AN INSPIRATION TO THE REST OF THE SOLDIERS
IN HIS PLATOON AND COMPANY. HIS ACTIONS GREATLY
ASSISTED HIS COMPANY IN SUCCESSFULLY DEFENDING
THE POSITION AND INFLICTING HEAVY CASUALTIES ON
THE ENEMY. AT DAYLIGHT PRIVATE MITCHELL COULD
HARDLY STAND FOR LOSS OF BLOOD, HIS COMPANY
COMMANDER ORDERED HIM TO REPORT TO THE MEDI-
CAL OFFICER WHO HAD HIM EVACUATED BY HELICOP-
TER IMMEDIATELY.

Award of

The Military Medal

To

M800022 Lance-Corporal Smiley Douglas

Princess Patricia's Canadian Light
Infantry

ON THE MORNING OF 25 of APRIL 1951, 2 BATTALION, PRINCESS PATRICIA'S CANADIAN LIGHT INFANTRY WAS HOLDING A POSITION IN AN AREA THREE MILES NORTH OF KAPYONG, KOREA. PART OF THE DEFENCES OF TACTICAL HEADQUARTERS WAS A FIELD OF NO. 36 GRENADES SET WITH TRIP WIRES. AT APPROXIMATELY 0800 HOURS A PLATOON SERGEANT FROM "B" COMPANY LEFT THE RECOGNIZED PATH AND LED HIS MEN INTO THE FIELD OF BOOBY TRAPS. ONE GRENADE EXPLODED SERIOUSLY WOUNDING ONE MAN AND KILLING AN-OTHER. TWO MEN WERE CLOSE TO ANOTHERGRENADE WHICH HAD BEEN TRIPPED AND SMOKING, LANCE-CORPORAL DOUGLAS YELLED AT THEM TO LIE DOWN, RUSHED FORWARD AND GRABBED THE GRENADE IN AN ATTEMPT TO THROW IT AWAY. IT EXPLODED IN HIS HAND, BLOWING HIS HAND OFF. LANCE-CORPORAL DOUGLAS, BY HIS BRAVE ACT AND COMPLETE DISRE-GARD FOR HIS OWN SAFETY UNDOUBTEDLY SAVED THE LIVES OF THE MEN IN QUESTION.

Award of
The Military Medal
To
M800036 Private Kenneth Francis Barwise
Princess Patricia's Canadian Light Infantry

PRIVATE BARWISE, D COMPANY, 2ND BATTALION, PRINCESS PATRICIA'S CANADIAN LIGHT INFANTRY SHOWED OUT-STANDING COURAGE DURING THE KAPYONG BATTLE, 23-26 APRIL 1951. DURING THE NIGHT 24-25 APRIL 1951, 12 PLATOON OF D COMPANY WAS COMPLETELY OVERRUN AND THE REMAINING PLATOON AND COMPANY HEAD-QUARTERS WERE SURROUNDED AND CUT OFF. PRIVATE BARWISE PLAYED AN IMPORTANT PART IN THE DEFENCE OF COMPANY HEADQUARTERS AND DURING THE NIGHT HE WAS CREDIT4ED WITH KILLING SIX CHINESE AT VERY CLOSE RANGE. ON THE MORNING OF 25 APRIL 1951 REALIZ-ING THE SERIOUSNESS OF THE SITUATION IN D COMPANY AREA , HE MADE HIS WAY ALONE TO C COMPANY AND LED A PLATOON OF C COMPANY INTO 12 PLATOON LOCATION TO CLEAR OUT THE ENEMY. DURING THE PLATOON ATTACK HE PERSONALLY RE-CAPTURED ONE VICKERS MACHINE GUN AND DESPITE ENEMY SMALL ARMS FIRE BROUGHT THE GUN INTO ACTION COVERING THE PLATOON ASSAULT. LATER THE SAME MORNING 10 PLATOON REPORTED THEY WERE RUNNING SHORT OF AMMUNITION. PRIVATE BARWISE VOLUNTEERED TO CARRY AMMUNITION FORWARD AND RUNNING THE GAUNTLET OF SNIPER AND SMALL ARMS FIRE DELIVERED 12 BANDOLIERS AND 2 BOXES OF GRENADES TO THE HARD PRESSED PLATOON. DURING THE AFTERNOON HE LED A PARTY OF AMMUNI-TION BEARERS AND STRETCHER BEARERS TO 10 PLATOON AND ASSISTED IN THE EVACUATION OF THE WOUNDED. TIME AFTER TIME DURING THE PERIOD THAT HIS COMPANY WAS UNDER ATTACK PRIVATE BARWISE VOLUNTARILY EX-POSED HIMSELF TO ENEMY FIRE WHILE UNDERTAKING SEVERAL DANGEROUS MISSIONS. HIS BRAVERY AND COM-PLETE DISREGARD FOR PERSONAL SAFETY UNDER FIRE WAS AN INSPIRATION TO HIS COMRADES AND CONTRIB-UTED LARGELY TO THE SUCCESSFUL AND THE GALLANT STAND MADE BY THE BATTALION AT KAPYONG.

EXTRACTS FROM
WAR DIARY

2nd Battalion PPCLI

KOREA

April 23rd - April 30th
1951

236 - 8	Apr 23
238 - 9	Apr 23, 24
239 - 41	Apr 24, 25
242	Apr 26
243	Apr 27, 28, 29
244	Apr 30

WAR DIARY

A.F.M. I.
A.F.J 218
600m-7-42 (A.I)
H.Q. 1772-39-1658

Original duplicate and triplicate
to be forwarded to O.i/c 2 nd
Echelon for disposal

Instructions regarding preparation of
War Diary (which will be kept from the
day of n obliteration, creation or
embodiment), are contained in F.S. Re gs
Vol 1.
Title pages will be prepared.

Place	Date	hour	Summary of Events and Information	Remarks, references, appendices and initials
Corps reserve area Korea	23 Apr		Battalion activities still confined to interior economy despite disturbing reports of enemy activity on the front.	
			Last night at 2100 hrs a strong enemy force launched an attack against elements of the 2nd ROK Regt in the vicinity square 7118 and 7418 and by 2215 hrs had penetrated to the 15 East-West grid line causing a withdrawal throughout the entire sector. By midnight HQ 6 ROK Div could no longer give locations of their units and in the opinion of the US 9.Corps Commander the situation had collapsed beyond control of the 6 ROK Div.	
			At 0800 hrs Lt-Col J.R. Stone and the IO left for Bde and upon returning at 0900 hrs a Bn "R" Group was called for 1100 hrs and the Coy Commanders, MMG Officer, Mortar Officer, Sigs Officer and Arty Officer left for a recce of the position the battalion was to occupy tonight.	
			Due to taking the wrong road at the start the "R" Group did not return from it's recce of Hill 677 MR 685935 until 1730 hrs.	
			The Bn "O" Group was called at 1800 hrs and the CO outlined and passed his final orders.	
			The Bde position will be as follows 1 Middlesex are to occupy the high ground vicinity Hill 794 in square 6996 with 3 coys, 1 coy of the 1 Middlesex is to be detached to support 1 troop of the 16 NZ Fd Regt which will be in the vicinity of TOKAE-RI in support of 19 Regt 6 ROK Div. 2 PPCLI will occupy the high ground extending from the MSR West to Hill 677 square 6893. 3 RAR plus the 72nd Tank Coy will occupy high ground in squares 7293 and 7393.	[signature]

WAR DIARY

Instructions regarding preparation of
War Diary (which will be kept from the
day of a mobilization, creation or
embodiment), are contained in F.S. Regs
Vol 1:
Title pages will be prepared.

Original duplicate and triplicate
to be forwarded to O.i/c 2 nd
Echelon for disposal

A.F.M 11
A.F.G 218
(600m-7-4- (SAC)
H.Q. 172-39-1658

Place	Date	Hour	Summary of Events and Information	Remarks, references to appendices and initials
Corps reserve area	23 Apr	(Cont'd)	The 1 KOSB will relieve the 1 A & SH vicinity Hill 225 at MR 717290. At 1900 hrs the battalion moved off and with the exception of The Hq and the mortars was in position at 2200 hrs. Due to narrowness of the road, the half tracks of the mortars were unable to move quickly and Tac HQ was not in position at MR 659926 until 0400 hrs 24 Apr. A Coy went firm on high ground at MR 700935, B Coy at MR 682947, C Coy at MR 692938, D Coy at MR 682933.	
			At 2000 hrs the 3 RAR were in position in squares 7293 and 7393, their Tac HQ was in the village of SOKCHANG-NI at MR 724927, the 72nd tank coy was deployed in the valley and on the high ground just East of their Tac HQ. At 2100 hrs the 1 Middlesex, influenced by the rapid withdrawal of the 6th ROK Div, and fearing for the safety of their detached coy withdrew from their assigned area to the high ground dominating a bend of the KAPYONG River in squares 6991 and 7091. By 2200 hrs leading elements of the 118th CCF Div were heavily engaging the 2 Australian coys on the low ridge line extending North-East from the village of SOKCHANG-RONG at MR 725940. Failing to dislodge the Australians at this point the attacking Chinese force which now constituted nearly 2 full Regts diverted their main attack to the Australian coys holding the high ground leading to Hill 504 square 7493. The attack continued without letup throughout the night, and by 0900 hrs with his communications disrupted, his CP continually over-run by small forces of Chinese, and without the support of the 42 inch mortars, or of the 1 Middlesex coy assigned to protect his left flank, Lt-Col Ferguson MC, Commanding the 3 RAR was forced to relinquish command to his coy comdrs to bring their coys out as best they might.	
			The 72nd tank coy made 11 trips to the the 3 RAR positions to evacuate wounded to the 3 RAR HQ now in position at MR 702914.	

A.F.M L:
A.F.W 218
600m-7-L2 (542)
H.Q. 172-39-1658

Original duplicate and triplicat
to be forwarded to O.i/c 2 nd
Echelon for disposal

WAR DIARY

Instructions regarding preparation of
War Diary (which will be kept from the
day of mobilization, creation or
embodiment), are contained in F.S. Regs
Vol 1.
Title pages will be prepared.

Place	Date	Hour	Summary of Events and information	Remarks, references to appendices and initials
Corps reserve area		23 Apr (Cont'd)	The evacuation of wounded was completed by 1400 hrs 24 April 51 and it was shortly to be the turn of the 2 PPCLI to bear the brunt of the Chinese attack. Australian casualties numbered 155 killed and wounded for the period of 2100 hrs 23 Apr to 1400 hrs 24 Apr 51.	
Tac Hq	24 Apr		MR 699926. Tac HQ and the mortars were in position by 0400 hrs. Coys dug in as rapidly as possible in preparation for heavy attacks that were expected that night. Throughout the day, reports continued to come in from the forward coys of an enemy build-up all along the battalion front.

By 0730 hrs elements of the 118 CCF Div had infiltrated the Bis area at least as far as the village of TUNGMUDIE MR 709922 and to meet this threat Lt-Col Stone moved B Coy from it's extended position ahead of D Coy, on to the hill feature protecting the back door to the battalion area. B Coy was in position on the hill feature at MR 706927 by 1100 hrs.

Tanks of 72 tank coy by this time engaged in supporting the withdrawal of the 3 RAR and evacuating their wounded opened fire on B Coy as they occupied the hill feature, wounding one man slightly. By 1300 hrs continual reports were coming in from B Coy of increasing enemy activity in the area of the village of NABCHON at MR 708928. B Coy continued to prepare it's newly occupied position as rapidly as possible in anticipation of an attack that night.

At approximately 2130 hrs Major C.V.Lilley MC, OC B Coy reported a concentration of 400 Chinese on the flat ground below his forward platoon position and asked for arty and mortar concentrations on this area, by 2200 hrs the forward platoon commanded by Lt H. Ross was being engaged with increasing ferocity and by 2230 hrs Major Lilley reported that his forward platoon had been partially over-run and was pulling back into the main coy defense area vicinity MR 706927.

(Cont'd) | |

238

WAR DIARY
OR
INTELLIGENCE SUMMARY

(Erase heading not required)

Summary of Events and Information

Instructions regarding preparation of War diary (which will be kept from first day of allotment, eutimise or embodiment), are contained in F.S. Regs. Vol. 1.

This page will be prepared.

Original, duplicate and triplicate to be fwd to O. I/c 2nd Echelon for disposal.

Place	Date	Hour	Summary of Events and Information	Remarks to appear init
Tac HQ	Apr 24	Cont	By 2300 hrs the greater part of the over-run platoon had managed to return to the coy defense perimeter. Due to the fierce nature of the fighting, the darkness, and confusion of the withdrawal exact casualty figures were difficult to obtain.	
			At the same time as the attack was in progress on B Coy positions a small body of Chinese attempted to infiltrate the battalion area by approaching up the valley behind Tac HQ. The machine guns of the mortar platoon engaged this enemy and succeeded in beating off this threat, with unknown results. Shortly afterwards a large body of Chinese were seen fording the KAPYONG River MR 702919. The bright moonlight silhouetted the Chinese and gave the 50 calibre machine guns on the half tracks a good target.	
	25		At 0130 hrs D Coy reported considerable movement in their Coy area, particularly in the 10 platoon area, and called for arty and 81mm Mortar DF fire. By 0200 hrs it was apparent that a considerable force, later estimated at 200 men, was moving against D Coy. The axis of their attack lay along the ridge line leading to Hill 677 from the WEST. 10 platoon commanded by Lt MG LEVY (was the western-most platoon of the Coy and by 0230 hrs was heavily engaged from 3 sides by an overwhelming number of Chinese. The attack developed so rapidly and attained such a momentum that the MMG section supporting 10 platoon from 12 platoon was over-run and the gun temporarily lost to the enemy. In this brief action both members of the MMG crew were killed at their gun which was later recovered was found to have an unexpended portion of the belt still in position. Without the support of this MMG section the position of 10 platoon would have been even more desperate than it was.	
			By 0300 hrs 10 platoon was cut off and 12 platoon was completely over-run and had withdrawn to Coy HQ. Lt MG LEVY asked for close in mortar and arty support. The acting Coy Commander, Capt JGW MILLS, realising that his outnumbered Coy must have some relief called for the support requested by Lt LEVY bringing fire to bear very close to his own Coy positions. Most of this fire was concentrated on the most heavily engaged platoon of the Coy. This stratagem was successful in driving off the attacking Chinese however, the Chinese continued to engage D Coy until 0700 hrs.	
			The Chinese continued to attempt an infiltration of the battalion area through D Coy despite the arty and mortar fire. Each time arty engaged them they were	

WAR DIARY

OR

INTELLIGENCE SUMMARY

(Erase heading not required)

*M.F.M. 11
A.F.C. 2118
6000—1/₂ 9431)
H.Q. 1*.

Original, duplicate and triplicate to be forwarded to O. I/c 2nd Echelon for disposal.

ons regarding preparation of War
h will be kept from first day of
creation or embodiment), are con-
Regn. Vol. 1.
es will be prepared.

Date	Hour	Summary of Events and Information	Remarks, references to appendices and initials
Apr 25		forced to withdraw, but continued to engage D Coy with accurately sighted MMG and Mortar fire. With the approach of day light the Chinese withdrew and 12 platoon re-established its position between Coy HQ and 10 platoon.	
		Throughout the day the Chinese continued to maintain their harassing fire on 10 platoon and the remainder of D Coy. Supplies were brought up under fire and at one time it was thought that 10 platoon would have to be withdrawn from its exposed position, but at last light 10 platoon was still on its lonely hill well out from the rest of the Company. Chinese long range AW fire made the Coy position uncomfortable throughout the day and night, but by the next morning Chinese pressure was completely removed and remained so until the battalion was relieved.	
		MR 699926, Pte BARWISE risked his life leading Lt WHITTAKER's platoon from C Coy in a successful attempt to recapture the MMG lost the previous night.	
		With the battalion surrounded and in need of supplies and ammunition Lt Col STONE called for an air drop the air drop took place at 1030 hrs and was very successful. Supply trains were organized and deliveries were made to the Coys as rapidly as possible.	
		By 1400 hrs patrols from B Coy reported the road at the base of the battalion position clear of the enemy and Lt Col JR STONE requested that further supplies and reinforcements be brought up by vehicle as rapidly as possible.	
		The coys continued to improve their positions in case of a delay of the battalion's relief and in anticipation of continued Chinese attack.	
		Elements of the 1st Cav Div were to move up the valley and counter-attack briefly in the area NORTH of our present position. Probable date of the 28th Brigade relief is the 26 Apr 51.	
		Enemy activity on the battalion front was limited to light patrolling without any penetration of the battalion perimeter.	
		With the relief of the 1 A and SH by the 1 KOSB to-day the changeover from	

WAR DIARY

OR

INTELLIGENCE SUMMARY

(Erase heading not required)

Summary of Events and Information

A.F.C. 2
sent-V
E.G. 15

Original, duplicate and triplicate to be forwarded to O. l/c 2nd Echelon for disposal.

Remarks, refs to appendicies initials

Instructions regarding preparation of War [...] (which will be kept from first day of [...]sation, creation or embodiment), are contained in F.S. Regn. Vol. 1.

the pages will be prepared.

Date	Hour
Apr 25	

the 27th --- to the 28th BCB is complete. In a special order of the day Brigadier BA BURKE turned over to 28 Brigade and commended the traditions of 27 Brigade and of those units of the Commonwealth Forces remaining with 28 Brigade in Korea.

At 1900 hrs warning order was recieved from 28 Brigade for the proposed withdrawal on the 26 Apr 51.

Capt DE HARRISON promoted to Major, Coy Commander of C Coy.

WAR DIARY

OR

INTELLIGENCE SUMMARY

(Erase heading not required)

Summary of Events and Information

Original, duplicate and triplicate to be forwarded
to O: I/c 2nd Echelon for disposal.

Instructions regarding preparation of War
....which will be kept from 1st day of
.... in treatment or embodiment), are con-
.... L Regn. Vol 1.
...ges will be prepared.

Date	Hour		Remarks, references to appendices as initials
Apr 26		MR 699926. At 0700 hrs CO received definite orders to the effect that the relief would take place and that it was to be complete by 1630 hrs. The relieving battalion is to be 1 Bn, 5 RCT, 1 Cav Div. The order of the move in the Brigade will be KOSB, 1 Middlesex, 2 PPCLI, and 3 RAR. The battalion order of move C, B, A, Tac HQ and D Coy, 81mm and 4.2 inch mortar. The area to which that battalion moved was vicinity village of NONGOL at MR 623793 sheet 6627 II. Tac HQ was established in the vicinity village of NONGOL. C Coy went on to Hill 260 at MR 627804. B Coy to high ground vicinity MR 623805. A Coy went on high ground vicinity MR 615796 and D Coy arrived at 2000 hrs took up a position on the hill feature at MR 624791. 81mm Mortars and F Echelon went into position at MR 624795. D Coy arrived late due to the slowness of the relieving force in arriving D Coy's area.	
		The anticipated axis of the Chinese advance was down the CHOJONG River valley from the NORTH-WEST. This was the axis of withdrawal of the badly mauled elements of the 21st RCT, 24 Div. The 19 RCT, 24 Div held the high ground due West from the town of CHANGGONG-NI, MR 610772. 28 Brigade was to from the rear guard to cover the withdrawal of the elements of 24 Div retreating from the vicinity of HIGM-NI, MR 548866.	
		No activity throughout the night and a continued and orderly withdrawal is scheduled for tomorrow.	

N.F.M 1i
A.F.C 218
600m-7-46 (3421)
H.Q. 1772-39-1658

Original duplicate and triplicate
to be forwarded to 0.i/c 2 nd
Echelon for disposal

WAR DIARY

Instructions regarding preparation of
War Diary (which will be kept from the
day of mobilization, creation or
embodiment), are contained in F.S. Regs
Vol 1.
Title pages will be prepared.

Place	Date	Hour	Summary of Events and information	(Remarks, references and appendices and initials)
HANGOL Korea	27 Apr		MR 623794. To-day the battalion moved further back to vicinity HAL-DONG sheet 6626 1 and occupied another rear guard position on the high ground in squares MR 5370, 5470. The battalion arrived in it's new area at 1630 hrs and occupied previously un-recced areas in the dark and driving rain. The coys spent the night digging in. The night passed without activity.	AMMcK
HAL-DONG Korea	28 Apr		At 0700 hrs a message was recieved from 28 Bde HQ in forming the CO that the Bde was being withdrawn to a Corps reserve position in the vicinity of INGITONG MR CS 6947 sheet CHUNCHON 1/250,000. At 0900 hrs the battalion moved off accompanied by our 4.2 inch mortar support coy and arrive in the Bde rest area at approximately 1530 hrs. The men extremely tired by this time, and very much in need of an opportunity to rest, clean their equipment and dry out their uniforms.	AMMcK
	29 Apr		MR CS 6947. Battalion activities confined to interior economy and rest throughout the day. At 1300 hrs the CO was informed of an impending move into an area East of our present location which the battalion had previously occupied. At 1430 hrs the CO left for an air recce of the area to which we were scheduled to move. At 1600 hrs he returned to camp and called for an "O" Group at 1630 hrs at which he gave preliminary orders for a move sometime tomorrow, or the day after. Major Tighe 2 i/c battalion took Coy Comdrs on a recce of battalion defensive positions in the YANGPONG area.	AMMcK

243

WAR DIARY

N.F.M.1
A.F.C 218
600m-7-4C (5421)
H.Q. 1772-39-1658

Original duplicate and triplica
to be forwarded to O.i/c 2 nd
Echelon for disposal

Instructions regarding preparation of
War Diary (which will be kept from the
day of a mobilisation, creation or
embodiment), are contained in P.S. Re ga
Vol 1.
Title pages will be prepared. —

Place Date	Hour	Summary of Events and Information	Remarks, references to appendices and initials
Corps reserve area Korea	30 Apr	ME CS 6947. Another day spent on interior economy and resting the battalion under Major H.D.P. Tighe N.D.P. Tighe for a preliminary recce of the new area. A recce party was despatched tomorrow.	
		At 2345 hrs the orders for the battalion move tomorrow were changed and the battalion is now to take up defensive positions on the HAN River vicinity square ME 4360 on the TOKTO sheet near the village of TOKSA-RI, they will relieve 1 Bn 19 ROK 24 Hrs	

(H.D.P. Tighe) Major M C
A/CO
2 PPCLI

APPENDIX "D"

KAPYONG

A Speech by Colonel JR Stone, DSO 2 bars, MC
To
The Officers of Third Battalion PPCLI
December 18, 1973
Excerpts from Colonel Stone's seven page speech
Page 4 (188) paragraphs two and three

"Platoons are to be Mutually Supporting."

"Hill 677 is about a mile and a half across, gullied, wooded and impossible to defend in the classic manner of deploying companies to support each other. <u>Each company had to develop it's own defended locality, the platoons to be mutually supporting.</u> The gaps between companies would have to be covered, to some extent, by defensive fire tasks of the Medium Machine Gun (MMG) section, the battalion 81mm mortars, the US mortar company and the New Zealand 25 pounder (artillery) regiment.

"I issued orders in the late afternoon of April 23 and we commenced moving into position that afternoon. <u>The defensive plan followed the lines of my appreciation in that companies were in individual localities, deployed so that platoons were mutually supporting.</u> Our six Vickers MMGs were deployed by sections giving depth to the defence, and covering the gaps in-between companies. A company of the US 120mm mortars supported with defensive fire task but when the battle got hot on the Australian front the FOO from the US mortars walked out and never a "pop" did we get from him. The New Zealand artillery regiment had far too big a front to cover but they gave it their all."

245

APPENDIX "E"

WITNESS STATEMENTS

12 Platoon Patrol - Mass Execution-Gumcochyi Patrol, May 1951

I find it difficult to remember much about the details of this patrol, though a few points stand out in my memory.

Our platoon commander was Lt. Gray. The whole platoon went on this patrol. It seemed to me we went an awfully long way out in front our battalion position. It was a hot day we were still wearing our winter uniforms.

I remember clearly... enemy soldiers all in three lines... Like a platoon. There were a lot of them. All dead. They were in a sort of sitting position, rigidly upright, all of them. It was not natural. What I remember most was the awful stench of death. I did not like it. I remember circling a long way out from them, because I could not stand the smell.

James Wanniandy

James Wanniandy

131104 15411 87th Avenue

Edmonton, Alberta, T5R 4K3

February 28th, 1998.

To Whom it May Concern - 98 02 12

Statement of Pte (S/Sgt) George Nestor
"Gumcochyi" Patrol, Korea, May 1951
Lt. Hub Gray, 12 Pl, "D" Coy 2nd Bn PPCLI

I was a member of 12 Platoon, but at the time was attached to "D" Company HQ, as runner. I was made aware of the patrol the day prior when the order came down to Capt Mills. Capt Mills was in command in the absence of Major Swinton, who was in charge of the Brigade NCO School.

I have read the report, written by Hub Gray, of the "Gumcochyi" patrol, made by 12 Platoon, "D" Company, during the first half of May 1951. I concur that the contents of the report are essentially as I remember it.

Captain Mills selected 12 to make the patrol. Being aware of the patrol, I was present the next morning when the platoon boarded tanks of the American 73rd Heavy Tank Battalion. I went to wish my buddies luck.

The information brought back at the end of the day was a hell of a surprise to all of us. They had found a whole platoon of enemy soldiers dead in some sort of mass formation. The information caused one hell of a buzz amongst us because of the queer way in which they all died at one time, on their knees sitting on their haunches. Gray wrote a report for Mills, saying he believed they died from some form of chemical warfare. That report caused a lot of concern - was it going to happen to us - when? We expected that there would be another patrol to further investigate the whole thing, but nothing happened. After a week, it faded away; we were preparing to move off of Line Golden, in pursuit of the enemy.

George Nestor
6033 Camass Place
Duncan, BC, V9L 3Z1

Statement - Pte (Sgt) C. (Neil) Neufeld

"Gumcochyi" Patrol, Korea, May 1951.

We were on Golden Line, when 12 Platoon took this patrol. I remember we were happy to be given a ride on the American Tanks, instead of walking all those miles in front of our position. The weather was very hot; we still had our winter gear on. The tanks pulled in just after breakfast, if that's what you can call "C" rations.

Someone put their foot on the exhaust pipe and in a few seconds darn near burnt the bottom of their boot off. Best Hot Foot I have ever seen.

At Gumcochyi the tanks parked and our patrol took off on foot. We were to find where the enemy had dug in. Hub Gray took a photograph of my section moving off along the railroad tracks, with the smashed up rail station behind us. I was fourth in the photo, carrying my Bren Gun, and two hundred rounds of ammunition. We were about two hours out when we sighted the enemy.

After pausing to examining the lay of the land, Lt Gray sent my section onto the right flank to give covering fire while the other two sections moved forward in an attack formation. The enemy formation was in the middle of a broad valley. There was no firing. The enemy troops were in line like an oversized platoon. All dead, sitting upright. Bloody peculiar, I thought. The men talked about these enemies dead for sometime afterward.

I saw a lot of strange things in Korea, this just added one more event to my war. To me it was all part of 'another days work.

Neil Neufeld
Apt. A 101   8620 Jasper Avenue, Edmonton AB

APPENDIX "F"

PLACEMENT NOMINAL
ROLL - KAPYONG

2Bn PPCLI,   EFFECTIVE 23/25 APRIL 1951

If you can position anyone not included herein in their platoon etc.
please notify Hub Gray,
c/o PPCLI Archives, Museum of the Regiments
4520 Crowchild Trail, Calgary, AB, T2T 5J4

The Battalion rest area prior to the battle was near the town of Chung-chon-Ni, MR 688886, Sheet 6727-4, which became "B" Echelon. "A" and "B" Echelon withdrew their positions a number of time once the battle was joined.

Note: *KIA* - Killed in Action, Kapyong, April 23-5

KIA & Date - Killed in Action, at another time.

COMMANDING OFFICER

LCol   Stone   James Riley, DSO 2 Bars, MC.

Awarded his third DSO for service in Korea.

The troops nicknames "Stone Head or Salmon Head." Defined by a Time Magazine headline in 1950, as **"The Bald Headed, Beak Nosed, Eagle**." Stone did not seem to care for this designation, thereafter reporters were seen to be a scarce commodity.

Those who served with Stone in Italy, at Ortona, have stated that he was **"The Epitome of the fighting human leader."**

Exercise Sweetbriar (1949-50) in the Yukon. Combined forces of the Canadian and American Armies. When **MGen Chris Vokes**, CO Western Command, Stone's old 1st Division Commander, heard he was to be escorted by **LCol Big Jim Stone of Ortona**, he is reported to have said, **"Me' God! Who is going to protect me!?"**

Kapyong, 0300 hrs April 25th 1951, the 2Battalion was surrounded by the Chinese. RSM Les Grimes took all available soldiers at Tac HQ outside to form a perimeter defence. Big Jim Stone sitting at his desk, grasping a rifle across his knees, virtually shaking with anticipation and said,
"Let the Bastards come!"

Pte   LaFramboise RX - LCol Stone's driver.

2IC   Major Tighe Henry HDP MC A Echelon, Tactical HQ

Adjutant   Captain Turnbull   Gorden J   "Bugs Bunny"

Asst Adj   Lieut Beaucuchamp, AC   "Shammy"
Sgt   Church   AJ   Desrosiers   JJ
        Essex   RJ
        Bn Orderly Room clerk   Cpl Ellis   Jud
RSM   Grimes Les F   A superb RSM, always a gentleman. "Daddy"

Intelligence Section
Lieut   McKenzie   APP
Sgt   Smith   GSL
Cpl   Rawlinson   L/Cpl Crocker, HR
Pte   Canfield   Mel: Making Notes of the conversations
        between Tactical HQ and the Companies, for entry into the
        War Diary.
        Kawanami   M   Ratinosky   Andy   Walsh   Harley

HEADQUARTERS COMPANY
Major Grant   Don W "Punchy"   "B" Ech   LOB
CSM   Falconer   J   "House"   LOB
CQMS Clarke   CW   LOB
Pte   Gallamore   VB   Smith   Roy   LOB

Cooks
Sgt.   Gordon MC

Medical
Captain Fitzgerald   Kieth   E MO   Tac Hq   RAP
Sgt   Pay   George J
Sgt   Gilbert   WB   Sanitation
Cpl   Anderson   Kostis   DG   Shuler WJ
L/Cpl   Marsh   KB   Swan   Jack

Pte	Copley	Donald R	
	Miles	JW "Doc"	Stewart

Quartermaster

Capt	Edwards	Murray C	Tac HQ

Promoted to QM on the 22, taking over from Captain Paddy Pyne

RQMS	England	CL
S/Sgt	McLennan	PD

Padres - Catholic

Capt	Valalee	Joseph	A Echelon and Tactical HQ

Moved up to F Echelon with Major Tighe. One night, by accident, he drove into an encampment of about 50-armed enemy soldiers. Valalee had been a missionary in China for 17 years. When they tried to take Valalee prisoner, he promptly stood up in his jeep and in short order delivered "A Hell of a Blood and Thunder Lecture" in Chinese, sat down, turned around and drove off. He was later quoted as saying that the enemy soldiers look absolutely stunned. So was Valalee.

C of E

Capt	Cunningham	RGC	A Echelon and Tactical HQ

Both Padres came to Tactical HQ, with Major Tighe, noon on the 24th.

Signals

Capt.	Combe	Edwin G	"Ed"	Tac HQ
Lieut	Keay	JF	"Ferdie"	A Ech LOB
Sgt	Sinclair	Elmer	James	
	Henry	Lineman		Tac HQ
	Siefret	J		
L/Cpl	Montgomery	JH	Storeman	A Ech LOB
L/Cpl	CrockerH	Ray	1900 set, Bde net	Tac HQ
Pte	Aylwin	Louis		
	Balinson	Morley		
	Irvine	James C		Tac HQ
	Parrington	Wm D		
	Polnuk	Adam E		Tac HQ
	Richardson	Norm F		

Transport

Lieut	Inglis	HR		"Downtown Harry"
CQMS	Trenter GS	*KIA 11 Oct 51*		
Sgt	Ferguson	JCW	Selkirk	I
Cpl	Riel	A Louis	Seifert	J
	Wilkinson	RC		
Pte	Brignell	R	Poupart	AG

LAD section: (Light Aid Detachment)
RCEME

Sgt	Goodmundson	Johnny I	Decoene	JJ
Pte	Croucher	Gordon L	Hoffman	CC
RCEME

Paymaster

Capt	Shaw	John A		LOB
Sgt	Bergen JW			

Welfare

Lieut	Campell	W J	"Bill"	LOB

Dental

Capt	Nesbitt	Frank M	LOB
Sgt	Flesher	LG	

Legal

Captain	Hanaway	LM MC	"Chub"	LOB
Driver	Pte Wagaczyk			

Regimental Police

Sgt	Larson	William	Provost Corps

Made the Recce of the withdrawal route.

L/Cpl	Hanson	Bill		
L/Cpl	Hibbs	DF		
Pte	Brazil	Walter R	Ryder	John A

Armourer

Sgt	Brown	RJ

SUPPORT COMPANY

Major	Henderson	Gordon "BB Eyes"	Battle Adjutant
CSM	Rudd	Jack A "Scudd"	
CQMS	Sundman	CE "Sonny"	

Medium Machine Gun Platoon,
Flame Thrower Section, Sniper section

Capt	Foulds	Andy		
	Lee	Jung Ok	Korean, Interpreter	
Sgt	Shearer	A		
Cpl	Cunningham	ERM		
L/Cpl	Burns	DW		
	Carr	Maurice	*KIA AT 12 PL*	
	MacDonald	Bruce	*KIA AT 12 PL*	
	MacKenzie	Bob D	Mitchell	
	Paquet	Joe W	Richardson	

Sniper section

S/Sgt	Gawthorn	Ken	Cassidy	ABB

Pioneer Patoon

Lieut	Hurst	Lorne L		
Sgt	Taplin	Al		LOB
A/Sgt	Pennell	DM	"Red"	

#1 Assault Section

Cpl	Douglas Smiley**			
Pte	Beattie	Bill	Cote	BN
	Dunn	Joe, Driver	Hoffman	CC
	Long	Bud	"slim" White	Red
		Jeep "Jiggs"		

** Awarded MM. An outgoing patrol, B Coy tripped a #36 grenade booby trap. Douglas dived to toss the smoking grenade away, time had expired, his right hand was blown away, legs badly wounded.

#2 Assault Section

Cpl	McQuaig	AL	"Sleepy"	
L/Cpl	Potrias	JG	Welch	W Ken
Pte	Albert	G	Dionne	HF
	Lougheed	GV	Webb	SR
		Jeep "Violet"		

#3 Assault Section

Cpl	Repay	Harry
Cpl	Cook	AW
Pte	Albert	AG

	Long	ME	"Slim"
	Wall	Jim,	Driver
	Walker	W Don *KIA*	
			Jeep "Bugaboo"

Trades Section

Cpl	Deleeuw	A			
A/Cpl	Anderson	J Carl	"Boxer"		
L/Cpl	Cardas	C			
L/Cpl	Inglee	H			
Pte	Andereson	CRI			
	Black "Blackie,"		Driver	Blacquiere	LF
	Dugray	AG,	Driver	Howard	WG
	Lynch	AL			
	Running	Howard			

RCEME Mechanic - L/Cpl Hoffman Cy. - MiD, April 12, 1952.

RC Engineers -

Pte	Powell	Tommy

Anti-Tank Platoon nicknamed "Constant Force"
Complete Nominal Roll, April 23-25: Courtesy of AM Sim,

Lieut.	Constant	AH	"Rick"		
Pl Sgt	Sims	AM			
Gun Sgt	Myhre	WE			
Cpl	Clarke	A		MacAulay	SV
	Mills	F		Muise	JP
	Pothier	CL		Shuman	SH
L/Cpl	Kadey	LG		MacNeil	JA
	Martin	PA		Shea	HC
	Woodside	DM			
Pte	Alward	FL		Atcheson	KD
	Anthony	RK		Barr	LR
	Beadle	JV		Buckland	MP
	Burk	LE		Burton	FJ
	Butts	LL		Campbell	HE
	Carriere	JE		Christie	AM
	Doan	DG		Jackson	BC
	Jobagy	JP		Jones	CH
	Jones	JW		Kendall	J
	Lamb	RJ		Moratto	E
	Murdoch	JL		MacAulay	WB
	McGrath	AF		McIsaac	DH

Nicholson	AE	Nystrom	AB
Ohling	RF	Oldford	AJ
Randall	GH	Raphael	JM
Readman	JL	Simon	CC
Stewart	CM	White	HR
Wilson	H	Wolfe	E

Initially supplied with 17 pounder Anti-Tanks guns, they were not maneuverable in the hills of Korea. For a time they fulfilled a reconnaissance role, nicknamed "Constant Force." In late April 1951, after Kapyong American 75mm Recoilless Rifle Anti-Tank weapons were employed.

Mortar Platoon

Capt.	Hill	Lloyd	"Mother Hill"	
Lieut.	Gray	Hubert A	"Hub"	

Comd 4 MMG's,4 HMG's at Kapyong.
Apr 26 Comd of 12 Pl, "D" Company.

Sgt	Shields	JW	Hendrick	C
Cpl	Hudson	PE	"Pappy"	
Cpl	Plouffe	GL		
RCEME	Craftsman	Hoffman,	Robert J.	(Mechanic)
L/Cpl	Cook	George	Black	George
Pte	Anthony	RK Bob	Baker	GL
	Brydon,	Harry B	Burns	GJ or HL?
	Chrysler	WJ	Cruise	AJ
	Cuzboka	Michael	Harris	TD
	Lusty	RG	Morris	
	Robertson	Robbie	Smillie	SR
	Zarlarski	M		

A COMPANY

Major	Flint	George AF	"GAF"	"Cough-Cough"
			LOB	Jr NCOs School On R&R
Captain	Browne	Owen R	Acting OC	
CSM	Acton	Doug		
CQMS	Clark	Pat (?)		

1 PL

Lieut				
Sgt	Wellington	WOG		
Cpl	Arnold	JE	Crooks	SG
	Dunbar	AN		

L/Cpl	Gladden	JD		Lee	William
Pte	Andersen			Austin	AG
	Blank	GR		Cuipka	OE
	Davis	ARM		Gibson	DN
	Johanson	Dan		Johnson	DL

2PL

Lieut	Munro	Brian	
Sgt	Prince	Tommy	MM, Silver Star
			(Devil's Brigade WW II)
Cpl	Baker	OB	Bishop	John R
L/Cpl	Bastien	RE	
Pte's	Allen	IF	Bourgon	RJ
	Carneg	RF	Cassidy	"Butch"Clark
	Cormier	DJ	Murphy	MM
	Ross	D	Reimer	LD
	Soloman	

3PL

Lieut	Regan	JJ Jack	
Sgt.	Shearer	A	
Cpl	Barker	OP	Moores	LE
	Paille	John E	
Pte	Alexanderson	KF	Arsenault	CJ
	Baron	NN	Charman	WJ
	Clattenberg	Ralph	Clark	GS
	Coutts	Norm	Crumley	JWB
	Cumming	Bob	D'Arcis	JR
	DelFaco		Deitzer	JC
	Dunbar	GW	Fraser	DG
	Gibson	DN	Jones	

B COMPANY

Major	Lilley	C Vince, MC CD	"The Black Prince"
Capt	Pyne	PM CD	"Paddy"
CSM	Goldsworthy	GJ	"Little Jesus"
CQMS	Ferris	Ralph	
Cpl	Price	Dick LOB, Sinus problem, Stretcher Bearer

4 PL

Sgt	Newcomb	CH	"Pappy"	LOB R&R
A/Sgt	Cpl Query	EW	"Chick"	
L/Cpl	Denne	William H	L/Cpl Don	F Hibbs

*Long	ME	(*Twins)	*Long
Crook	John S	Davis	ARM
Doyle	CP	Golden	
Graham	JR	Green	AE
Hegberg	AE	Perley	RJ
Reid	BC	Whalen	Jim W
Wilmot	WJ	Cometu	PJ
Do Yhe			

5 PL

Lieut	Petrie	Charles A		
A/ Sgt	Cpl O'Brien			
Cpl	Moores	LE	Evans	GR
	Denne	WH		
Pte	Cadrez	JO	Carde	JO
	Dore	E	Dunphy	MA *KIA 11 July*
	Doherty	JK	Gowing	LM
	Henry ??		Kozak	A
	Lachance	DDJ	Menard	RW
	Mitchell	TB	Mitchell	R
	Murphy	M	Nelson	JH
	O'Dwyer	pm	Potts	E
	Reaume	Dell	Whalen	JW

6 PL

Lieut	Ross	Harold T	"Scarface"	
Sgt	Ulmer	Roy W		
Cpl	Szalahetka	HA	*KIA 29 June*	
Cpl	Evans	GR	*KIA*	
Cpl	Wabasca	A	L/Cpl Cook	J
Pte	Black	GJ	Butts	LL
	Campbell		Disobato	WR
	Dobbs	K	Eberts	RA
	Fielding	L	*KIA*	
	Hayes	CA	*KIA*	
	Hegberg	EA	Hibbs	D
	Lamey	RJ	Levesque	RW
	Marsh	K	Mitchell	WR**
	Morrow	Don	McCall	JK
	Nelson		Reaume	A
	Richardson	Ed	Tolver	RGH *KIA*

**Awarded the DCM, Kapyong. Though twice wounded he continued to man his Bren gun throughout the night. Three times he charged the enemy forces.

C COMPANY

Major Harrison   Del   "Snuffy"

Succeeded Major George, who was later awarded a DSO, Korea, serving with the 1 Battalion PPCLI. Evacuated April 25, he was posted to 3 Battalion PPCLI, Fort Lewis, USA.

Capt	Campbell	Jack D	"Jock"	R&R
CSM	Renwick	Rick		R&R
CQMS	Melnechuck	Mike	Acting CSM	
CQMS	Newcomb	CH		
Cpl	Shields	JW	Forward Mortar Controller	
Pte	Oshanski	Nick		
	Mercer	L.		

Major George, when commanding, established a "Defence Unit," 12 men, recruiting four from each platoon.

L/Cpl	Klyne	RE		
	Kirkhoff	"The Dog"		
Pte	Ilton	LW	Leach	AG
	Ward	John	Worsfold	Don

60mm Mortar section - C Coy HQ

Cpl	Klein	AJ		
Pte	Leach	AG		
Pte	Pickett	Fred	Worsfield	Don S
	Ilton	LW		

7 PL

Lieut	Entwistle	JLC	"Mert"	
Sgt	Brister	Jimmy		
Cpl	LaPointe	RE	Umperville	Ken
Pte	Howe	Chris	Green	AE
	Kolanchey	John	Lynch	Al
	LePage	JGR	Mahood	Vic J
	Meeter	Rod	Moore	KB
	Murray	RG	McDade	Ed
	McNeill	FR	Towestego	Steve

8 PL

Lieut.	Deegan,	Johnny

Sgt	McCuish	DA	DCM			
Cpl	Denne	William H		"Chicago Bill"		
L/Cpl	MacDonald					
Pte	Kelin	AJ		LaChance	DDJ	
	Gilmour	Ron		Moore	SWJ	
	Moreau	RJ		Munn	C	
	Thorsen	CH		Herman		

9 PL

Lieut	Whittaker	RD Troops nickname: "JD" (Juvenile Delinquent)		
Sgt	Tuttle	LA		
Cpl	Bolongo	JA		
	Dunphy	Kerry J - LOB NCOs School		
Pte	Downey	Tom	Glasner	DA
	Hansen	W	Nadeau	R
	Perley	RJ	Sandor	Paul
	Stephens	WR	Thomlinson	GE
	Thorsen	H	Turner	R
	White	Fred	Worsfold	Don

D COMPANY

Major	Swinton	RK Bob, MC	LOB	On R&R
Captain Mills**		JGW Wally		Acting OC

**Awarded MC - For relaying to tactical HQ, calls for supporting fire, originated by Lieut Mike Levy of 10 platoon.

CSM	Morris	Edwin H	"Eddy"
CQMS			
Pte	Nestor	George Coy HQ runner (Seconded from 12 Pl)	
Pte	Barwise**	Kenneth	60mm mortar
Pte	Grison	Jean Bernard	Operated the 300 set to Tac HQ.

**Awarded MM. Barwise at about 0700 April 25, twice ran 75 meters to retrieve bandoliers of .303 ammo at 12 Platoon west, abandoned position. He was shot at by Chinese snipers. Later Barwise and L/Cpl J Wanniandy recovered the disabled Vickers MMG at the same position, an escort was provided by Lieut Bob Whittaker's 9 Pl.

10 Pl

Lieut	Levy	Mike, (MiD Malaya, 1945)	
A/Sgt Cpl Watson		JI	
Cpl	Clouthier	Leroy "Roy"	Comd fwd section

Cpl	Andrews	JI	"The Enforcer" Sec Comd	
Cpl	Woodcock	N		
L/Cpl	White	Bill	Reserve Section Acting Sec Comd	
L/Cpl	Bortolotti	LE		
L/Cpl	Edmond	AM		
Pte	Allen	Bill	Ash	Tom
	Baxter	CR	Bordeleau	Jerry GF
	Cote	Bernie	Cometu	PJ
	Delroy	GAF	Densmore	BH
	Dionne	HF	Gifford	RF
	Hughes	KA	Nash	
	Nuible	A	Phiffer	Rudy
	Simpson	WH	Smith	RG
	Stein	Ken	Walker	GL
	Whalen	JW		

11 Pl

Lieut	Pearson	John		
Sgt	Markell	D		
Pte	Wotton	TB	*KIA*	Bren Gunner
	Lessard	JML	*KIA* ***	No 2, Bren
	Baker	DT	Harris	AH
	Price	Harry	Polnuk	AE
	Pourart	AG	Steele,	Harold J
	Shergold,	KJ	Simpson,	Neil
	Williamson	SP		
	Young,	Ronald *** *Claimed KIA at both 11 and 12platoon.*		

12 Pl

Sgt	Holligan	BW	Acting Platoon Comd, Seconded from 11 Platoon

13 Feb 1958. Holligan rescued a Patricia Paratrooper whose parachute became entangled outside the rear exit of a C119 aircraft; Exercise Bulldog, Canada. Holligan risked his life to rescue the soldier and was awarded the **George Medal**. The Medal was **presented by HM The Queen, 1959**.

Lieut. Lee Hill, was wounded, April 14. Lieut Hub Gray took command April 26.

Cpl	Lightfoot	H
Cpl	Dunbar	AN

L/Cpl	Wanniandy	JW			
L/Cpl	MacDonald				
MMG	Carr	Maurice	**KIA**		
&	MacDonald	Bruce	**KIA**		
		Killed manning the Vickers MMG			
L/Cpl	Edgely	HV	**KIA, 6 June**		
L/Cpl	Sharp				
Pte	Boldt	P		Bordeleau	GF
	Brown			Dempsey	CJ
	Embree	JW		Gallant	VL
	Gifford	RF		Goodwin	WI **KIA,14Oct**
	Hughes			McIssac	DH
	McRae	FJ		McAvena	K (age 14)
	Overland	AN		Rivard	CM
	Sauve	AJ		Sarty	WE
	Shaver	RW		Shergold	KJ
	Sparks	TC			
	Neufeld	C	"Neil"	Bren LMG, his # 2:	
	Lessard	JM	**KIA*** LMG**		

*** Claimed KIA at both 11 & 12 Pl.

SECOND BATTALION PPLCI LIAISON OFFICER, 27 BRITISH COMMONWEALTH BRIGADE HEADQUARTERS.

Lieut	Middleton	Rod M	Initial six weeks, Comd of 12 PL.

BATTALION JUNIOR NCOs SCHOOL
INSTRUCTIONAL STAFF, B ECHELON, SECOND COURSE, APRIL 1951.

Major	Flint	George A	"Gaff" or "Cough, Cough"	LOB R&R

Chief Instructor

Lieut	MacLeod	DG	"Bud"	(5 Pl)	LOB

MacLeod later enjoyed a unique posting:
6147 TACTICAL CONTROL GROUP (MOSQUITO), 5TH AIR FORCE, UNITED STATES AIR FORCE.
See Chapter 19, page 320.

JR NCOs SCHOOL INSTRUCTORS - continued:

CSM	Coutts	JC	"Jimmy"	LOB
Sgt	O'Brien	WA		LOB
Sgt	Rushton	Roy	(10Pl)	LOB

Sgt	Moran	Frank B		LOB
Cpl	Dunphy	Kerry		LOB
Pte	Black	George	Bugler	LOB

Course Candidates

The course was completed. An administrative problem developed. Course reports were not written on the required Army forms as they were not available. Lieut MacLeod on completion of the course wrote up individual reports and handed them to Major Don Grant, Commanding HQ Company. Grant initially stuffed them under his bed, for safe keeping, prior to forwarding them to the adjutant for processing. The documents somehow went astray. Ottawa, not having copies of the reports in hand, refused to recognize the "earned" qualifications. The graduated Junior NCOs all had to enroll in a similar course when they returned to Currie Barracks, Calgary, to qualify for the increased pay in rank, again run by Lieut Bud MacLeod! There were about 31 on the course. It was a typical Canadian Army SNAFU or FAFU.

Haley	LA	McCuish*	DA
MacKenzie	DE	MacKenzie	TA
Sauve	AJ	Tuttle	LA

*Later as a Sergeant he was awarded a Distinguished Conduct Medal (DCM). Still later in Canada, he held up a taxi driver in Toronto, and served time. His DCM turned up in a Florida pawn shop.

REINFORCEMENT OFFICERS, KAPYONG

Lieut	Botting	Gerry	LOB	Lost

At B Echelon a jeep was assigned to take Botting to the Battalion, to be posted to a rifle Company, but to first report to A Echelon, which was on the move and they could not locate it. Botting later took over 11 Platoon from Lieut John Pearson, in August. John fell over an embankment to land on his head and was given a medical discharge.

Lieut	Skelly	George	LOB	B Ech

Skelly had been at B Echelon, for two days awaiting assignment to a Rifle Company. "We had a party every night at Major Grant's infamous 'Banglestein's Bar'." The lore of Banglestein has been preserved in an appropriate song. The song so impressed Skelly that to this day he can sing every verse by heart. When the battle began B Echelon packed up and withdrew and continued to move several times. After Kapyong Skelly took command of the anti-tank platoon from Lt. Rick Constant, who injured his back falling off a truck during the withdrawal from Hill 677.

Killed at Kapyong:

Carr,	MS	Private	29
Evans,	GR	Corporal	23
Fielding,	LT	Private	23
Gladu,	LP	Private	19
Hayes,	CA	Private	21
Lessard,	JM	Private	23
MacAshill,	E	Corporal	23
Macdonald,	BM	Private	20
Marshal,	WJ	Private	22
Tolver,	RGH	Private	26
Walker,	RL	Private	23
Wotton,	TB	Private	22

KAPYONG REMEMBERED
Placement Nominal Roll - Kapyong (Only)

For inclusion of your name in the Kapyong Placement Nominal Roll, PPCLI Archives, Calgary, Alberta, please forward:

Name_____

Rank _____

Regimental Number _____

Company - Platoon _____

Position_____

Name of your OffIcer_____

NCO(s) _____

Others _____

Served from 19_____Retired19_____

Rank_____

Address_____

_____'Phone_____

E/mail _____

FAX _____

Mail to:

Hub Gray,
c/o PPCLI Archives, Museum of the Regiments
4520 Crowchild Trail, Calgary, AB, T2T 5J4

APPENDIX G

British Commonwealth 27th - 28th Infantry Brigades Korea, April 1951

Commonwealth Units	Short Text Reference
Second Battalion, Princess Patricia's Canadian Light Infantry	2PPCLI, Patricias or Second Patricias
Third Battalion The Royal Australian Regiment	3RAR
The Argyll and Sutherland Highlanders First Battalion	A&SH
King's Own Scottish Borderers Regiment	KOSBs
First King's Shropshire Light Infantry Regiment	KSLI
First Battalion The Middlesex Regiment (Duke of Cambridge's Own)	MX
16th Field Regiment, Royal New Zealand Artillery	16RNZA

STATED TIMES
The times stated herein and those of the War Diary may differ. Where it appears appropriate I have utilized the time provided by a veteran. *All times, whatever the source, are approximations.*

MAP REPRESENTATIONS.
Maps are drawn from a variety of sources, therefore the placement of formations may vary from map to map. All placements are approximate.

MILITARY FORMATIONS - TERMINOLOGY
Applicable in Korea, 1951

Echelon
There are three echelons in an Infantry Battalion. The composition may vary according to conditions and operations. The final decision is that of the Commanding Officer. At Kapyong:

F - Echelon- **"The Cutting Edge of the Army."** The Poor Bloody Infantry, forward fighting soldiers. Tactical Headquarters, four Rifle Companies and Support Company. (Detailed under Battalion)

A - Echelon - **Administrative -** Positioned one to three miles behind *F* echelon. There were times when A Echelon, due to the insurmountable mountainous terrain, was as much as ten miles behind the fighting line. At Kapyong it was initially about 4km to the rear, however, because of the flow of the battle it moved about six times. Under battalion control at Kapyong. Commanded by the second in command of the battalion. Personnel: Second in command of companies, padres, adjutant. Elements of transport, ammunition, supply, rations, petrol etc.

B - Echelon - **Administrative** - About 20 miles behind the front line Infantry at *F* echelon. Under Divisional or Brigade command. Assistant adjutant, assistant signals Officer, administrative elements, further transport, army stores etc. At Kapyong A and B were initially together at the rest area. There is some discussion as to their varied placements as the battle raged and the army withdrew.

Adjutant
Personnel - administrative officer of the battalion.

Air Observation Post (AOP) - An unarmed light aircraft of the US Army. Accompanied by an artillery officer observer, flying low over the forward fighting areas and behind the enemy lines, relaying fire orders to artillery batteries. Also passing along intelligence information.

Armour
Company A, 72 Heavy Tank Battalion, US Army. Fifteen M4A3 Sherman tanks. Assigned to the Australians.

Artillery at Kapyong

BRITISH BRIGADE ARTILLERY
16 Field Regiment, Royal New Zealand Artillery (16RNZA). Equipped with 25 pounder British designed field guns. The Regiment is divided into three batteries, each battery composed of two troops, each troop having 4 guns. Total 24 guns.

- Battery Commander (BC). In battle he is stationed at the Infantry Battalion Tactical Headquarters, passing orders to his battery gun line. At Kapyong the 16RNZA gun line on the 24 April, was initially located near the eastern base of Hill 667. As the Chinese advanced they were later relocated about four km south of the Patricia's Tactical HQ, just south of 27th Brigade HQ.

- Forward Observation Officer (FOO). Positioned with the front line infantry companies. Prior to the battle he is responsible for zeroing in the guns, establishing pre-registered targets; known as Defensive Fire tasks (DF tasks). During the engagement the FOO is passing fire orders to the Battery Commander at battalion Tactical HQ. The 16RNZA FOO with the Patricias had been continuously in action for 72 hours. He was with our forward infantry at C Company, but by 1800 hours the 24 April, he was exhausted, and retired to PPCLI Tactical HQ to sleep throughout the night.

AMERICAN ARTILLERY

Eight Inch Heavy Howitzers - There was one battery available to support 2PPCLI, after 1650 hrs the 24th. A battery consisted of four guns, and carried an inventory of 50 rounds. Normally they fired 1,600 to 2,000 rounds per month. If the infantry were engaged in continuing battle the number of fired rounds would increase considerably.

Armoured Support Battalion (ASB) - US Army. Equipped with Armoured Self Propelled 155 mm howitzers, having three batteries of six guns per battery, total 18 howitzers. The artillery shells contain Variable Time fuse (VT), which explode above ground, creating devastatingly wide spread aerial shrapnel bursts. VTs are said to be five times more effective than the ground burst 25 pounder. The 16RNZA later received VT fused artillery shells. The Battery Commander is stationed at the artillery firing line. The Forward Fire Officer (FFO) is with the front line infantry.

Field Artillery Battalion (FAB) - US Army. Consisting of three batteries, each having six 105 mm howitzers, total compliment 18. VT capability. The Battery Commander is stationed at the gun line, while the FFO with the front line infantry.

2 Chemical 4.2 inch Heavy Mortar Battalion. Assigned to 2 PPCLI - Company A, 3RAR - Company B
A Forward Fire Officer (FFO) and a radio man are stationed with the forward infantry.

Battalion   2PPCLI Kapyong - Establishment:

Battalion, Infantry - 942 men, full compliment. Commanded by a Lieutenant Colonel (LCol), Second in Command (2IC) a Major. Headquarters Company, four Rifle Companies and Support Company.

Tactical Headquarters (Tac HQ) - The Operational Command centre:

Commanding Officer, Regimental Sergeant Major (RSM), Intelligence Section, Signals, Quartermaster, Regimental Aid Post (RAP) Medical. Attached: 16RNZA Battery Commander.

Headquarters Company (HQ Company) - Many of the elements were engaged at tactical headquarters. The remaining troops of the company were at A or B echelons.

Rifle Company - Commanded by a Major, second in command a Captain. All second in commands are held in reserve at A echelon, ready to take over should the commander become a casualty or temporarily posted to another responsibility. Personnel 133. Company HQ - 13 men. In the text rifle companies are identified as: **A** company, **B**, **C** and **D**. Each company consists of three platoons.

Platoon - Establishment: 40 all ranks. One officer and one sergeant. Platoon HQ: 7 all ranks. Other ranks: 33 men, divided into three sections, each section having one Bren Light Machine Gun, two men manning. Soldiers carry the Lee Enfield bolt-action rifle, 100 rounds .303 ammunition, two #36 hand Grenades. Platoons are identified by numbers commencing with **1** in A company - ending with **12** in D company. Example: D company numbers are 10, 11 and 12. We were always short of reinforcements in Korea. During the battle at Kapyong D company was undermanned, having a compliment of 24 - 25 men per platoon.

Support Company - Commanded by a Major, who during the battle was designated Battle Adjutant, at Tactical HQ, gathering situation reports from the fighting companies to keep the commander abreast of the developing battle.

Pioneer Platoon - (engineers of the battalion), commanded by a Lieut. Three assault sections of 10 men each. Trades Section, carpenters and others.

Mortar Platoon - Commanded by a Captain, Second-in-Command a Lieut. Six 81 mm Mortars. Normal allotment of ammunition, 936 bombs, of which 20% are smoke. At Kapyong they inventoried almost two times the normal allotment. One .30 caliber and one .50 caliber machine guns mounted on each halftrack.

Medium Machine Gun Platoon - Commanded by a Captain. Six Vickers .303 medium machine guns, a Flame Thrower section and Sniper

Section. Machine gun crews are assigned to various rifle companies during battle, as are the snipers.

Anti-Tank Platoon, 50 all ranks. A Lieut, Platoon Sergeant and a Gun Sergeant. Initially they were equipped with 17 pounder anti-tank guns, which are not maneuverable in mountainous terrain. The platoon assumed an infantry reconnaissance role until they received American Ant-tank Recoilless Rifles in June of 1951.

3RAR
Originally assigned as occupation troops in Japan, they were reinforced and sent to Korea. The Australians refer only to Battalion Headquarters (BHQ), in their historical reporting of Kapyong, they do reference the term "Tactical HQ"

Brigade
Composed of three Infantry Battalions, an Armoured Regiment (tanks), an Artillery Regiment and supporting services. Usually 5,000 all ranks. In Korea the establishment for 25 Canadian Infantry Brigade (25CIB), being the sole Canadian army unit, was reinforced, totaling about 6,000 all ranks.

British Commonwealth Occupation Force (BCOF)
The occupation troops were Australian, located at Kure, Japan. This force was established at the end of World war II.

Division - Infantry

British Commonwealth Forces - Composed of three Brigades. approximately 18,000 all services, 65% of a Division are deemed front line fighters

South Korean - 10,000.

Chinese - 10,000 - 90% of the soldiers are front line fighters.

Corps Composed of three Divisions, approximately 58,000 men.

Machine Guns

Bren Light Machine Gun .303, British, magazine load, 30 rounds; however, if one loaded more than 28 rounds it would often result in a jammed magazine.

<u>Medium Machine Gun</u> (MMG): Vickers .303 caliber, belt fed, water cooled, British. Browning, .30 caliber, belt fed, USA.
<u>Heavy Machine Gun</u> (HMG), Browning .50 caliber, belt fed, USA.

Map Overlays - or Overlays
A sheet of plastic, marked with a grease pencil, showing future unit and sub unit locations and boundaries, to be laid over a map.

Navy, Army, Air Force Institute, (NAFFI)
Commissary (canteen services plus), Australian or British.

Orders Group (O Gp)- A gathering of subordinate commanders to whom Orders are being issued.

Reconnaissance Group (R Gp) - Consisting of those individuals the commander must consult/instruct in implementing his operational plans.

Regimental Aid Post (RAP). Medical Officer a Captain, Sergeant, Corporal Medical Assistants (Med As) and stretcher bearers. The Med As are posted to the rifle companies during battle to immediately attend to casualties.

25 Canadian Reinforcement Group (25CRG) - Japan. Receiving point for troops arriving from Canada, and returning from Korea.

A holding and a training centre for reinforcements awaiting posting to Korea, located at Hiro, a suburb of Kure, Japan. The battle training facilities were in mountainous terrain at Nippom Bara, the ranges at Hara Mura, Japan.

6147 Tactical Control Group, 5th US Air Force
To control Air Strikes between United Nations Forces front lines and the enemy. An important function was to eliminate casualties to UN troops, from "friendly fire." Tasks - locate enemy formations and to identify them for fighter/bombers. Crew: An American pilot accompanied by an officer from an infantry formation. Seventeen Canadians flew as observers. (Detailed chapter 19, page 197).

APPENDIX "H"

ERRONEOUS PUBLICATIONS

Publications, commencing with the Patricias official history, Volume Three, 1957, have failed to detail the reality of the actions taken by decision makers, at D Company. Examples of the representations of various authors, is listed below.

"PPCLI, 1919 - 1957, VOLUME III,"
by the official historian, C. R. Stevens.

Page 302, paragraph 2, line 4: *"Lieutenant Levy and his men disappeared in a swarm of enemies and the Chinese swept on to 12 platoon."* Unfortunately this erroneous report contained in the Patricias official history has been frequently referred to. While the enemy reached the foremost trenches they never penetrated 10 Platoon's position. I do believe he mistakenly reversed the rolls of 10 and 12 platoons.

"STRANGE BATTLEGROUND"
Queen's Printer, Ottawa 1966 - Lieutenant Colonel Herb Wood.

"At this point Captain Mills requested the artillery to lay down offensive fire....", page 77. True, as far as the statement goes, but not taken into account was the fact that these requests for supporting artillery fire originated with Levy of 10 Platoon. Levy's actions are recorded in the 2 PPCLI War Diary. Levy addressed the signaler at D Coy HQ via the Walkie-Talkie, who in turn informed Mills, who then requested Stone's permission for the fire order, he would not execute on his own. Levy's fire orders were then directed to the 16 RNZA Battery Commander located at the Patricias Tactical. HQ. For some five hours the enemy's action centered upon destroying 10 Platoon as a prelude to overrunning D Company. At no time during the battle did Mills address Levy directly. Mills, due to the mountainous terrain and his positioning of his HQ, was denied a view of any of the engagements of 10, 11 or 12 Pls throughout the battle.

"CANADA'S GLORY,"
Arthur Bishop, 1996.

Reporting upon a selection of Canada's historic military actions. Page 298, *"At this point Captain John Mills, the company commander, who seemed to be everywhere, encouraging his men, called for supporting fire."* At this late date accounts appear to delivery "expansive statements." The truth is that 10 Platoon, cut off from the remainder of the company, virtually alone, fought an aggressive enemy to a standstill. The roles played by Mills, Levy, Pearson, Holligan, and other formations during the battle have been revealed in the main body of my text.

"MARCHING AS TO WAR"
Pierre Berton - 2001

The Mills myth is repeated, page 560.

Fifty years on, erroneous commentary continues to mistakenly credit Mills with originating the order for friendly artillery fire to descend upon 10 Pl.

OTHER MISREPRESENTATIONS
CANADA

A number of books published about Korea have unfortunately named personnel incorrectly, placed individuals in the battle when they were not present. Myths have thus been created and perpetuated. It is sometimes difficult for the reader to separate novel "fiction," from reality. Errors have only seen the light of day because the writer(s) did not take the time to thoroughly confirm their "historical facts" with the available originating individuals.

APPENDIX "J"

CANADIAN BRAVERY DECORATIONS

DENIAL - RETROACTIVE RECOGNITION OF BRAVERY - CANADA
RETROACTIVE RECOGNITION OF CANADIANS - FOREIGN
DEFINING COMBAT DESIGNATION

I commenced my research with the intention of gathering enough information to design what might become the Citation for a retroactive award of the Military Cross (MC) to Lieut. Michael G Levy, (Major Retired) who commanded 10 Pl at the Battle of Kapyong, April 23 through 26, 1951. In my opinion, he was the foremost unrecognized defender of D Coy. At a meeting in Victoria, on 26 November 1996, a selection of fellow veterans wholeheartedly endorsed my proposal.

In my quest I was greatly encouraged by the then Colonel of our Regiment, Major General CW (Bill) Hewson, CMM, CD, (Retired), who contributed years of support of my efforts. Unfortunately the Canadian Army regulations stipulate that awards will not be considered two years after an action or incident no matter how deserving the recipient. Hewson, upon enquiring on a no name basis, was informed by National Defence Headquarters, that exceptions to the current policy would not be entertained. He then took up our cause with Lieut General J Gervais, (Retired), Second Secretary at Government House, Ottawa. Gervais read one of my earlier drafts and contacted the British awards authorities, who advised that if the Canadian award body approved a retroactive award for Levy they would give it due consideration. The British later noted that they could not locate the Gazette record of Levy's Mentioned in Dispatches (MiD), awarded in Malaya while serving in Special Operations Executive (SOE) Force 136. Due to a backlog of work it was not published until the 25 September, 1947.

Over the ensuing years it became evident that the possibility of a retroactive decoration for Levy was highly improbable.

Gervais advised the best they could do, would be to provide a Governor General's Certificate. A war veteran receives his defining accolades from peers who have served in action. It is through the acknowledgment of medals - ribbons that he exhibits on his chest, not through a piece of paper hidden in the memory hall of an individual home, that he receives his recognition. So while the Governor General's Certificate may be most honourably awarded to a very deserving Boy Scout, to my mind it simply does not rank with the herculean efforts exhibited by Levy and his troops during the momentous Battle of Kapyong.

Decorations Awarded in Korea

DSO Distinguished Service Order - Usually LCol and above
OBE Member of the Most Excellent Order of the British Empire
      ("Well Done Old Boy")
MC Military Cross - Commissioned Officer and Warrant Officers
DCM Distinguished Conduct Medal - Other Ranks
MM Military Medal - Other Ranks
BEM British Empire Medal - Other Ranks ("Well done Old Boy")
MiD Mentioned in Dispatches - Recognition, no medal, all ranks

Medals awarded in Korea to Canadians:

		Awarded	2PPCLI
DSO	LCol	5	1
	Major	3	--
OBE		58	--
MC		33	1
DCM		7	1
MM		53	2
BEM		21	--
Total		**171**	**7**

Stone was awarded a second bar to his DSO.

Awards Decisions
The assignment of medals falls into two categories. There are those awarded at the time of an action. There are also medal allotments, which the troops would say, "Came up with the rations." A government sacrificing its young men in wartime strives to ensure that heroes are properly recognized for their heroics, and this is partially for public

relations on the home front. Thus at times a quota of medals is assigned to a unit, and are officially designated "*a periodic award.*" This does not necessarily mean the recipients are any less deserving. Some citations in Korea fell into this latter category. In any case, award decisions are the prerogative of the Commanding Officer. Platoon or company commanders will forward recommendations, the Commanding Officer accepts or rejects. No system is perfect.

CANADIAN BRAVERY DECORATIONS

"Canadian Bravery Decorations are to accord recognition to all Canadian citizens and other persons who perform acts of courage."

Canada terminated the awarding of British military honours on 1 June 1972, with the adoption of Canadian Honours. Thus Canadian troops were decorated for bravery in operational events, after 1972 and prior to 1993, were awarded the same decorations as those awarded for Canadian civilian events. In 1993 Canada instituted bravery decorations for the military.

Military

Victoria Cross
Canadian version - To recognize acts of valour, self-sacrifice or devotion to duty in the presence of the enemy. None have been awarded to date.

Star of Military Valour
For distinguished and valiant service in the presence of the enemy.

Medal of Military Valour
For acts of valour or devotion to duty in the presence of the enemy.

The Commanding Officer initiating the award must submit the recommendation within 30 days of the incident. Nominations are forwarded to the *Military Valour Decorations Committee.* On acceptance the Chief of the Defence Staff forwards the recommendation to the Governor General for final approval. It must be received at Government House with two years of the incident.

Military and Civilian

Cross of Valour

For acts of conspicuous courage in circumstances of extreme peril. All Canadian citizens, both civilians and military, are eligible.
Two were awarded soldiers/sailors for civilian events.

Star of Courage
For acts of conspicuous courage in circumstances of great peril.
A couple were awarded in Cyprus in 1974 to the Airborne Regiment.

Medal of Bravery
For acts of bravery in hazardous circumstances.
Awarded in 1974 in Cyprus.

Consideration is not given to incidents which occurred more than two years prior to the date on which a proposal is first submitted. Recommendations are considered by the *Canadian Decorations Advisory Committee,* prior to being submitted to the Governor General for approval. The committee is composed of the following or their designated alternative member:

> Clerk of the Privy Council
> Secretary to the Governor General
> Under secretary of State
> Deputy Minister of National Defence
> Deputy Minister of Transport
> Commissioner of the RCMP
> Dominion Fire Commissioner
> And not more than three other members appointed by the Governor General .

RETROACTIVE RECOGNITION OF CANADIAN SERVICEMEN, (AND OTHER NATIONALS) BY FOREIGN GOVERNMENTS APPROVED BY THE CANADIAN GOVERNMENT

France recently honoured a number of Canadian airmen for their actions in the Second World War over France. The Canadian government welcomed the awards and authorized the recipients to accept them. The French also honoured veterans from the First World War, who attained 100 years of age. Again Canada gratefully approved. The United States has undertaken a programme of recognition for actions taken by its soldiers in the Second World War, and later. Two Medals of Honour awarded for action in 1966 in Vietnam, authorized 10 July

1998 and 8 February 2000; and one Medal of Honour for 1945, again awarded in 1998. The US also awarded 32 Medals of Honour to deserving former soldiers of Japanese ancestry. I find it ironic and deplorable that foreign governments are willing to review heroic endeavours and pay tribute to those servicemen who are deemed deserving, yet Canadian authorities stand aloof. They refuse to honour their deserving sons from the past who willingly gave so much for our country's freedom and have never been officially recognized. A decision executed by men who have never been in battle?

DEFINING COMBAT DESIGNATION

And finally while discussing medals. In a war zone one has to be in attendance only one day to earn entitlement to wear the appropriate campaign medal-ribbon. That is as it should be. Individuals are unfortunately wounded on their one and only day in battle. It also means that administrative types from military HQ in Ottawa, or elsewhere, not involved in combat, must attend the war zone 30 times, stay but 24 hours and head home, thus earning entitlement to display the campaign ribbon. There are many Canadians, mostly officers, wearing the Korean ribbons, but yet they *never* heard a shot fired, having never participated in actually fighting a war!

American servicemen have a defining badge that identifies those who have served in battle in a war zone. It is called *Combat Infantry Man's Badge (CIB)*, thus segregating out the non-combatants. Many senior American military officers, during field exercises, having earned rows of ribbons, will with pride, wear only The Combat Infantry Man's Badge.

Canada should honour all those who have made sacrifices for their countrymen in battle, by adopting a Defining Combat Designation.

Private Penny & Friend (photo: Hub Gray)

APPENDIX K

SPECIAL ORDER OF THE DAY
BY
BRIGADIER B. A. BURKE, D. S. O.
COMMANDING
27 BRITISH COMMONWEALTH BRIGADE

27 British Commonwealth Brigade ceases as such to exist, but this is far from the case in respect to its units and personnel. The British personnel revert to the 27th Infantry Brigade, and those of the Commonwealth become absorbed into the 28 British Commonwealth Brigade.

The bonds of friendship formed in battle between British, Australian, Canadian and New Zealand and Indian soldiers of all ranks in the 27 British Commonwealth brigade during the last months can never be severed, and must be of lasting service to King and Commonwealth, which they serve.

It has been my pride and honour to command this Brigade for the past month, spent nearly all in action as usual, and I venture to think that the splendid stand, and wholesome destruction of the enemy during the past action, will rank amongst their finest achievements and has appropriate finale.

On behalf of the British personnel who now depart Korea, I wish you all members of the Commonwealth who remain the very best in the future, good fortune, and sincere and deep thanks for the friendships found and formed.

B.A. Burke

25th April 1951

Brigadier
Commanding 27 British Commonwealth Brigade

1 MX	camp
1 A & SH	27 Bde Sigs
2PPCLI	16 Fd Regt RNZA
3 RAR	60 Indian Airborne Fd Amb
	War Diary (2)

Kure, Lieut's Bud mcLeod, Mert Entwhistle (photo: Hub Gray)

Appendix "L"

CONTRIBUTORS
and others

Position at Kapyong - Military Service - Present Day

BARWISE, Kenneth, MM, Pte, 60mm Mortar, D Coy. 12 Pl west
Pentiction, BC
CASF & CAAF 1950-80. Awarded the Military Medal, Kapyong,
Korea, April 1951. Patricias to 1955, Army Service Corps to retirement.
Retired Corporal.

BEAUCHAMP, Shammy Lieut, Assistant Adjutant, LOB B Echelon
Deceased. Served in WWII and Korea.

BOTTING, Gerry, Lieut. reinforcement, searching for B Echelon
Prescot, ON
CASF & CAAF 1950-74. Retired Major. Served: Korea, USA,
Germany, England, Ghana, Kashmir. Retired 1974. 1974-89, moved to
the Civil Service and continued former Army employment, Project
Coordinator for Deputy Chief of the Defence Staff.

BOURGON, Ron, Batman, 2 Platoon, A Company
St. Eugene, ON & Florida, USA.
1950-53 CASF & CAAF, Served Korea. LLB 1955. Worked for a law
firm. Formed his own collection agency, Collection Bailiff. 1969
Bought two farms, 1,000 acres.

BROWNE, Owen, Captain, 2IC A Company
Deceased
Served in WWII, Loyal Edmonton Regiment. Retired in the 1970s with
the rank of LCol.

CANFIELD, Mel, Pte, IO Section. Tac HQ
Chilliwack, BC
CASF & CAAF1950-73. Retired Captain. Served: Korea, Germany,
Vietnam. Federal Prison Service 1973-86. Marriage Counseling 1980
to date. Contacted MS in 1980, Mel is confined to a wheel chair.

CHRYSLER, William, Driver, Mortar Platoon
Fort Erie, On.
Discharged 1952. Worked for Horton Steel 24 years, assembling storage tanks in Singapore, Korea, Indonesia, Malaya. In 1980 worked at Inchon, Korea, where he met and married his second wife.

CLOUTHIER, LeRoy, Cpl, # 1 section, 10 Pl D Coy.
Edmonton, AB
CASF & CAAF 1950-74, Retired Sergeant. Served: Korea, Germany, Egypt, England (SAS), USA Ft Benning, Georgia. 1974-75, Managed Officers and Sergeant Mess.

COOMBE, Ed Captain, RCSC, Signals Officer, at Tac HQ, operating wireless set to Coys.
Calgary, AB
Canadian Army 1935-65. Retired Major. Served: WWII, Italy in the Artillery and NW Europe, later Corps HQ. Korea 1950-51, RCCS. City of Calgary 1965-71, retired as Assistant City Clerk.

COPLEY, Don, Stretcher Bearer. A Echelon, and Regimental Aid Post.
Vancouver, BC
CASF 1950-52. Served: Korea. Earned BSc, then a Medical Degree. RCAF 5 years, Medical Officer. Public Service, 6 years, Canadian Pension Commission. Civil Aviation, Health and Welfare to 1986. Retired. BC Workers Compensation, Retired 1999.

CROCKER, HA, Lance Corporal, operating #19 wireless on the Brigade radio net, Tac HQ.
Stoney Plain, AB
CASF - CAAF 1950 1975. Served in Korea and Cyprus, transferred to Army Service Corp late 1951, last eight years in the military. Served as a Pastor at a church in Burnaby BC. 1974-96, Pastor in the Manitoba Northwest Ontario District. Retired 1996, serves as a hospital pastor.

CROUCHER, Gord L, Private, HQ Company, B Echelon.
Kamloops, BC
CASF-CAAF, 1946 - 69. 1953 RCEME. '56 to Engineers, Sgt Photographer. Served: Cyprus, Middle East, Retired Sgt. Militia, to Captain. 1969. News photographer Vancouver Province, 1976 -86 PR CPR Air. As an Army Photographer and for CP Air PR, he traveled the world. Editor of the KVA Newsletter, "The Three Rice Burners."

CUNNINGHAM, Captain, Protestant Chaplain, B Echelon, AT Tactical HQ from about noon the 24th.
Deceased
Later became the Brigadier commanding the Canadian Army Chaplain Corps.

CZUBOKA, Michael, #2 Mortar man, 81 mm Mortars.
Winnipeg, Man.
CASF, CAAF, qualified parachutist. Discharged 1954, attended university, obtaining BA, MA, B,Ed, M.Ed. Enrolled COTC, qualified Lieut, three summers Cdn Army, Germany. A high school principal, Brandon, Superintendent of Schools, Winnipeg. Retired 1995. President Manitoba Association School Superintendents. 1996-7, Lecturer, at Ukrainian Universities, Ukraine. Published four books: among them; *Ukrainian Canadian Eh?; Why It's Hard to Fire Johnny's Teacher* - a book about teacher tenure that has been used by lawyers and school districts throughout Canada.

O'DALE, Bill, Private, B Echelon and Tac HQ Defensive Force
Sarnia, ON
1950 - 1952 CASF, Private. 1952- 1956 Polysar Sarnia, 1966-1974 CIL, 1974-1992 Petrosar (Nova).

DOUGLAS, Smiley, MM, A/Cpl, Pnr Pl, # 1 Assault Section
Elnora, AB
Awarded the Military Medal, after loosing a hand trying to defuse a grenade at Kapyong. Enlisted CASF August 1950, Retired Oct 51. Smiley rested for a time. In 1952 he resumed his previous employment driving a cat skinner. In 1955 he commenced farming and he is still working long days on his land. Everyone I spoke with commented that he is one of the most thoughtful and gentle people they know, that he carries no bitterness for his loss.

EDWARDS, Murray, Captain, Quartermaster, Tac HQ
Victoria, BC,
WW II, 1942-46. Private to Lieut, England. CASF & CAAF1950-69. Retired Major. Served: Korea, NATO Germany, Cyprus, Middle East Peace Commission. 1969-71U of Victoria, teacher's certificate. Army call out Cadet Services 1972-84.

FLINT, George, Major, LOB, Commanding the Battalion Jr NCO School.
Deceased

Served in WWII. Commanded A Company. Killed in Palestine 1958, serving in the UN Peace Keeping Forces.

FITZGERALD, Keith, Captain, MO, Tac IIQ
Deceased
Korea 1950-51. He later became a Brigadier General Commanding the Canadian Army Medical Corps. After retiring he worked as Medical Officer for Etobicoke, and later Toronto. A keen photographer, many of his Korean photographs are in the archives of the Patricias.

FOULDS, Andy, Captain, Comd MMG Pl.
Vancouver, BC
WW II, 1939-46. Sgt Artillery. Served: England; OCTU Canada, Infantry; Lieut, Italy, NW Europe. CASF 1950-51, Advance Party, Korea. 1952-81. Senior positions, Vancouver, Winnipeg, Toronto, Edmonton: Brewery, 7-Up Canada, Dickenson-Robertson Gp.

GRAY, Hub, Lieut - 2nd in Comd, Mortar Pl
Calgary, AB
CASF & CAAF 1951-1953. 1953-1978 Richardson Securities Of Canada, sales, management, Partner Europe & the Middle East, Alberta. 1978 - 1995 Independent Financial Consultant.

GRIMES, Leslie, RSM - Tac HQ
Hayle, Cornwall, UK
Korea 1950-51. Born in England, came to Canada, joined the Canadian Army 1931, in 1933 transferred to British Army. He served 8 years in India, in 1936 he was awarded the Northwest Frontier Medal. WWII, served two years in North-west Europe, one year in the Middle East. Civilian life in 1946. Joined 2PPCLI 1950. 1976 posted to Naples, Garrison RSM Canadian Forces, Middle East Staging Area. Always a gentleman, well loved by the military he served. He named his cottage in Cornwall, "Kapyong."

GRISON, Jean, Pte, D Coy HQ, 300 wireless set to Tac HQ,
Montreal, PQ,
CASF - CAAF 1950-55. Served: Korea. Studied electronics, TVs. Retired 2000. Raised 4 boys and 2 girls, 5 live in BC and one in Lethbridge.

HARRISON, Del, Major, Comd C Coy.
White Rock, BC
WW II 1939-45. Served: England, NW Europe, Pte to Major. 1946

Managed a bakery. 1947-50 Call Out, CAAF. CASF & CAAF 1950-69. Served Korea, Germany 2x, Palestine, Staff College Kingston. 1969-85, business manager of a High School, Vancouver. PPCLI Heritage Committee interviews.

HENDERSON, Gordon, Major, Battle Adjutant, Tac HQ
White Rock, BC
Royal Military College, Kingston, ON, 1937-1940. Indian Army 1940-44, Canadian Army 1944-69. Served: Korea, England, Germany. Retired Major. Stock broker 1970-1990.

HOFFMAN, Robert J. RCEME Craftsman, B Ech and Tac HQ.
Abbotsford, BC
1950-52 CASF, Medical discharge. Mechanic 1953-55. Finning Tractor 1955-64. 1964-69 Manager Heavy Equipment, Burnaby, BC. 1969-87 Apprentice and Industrial Trades, BC Government. Owned three Mobile Home Parks. Retired 2000.

HURST, Lorne, Lieut, Comd Pnr Pl
Edmonton, AB,
Deceased April 2002
WW II 1939-46. Served: England, NW Europe, Sapper Engineers - Captain to A/Major. 1950-56 CASF & CAAF, Served: Korea, Germany. Lieut-Captain. 1960-63 Call out Capt. 1963-66 Emergency Measures Organization. 1966-1987 Public relations Alberta Government; 1987, Vitamins and related products.

LAMEY, Paul, Pte, 6 Pl, B Coy
Peachland, BC
CASF & CAAF 1950-1954. Served: Korea. Various jobs for three years. Land Titles Office, City of Calgary 30 years. 1986 Retired to Victoria, '94 moved to Peachland.

LAPOINTE Rollie, CPl 7 Pl, C Coy
Victoria BC.
CASF & CAAF 1950 - 1954. Served: Korea. An inspirational soldier. BC Forest Products, 32 years.

LEE, Bill, Pte, A Coy.
Edmonton, AB.
CASF & CAAF 1950-54. Retired Cpl. Served: Korea. Independent businessman, Lethbridge, Calgary, Edmonton. Retired in 1973.

LEVY, Michael   G. Lieut, ComD 10 Pl, D Coy
Richmond, BC
Prisoner of War, interned by the Japanese, Shanghai, China 1942, escaped 1944. British Army 1944 - 48, Liicut - Captain India, Malaya awarded MiD. Hong Kong - War Crimes Tribunal 1946-47. CASF & CAAF 1950-1974, Served: Korea, Germany, Vietnam, Cyprus. Successfully completed US Marine Corps Command and Staff College. Washington DC, Canadian Defence Liaison Staff 1969-71. Retired Major. 1974, Contracted Department of National Defence, Protocol, Ottawa. 1975-6, External Affairs, Habitat, Vancouver. 1977 White-horse, Environment Canada. 1977-86, Public Works Canada, Vancouver. Retired 1986.

MACAULAY, S. Cpl. Anti-Tank Pl
Cardigan, PEI
WW II, 1941-46. Wounded in Italy, bone grafts and screws the leg. CASF &CAAF 1950-72. Sgt. Independent businessman, Calgary. 1981 retired to PEI, to care for his parents.

MACLEOD, Bud, Lieut, LOB, Bn Jr. NCOs School
Halfmoon Bay, BC
UBC COTC 1944-48. CASF & CAAF 1950-76. Served: Korea, Germany 2x, Canadian Liaison Officer US Army Alaska. Retired 1976. 1976-78, Call Out Commander, LCol Banff National Army Cadet Camp. Awarded the United Sates Air Medal, for his time as an Observer in a Harvard Aircraft over flying the enemy and our own front lines, Korea 1951, spotting targets for assault by fighter and bomber aircraft .

MELNECHUUK, Mike, A/CSM, C Coy
Kamloops, BC
Canadian Army WW II, 1939-47, Served: England, NW Europe. CASF & CAAF 1950-68. Korea, Germany. Retired Warrant Officer Class II. Commenced a wire fence business, which his daughter now administers.

MENARD, Bob, Pte, 6 Pl, B Coy
Salut Saint Marie, On
CASF 1950-51. Worked in Flin Flon Manitoba, Sault St Marie where he retired.

MIDDLETON, Rod, Lieut, 27th Infantry Brigade HQ, LO.
Calgary, AB

Command Contingent #2, Camp Borden 1949, former commander of 12 Pl, D Coy and LO to 27th Brigade Korea. CASF & CAAF 1950-76. Retired Major. Served: Korea, Germany, UK. Staff College India, Forces Staff College Norfolk Virginia. Manager Mewata Officer Mess, Calgary, for 13 years. National President, PPCLI Association 1984-89. 1989-2000 managed PPCLI Gallery, Museum of the Regiments, Calgary. Chairman PPCLI Heritage Committee 1995-to 2001. Director, Museum Regiments Calgary, April - September 2000.

MILLS, JG Wally, MC. Captain, A/Comd, Dog Coy
Edmonton, AB, Deceased 1 Feb 1995.
WWII:Sep 1939; Cpl Dieppe Raid 19 Sep 1942; Lieut, Aug 1944; served in England, discharged Sept 1945. Enlisted CASF & CAAF. Korea, awarded the Military Cross Kapyong, Korea April 1951. Served: Korea, Germany, Palestine, and Yemen. Retired Major Feb 1968. Business Manager, Edmonton School Board - 1970-1984.

MITCHELL, WR. Pte, 9 Section, 6 Pl, B Coy, # 1 Bren LMG
Deceased 1999, Vancouver, BC
Awarded the Distinguished Conduct Medal (DCM), Kapyong.

MORROW, DC. Pte, B Coy, 6 Pl
Moved - unavailable
Farmed near Drumheller, Alberta.

MUNRO, Brian, Lieut, Comd 2 Pl, A Coy
Victoria, BC
Comd Contingent # 2, Camp Borden 1949. CASF & CAAF 1950-82. Retired Major. Served, Korea, Viet Nam, Cambodia, Laos, Ghana, Israel, Lebanon, Syria. Cadet Services 1983-86, promoted to LCol, Commanded Cadet Camp Vernon.

NESTOR, George, Pte, D Coy HQ Runner, Bren LMG
Duncan, BC
CASF 1950 - 1953. Served: Korea. Longshoreman 1953 - 83, Vancouver Island. Recently returned to work as a host, Real Canadian Superstore.

NEUFELD, Neil, Pte, 12 Pl W, D Coy , #1 on a Bren LMG
Edmonton, AB,
CASF & CAAF1950-54, Korea, Private. 1960-66, 80th Field Artillery, Retired Sergeant. 23 years working for Stelco.

PEARSON, John, Lieut, Comd 11 Pl, D Coy
Vancouver, BC
Merchant Marine 1941-42. Australian Army 1943-46, Sapper. CASF 1950-51, Served: Korea. Lieut, medical discharge, 1951. LLB U of Manitoba 1953, Masters 1956. Practiced law 1953-63, Canadian Pacific Railway: Montreal, Winnipeg, Calgary. Practiced law in Winnipeg 1963-68. Davis and Company, Partner Vancouver 1968-86.

PENNEL, Red, A/Sgt, Pnr Pl
North Bay, Ontario
1939-45, Engineers, Sapper. Served, UK, Sicily, Italy, Holland. 1947-50 Ontario Northland Railway. 1950-69 CASF & CAAF, 2nd Battalion PPCLI. Served Korea and Germany, Retired Warrant Officer. 1971 External Affairs, Security PRC 5: India, Austria, Egypt, Italy, Retired 1981.

PETRIE, Charles, Lieut, Comd 5 Pl, B Coy
Ross on Wye, ENGLAND
WWII 1944-45, England, Germany, Airborne Signals. CASF & CAAF 1950-70 Retired Captain. Served: Korea, Germany. PDGE U of Victoria 1971, Taught maths and science in Wales for 8 years. PGCE Keele, UK, 1979. Retired.

REAUME, Del, Pte. 6 Pl, B Coy
Windsor, ON
1945 - 6 months infantry. 1950-52 CASF, Private. Work for 34 years at Ford and General Motors.

RICHARDSON, Ed, Pte, 6 Pl, B Coy
Whiterock, BC
CASF 1950-52. Served; Korea. Raised 5 kids. Construction, Hotels, Brewery, Vancouver Stock Exchange.

RUSHTON, Roy, Cpl, 10 Pl, D Coy
Westville, Nova Scotia
Canadian Army 1939 - 1945. 1st Canadian Parachute Bn. Parachuted into Normandy D-Day 6 hrs prior to sea borne landings. Parachuted across the Rhine March 24/1945. Served: England, France, Belgium, Holland & Germany. CASF August 1950; Served: Korea. Discharged Sep 51, medically unfit, retired Sergeant. Call Out with Army, WO2, for many years. Project manager with a housing authority at age 65.

SANDOR, Paul, Pte, 9 Pl, Bren LMG
Kennedy, Saskatchewan
CASF Aug 1950 - February 1952. Returned to the farm, and as of 2002, still farming.

SHULER, Bill, Cpl, Med A, evacuated casualties B-D Coys.
Chapeau, PQ,
Hitler Youth, Luftwaffe, Germany 1935-1938, emigrated to Canada 1938. CASF & CAAF 1950-73. Retired Major. Transferred to the Medical Corps 1962. Served: Korea, Germany, Alaska 2x, England, Royal Marine Commandos. Olympic movement 14 years.

SIM, Alex, Sgt, Anti-tank Pl
Kamloops, BC
WW II 1941-46. Gunner, artillery. 1944, Infantry. Served UK, NW Europe. 1947-50 Militia Call Out. 1950-69 CASF & CAAF. Retired Warrant Officer class II. Served Korea, Germany. President Clans and Scottish Societies of Canada. In 1976 Sim joined "Historical 78th Frazer Highlanders" and is an officer of the association.

SKELLY, George, Lieut, Reinforcement, B Echelon
Sun City, Arizona, USA
CASF & CAAF 1950-56. served: Korea. Resigned, Captain. 1956-61 U of Manitoba, Medicine. General Practitioner 1961-66. U of Minnesota 4 years, Radiology. One year fellowship Cardiovascular Radiology and Invasive Procedures. Practiced in Minnesota, retired 1987.

SWINTON, Bob, MC. Major Comd D Coy, on R&R.
Deceased
WWII, awarded the Military Cross. CASF, CAAF. Killed in Germany in an automobile accident early 1970s. One hell of a fine officer.

STONE, James Riley, DSO & 2 BARS, MC. LCol, CO 2nd Battalion PPCLI.
Victoria, BC
1939-46 WWII. Private, commissioned an officer in 1942, Stone rose to LCol, Commanding The Loyal Edmonton Regiment, September 1944. Served Sicily, Italy, NW Europe. Operated a Motel, Salmon Arm BC, after the war. Korea, 1950-51. 1950-58: CASF-CAAF. On return to Canada from Korea he qualified as a parachutist and commanded the 2nd Patricia's as a part of the Mobile Striking Force, the predecessor of the Canadian Airborne Regiment. In 1953 he became The Chief Instructor at the Royal Canadian School of Infantry, Camp Borden,

Ontario. Promoted to full Colonel in 1954, he commanded the Canadian Army Provost Corps, (Military Police). During his term he instituted a unique policy: newly appointed provost officers were required to serve six months in an infantry battalion to develop a better understanding of the rank and file soldiers. In 1995 Stone received The Order of Canada, for being the founding organizer, 1957, of the Military Police Fund for Blind Children. Said Stone: "It's the greatest accomplishment of my life."

THORSON, H. Pte, 9 Pl
Innisfail, AB

VALALEE, Jim, Captain, Catholic Padre
Deceased.
Possessed a great sense of humour. For 17 years he served as a missionary in China.

WALL, Jim, Pte, Pnr Pl, Driver
Winnipeg, MB
WW II 1942-46, Trooper and Guardsman. CASF & CAAF 1950-73, Retired Sergeant. Served Korea, Cyprus, Germany 3x. 1973-93, Administrator, Profession of Resident Doctors of Man.

WALKER, Vern, Pte 10 Pl, # 1 section D Coy
Address unknown

WANNIANDY, Jimmy, L/Cpl, Section Comd, 12 Pl W
Edmonton, AB
WW II 1944-45. CASF, CAAF 1950-__. First Nation's Canadian. Retired Sergeant. Passed away 18th April 2000.

WORSFOLD, Don, Pte C Coy.
Victoria, BC
CASF 1950-53. Served: Korea. Canadian National Telegraph eight months. RCN 1954-75, Retired a Master Warrant Officer. Sailed the seven seas. CP Steamships, BC Steamship Company 1975-90, 1ST Mate sailing on the Princess Marguerite Seattle - Victoria.

ABOUT THE AUTHOR

Born 27 August 1928, in Winnipeg, Manitoba. Married to Pamela Joy, with four married sons and ten grand children. Retired and living in Calgary, Alberta.

As a young man for years I had thought that I would join the Navy, for my father had run away to sea on square rig sailing ships at the age of 13, back in about 1894. As a child he entertained me with stories around Cape Horn and being shipwrecked by a Pacific storm, six days out of Sydney, Australia. His colourful sea tales inspired this Prairie boy to join the Sea Cadets.

I was always rather big for my age and in late 1944 and early 1945, I was accosted on the street by motherly types who accused me of being a shirker when there was a war on - after all, their sons were in the Army serving Canada; "Why aren't you!" I was 16, but this really got to me and one day, while still carrying my school books I went to the recruiting depot. The Sergeant at the depot on Yates Street, told me to go home, that the war would soon be over. I pleaded and finally he said that if I must do something I should join the Army Cadet Corps attached to the militia unit of The Canadian Scottish Regiment.

After qualifying as an officer at Camp Borden in 1949 I furthered my army relationship by serving with the regular force and attending various courses at the School of Infantry, Camp Borden, Ontario; 3 Inch Mortar, ABC Chemical Warfare and so on. Between courses I signed up for a variety of 'Call Out' engagements with the regular force. In this way I spent about two years continuously employed in army. I was on Exercise Sweetbriar for about nine months, which took place in the Yukon in 1950-51. We assembled at Camp Wainwright, Alberta, and I'll never forget it. One winter night the temperature hit the lowest I have ever experienced, -62 degrees. I was astounded the next morning to observe drivers lighting fires under their engines. We moved to Whitehorse where the 1st Battalion PPCLI and 10,000 American soldiers participated in the combined exercise. I was fascinated by the Patricia troops displaying their distinguishing parachute wings on their uniforms. I wanted very much to become a paratrooper, and later, after Korea, I qualified being a member of the 2nd Battalion. The Patricias were part of the Mobile Striking Force, the predecessor to the Parachute Regiment.

The RCMP Whitehorse detachment would not allow the American

Military Police (MPs) to carry Billy Sticks in the town; however, it was not an uncommon sight to see the US MPs carrying four cell flashlight harbouring a well defined "U" shape after being cracked over some un-fortunates soldier's skull.

I was the canteen officer for the Canadians, and I distinguished myself by making a rather bad show of it. I had over-ordered supplies of pop, candy bars and other confections. So, rather than taking it back to Ed-monton where it would take months to have the troops absorb the goods—which might then become stale, I disposed of the inventory by unloading it "cheap" to local merchants. With the financial proceeds I broke another law by returning south in a truck loaded with cases of over-proof rum. The local confection wholesaler in Whitehorse was understandably furious. I had a lot of explaining to do to a certain Army Service Corps Colonel at Headquarters Western Command; how-ever, the southern officers messes appeared delighted to quietly dispose of my contraband rum.

Military

Militia
Canadian Scottish Regiment, Princess Mary's, Victoria, BC,1946.
1st Command Contingent Course, Camp Borden, Sept 1948.
Commissioned a Lieutenant, Reserve Army, Oct 1949.
Exercise Sweetbriar 1949-50

Canadian Army Special Force (CASF)
Posted 2rd Battalion PPCLI, Oct 1950.
Posted 3rd Battalion PPCLI, Nov 1950
Reinforcement, 2nd Battalion PPCLI, Korea, February 1951.
-Second-in-Command of the Mortar Platoon - **Kapyong.**
-Commanded 12 Platoon, Dog Company.

Canadian Army Active Force (CAAF)
Long term 20 year commission, ZK 4348, May 1951.
2PPCLI, Korea, February to August 1951, British Commonwealth Occupation Forces Hospital, Kure, Japan, August 1951.
25 Canadian Reinforcement Group, Kure, Japan, Sept 1951.
2nd Battalion PPCLI, Curie Barracks, Calgary, Nov 1951.
Paratroop Course, Rivers, MB, Serial 122, 1952.
Part II, Lieut to Capt, Camp Borden 1952.
Resigned Commission CAAF, May 1953.

Milita
Captain, Queen's Own Rifles, Toronto
48th Highlanders - Toronto
Supplementary Reserve 1958

Business
Richardson Securities of Canada, 1953 - 1978.
Sales, Manager Managed Funds, Partner Research Dept,
Partner Europe and Middle East, Partner Alberta.
Independent Financial Consultant 1978. Retired 1995.

PPCLI Association:
Member, PPCLI Regimental Heritage Committee, 1998-2001. PPCLI
Association Finance Committee 2000-to date.

Hub Gray — 1953

Hub Gray — 2003

A CLOSING NOTE:

I have been asked if we built bunkers in 1951, during our time in Korea, and for the most part we did not. In the early months, we were not in static positions for the battalion was constantly on the move attacking and dislodging the enemy. Bunkers were not constructed at Kapyong. During May we spent 21 days on the Line Golden and did not employ bunkers as we were out of direct contact with the enemy - whom were 6 or more km to the north. A platoon was always positioned on a dominating hill, well in front of the battalion so as to warn of any enemy advances. Bunkers were not put to use in this instance. 12Pl, taking its turn spending a week on that forward position, found it very uncomfortable for it was overrun with ants. The Chinese and North Koreans, at this time, were still lacking in artillery.

Around Chorwon area, late August, the first bunkers came into being at company HQ, to facilitate Orders Groups at night. Charles Petrie and Brian Munro advise that they did not erect bunker protection during their time in Korea. Petrie took over a well constructed bunkered trench from the Americans in a paddy field. During the night the heavy rains came, the roof collapsed, and he was buried up to his neck with only one arm free, he had to be dug out. It was common to construct overhead covering for the protection from the rain. Petrie states that on nights free of rain he would sleep out in the open to be quickly alerted upon the distinctive "whomp" that signaled the enemy were unleashing artillery or rockets at this position.

BIBLIOGRAPHY

Barris, Ted. *Deadlock in Korea* - Macmilllan, Canada, 1999.

Breen, Bob. *The Battle of Kapyong - 3rd Battalion The Royal Australian Regiment, Korea 23-34, April 1951* - Army Doctrine Centre, New South Wales, Australia, 1992.

Bishop, Arthur. *Canada's Glory* - McGraw-Hill Ryerson Limited, 1996

Bishop, John R. *The King's Bishop* - by John R. Bishop with GW Stephen Brodsky. Mossy Hole Enterprises, 2000.

Blair, Clay. *The Forgotten War* - Random House Canada, 1987.

Berton, Pierre. *Marching as to War,* Doubleday Canada, 2001

Endicott, Stephen and Edward Hagerman. *The United States and Biological Warfare* - Indiana University Press, 1998.

Farrar-Hockley, General Sir Anthony. *Official History, The British Part in the KOREAN WAR, Volume II* - HMSO Publication Centre, London, 1995.

Hastings, Max. *The Korean War* - Romandata Ltd, Simon & Shuster, 1987

Hicky, Michael. *The Korean War* - John Murray Publisher, London, England, 1999.

McGibbon, Ian. *NEW ZEALAND & THE KOREAN WAR, Volume II* - Auckland University Press, in association with the Historical Branch, Department of Internal Affairs, New Zealand, 1996.

O'Neill, Robert. *Australia in The Korean Was, 1950 - 53, Volume II* - The Australian War Memorial and the Australian Government Printing Service, Canberra, 1985.

Stevens, CR. *Princess Patricia's Canadian Light Infantry 1919 - 1957, Volume III* - Historical Committee of the Regiment.

Wood, Lieutenant-Colonel Herbert. *Strange Battleground* - The Ministry of National Defence, Canada. Queen's Printer 1966.

2PPCLI War Diary, Korea, April 1951- PPCLI Regimental Archives, Museum of the Regiments, Calgary, Alberta.

PPCLI Archives - Museum of the Regiments, Calgary, Alberta.

History and Heritage, Department of National Defence, Ottawa

Department of Veterans Affairs, Charlettown, PEI.

Dr. David Bercuson, PhD, FRCS, LLB, Professor of Strategic Studies, University of Calgary, lent his personal files which he copied from DND records Ottawa, and 27 & 28 Brigade records, United Kingdom:

Transcript of an Interview between LCol GWL Nicholson, D Hist, AHQ, and LCol Stone, at 1630 hrs, 5 June 51

2 PPCLI Action Kapyong area - 23 to 26 Apr 51: dated Ottawa 25 Nov 54. By Capt APPMacKenzie (formerly IO, 2 PPCLI)

DND - Army. Article by Ronald Batchelor, of Reuters, 27 Brigade engagement, Kapyong: dated 26 April 1951.

The Kapyong Battle - Undated, unsigned: DND, 145.2P7013(D4),

War Diary British Commonwealth 27 Brigade, January - April 1951

War Diary British Commonwealth 28 Brigade, April - May 1951.

Impressions CCF Offensive, 22-26 April 1951, Lieutenant-General Sir HCH Robertson, KBE, DSO, Headquarters, British Commonwealth Forces, Japan - undated.

PPCLI Archives: HEADQUARTERS, 2ND CHEMICAL MORTAR BATTALION, APO 301, dated 12 July 1951. Reports of the actions of A & B Companies, supporting 2 PPCLI and 3RAR respectively, April 23-26, 1951.

MISSING RECORDS:

In Korea the Intelligence Section of our battalion wrote up the *"Radio Logs:"* a record of communications between Tactical HQ and the various companies. The SITRUPS from the companies, orders given by Stone and their timings were recorded. I was particularly interested in the dates of April 23-25, 1951. No record of these documents has been located in Ottawa.

History & Heritage, DND, Ottawa, did forward their record of supplements to the 2PPCLI War diary, *"ORDER OF BATTLE HIGH-LIGHTS,"* for the month of April 1951. Every day is represented with the unfortunate exception of April 23 to 25 - the time phase I was eager to access. These situation reports were sent to each battalion from 27 Brigade HQ, who in turn received them from Division HQ, and it is obvious that they originated at Eight Army HQ. These reports summarize: Enemy movements, formations, and strengths; engagements with the enemy; equipment captured; casualties both sides; conditions of UN Forces; intelligence from spies behind enemy lines; number of prisoner taken and intelligence gained from Prisoner of War interrogations. It is most disappointing that the higher command assessments of the Patricias Battle at Kapyong should be missing from this summary documentation.

INDEX

INDEX